VISIONARY DR

EXPLORING THE ASTROLOGI

Haydn Paul was born in 1952, and lives near Leicester with his wife and three children. He has spent many years exploring the transpersonal way, and has been a practising Astrologer for over ten years.

VISIONARY DREAMER

EXPLORING THE ASTROLOGICAL NEPTUNE

Haydn Paul

ELEMENT BOOKS

First published in 1989 by
Element Books Limited
Longmead, Shaftesbury, Dorset

Typeset in Linotronic Palatino by
Character Graphics, Taunton, Somerset
Printed and bound in Great Britain by Billings
Hylton Road, Worcester

Cover illustration by David A. Hardy

Cover design by Max Fairbrother

British Library Cataloguing in Publication Data
Paul, Haydn
Visionary Dreamer: exploring the astrological neptune
1. neptune. astrological aspects
I. title
133.5'3
ISBN 1-85230-122-8

Cover Image: *View of Neptune from Triton*

Artist's Notes

I was present in Pasadena at the encounter late in August 1989, and this scene is the result of a discussion with *Voyager* scientist Dr Garry Hunt, who believes that geysers are a viable possibility. The one shown here is high due to the low gravity and intermittently erupting in spurts. In *Voyager* images, dark streaks can be seen and here one of these is shown to be due to material falling back on the surface.

Both 'pink' and 'blue' ices (methane/nitrogen) are shown, and in the foreground the terrain has slumped due to subterranean (or subtritonian) heating caused by tidal effects, forming caves and a temporary 'lake'. Haze layers are visible and the sky around the distant Sun is deep blue. Neptune was found to have rings but these are too faint to be visible in these lighting conditions. Its most unexpected feature, a 'Great Dark Spot' (similar in size and nature to Jupiter's Great Red Spot) may be seen in the atmosphere of Neptune, here in crescent phase.

*I prefer to be a dreamer among the humblest
with visions to be realized, than lord among
those without dreams and desires.*

Kahlil Gibran

Visionary Dreamer is dedicated to my father, Dennis Paul, with love and appreciation for his steadfast presence in my life, his quiet care, support and loving concern. For having faith in a sometimes wayward son, I would like to simply say 'Thank you', and wish you a happy seventieth year, and many more to come.

Contents

Dreams . . .

FOLLOWING THE DISCOVERY of Uranus in 1781, the attention of the Western astronomers was turned towards studying that new planet in our solar system, and after several years of intense research into the orbital motion of Uranus speculation developed that there was another hidden planet still to be found. Mathematical calculations suggested that the perturbations in the orbital pattern of Uranus were not accounted for by the gravitational force fields of the known neighbouring planets, and so the search commenced to find the next unknown planet.

For both mathematicians and astronomers, personal dreams of fame and acknowledgement throughout history and the acclamation of the scientific community gave fuel to their endeavours. The hypothetical orbit of this mystery planet was difficult to determine, because the pattern of Uranus tended to be erratic, and to the scientific instrumentation and analytical tools of that time the planet often appeared to arrive either ahead or behind its calculated and predicted route through the zodiac.

After years of focused and prolonged effort, and through studying the orbital motion irregularities of Uranus, both John Couch Adams of England and Leverrier of France arrived at a set of mathematical calculations which predicted a probable location of the mystery planet. Leverrier persuaded the German astronomer Johann Galle to explore a specific region of the sky, and from the Heinrich D'Arrest observatory in Berlin on 23 September 1846 a giant planet was located extremely close to the calculated and predicted point.

Neptune had rejoined the modern pantheon of planetary gods. A billion miles further away from Earth than Uranus, Neptune was totally invisible to the naked human eye. It is one of the giant planets, although smaller than Jupiter, Saturn and Uranus. The

Neptunian orbit is very extended, with one Neptune year equalling a time span of 165 Earth years. There is some evidence that suggests Galileo had noted the position of Neptune in 1613, but had decided that it was a star, failing to recognise it as a member of our solar system. The Voyager space flight passed Neptune in August 1989, prior to travelling beyond Pluto and into the depths of space.

Neptune emerged into the collective consciousness at a time when Western society was passing through the early phase of the transformation of the Industrial Revolution. Great social changes were underway, the new impulses already clashing with the established social order, and Neptune reflected those dreams and aspirations of the masses that had been inspired by the earlier American and French Revolutions. The social structures of the Western states began to enter a period of flux, and by 1848, ideas of revolution were again flourishing and becoming fashionable as a wave of civil revolts erupted in Europe as an attempt to undermine the existing powerful social elite.

The publication of the Communist Manifesto in 1848 shortly followed the Saturn–Neptune conjunction of 1846, and revealed several Neptunian characteristics. These include dreams and visions of a universal utopia, the establishing of a unified collective state and the ideal of creating a perfect society founded on mutual communal feeling and solidarity, united within a common and collective cause and purpose. This emphasis on collectivist, communistic and pluralist tendencies associates Neptune with general 'left wing' attitudes, where under the glamours and illusions of any political philosophy, the elevation of idealistic principles is often achieved at the expense of the human being and his own freedoms and opportunities for personal development.

Neptune is connected to tendencies of subversion, deceit, manipulative devious behaviour and tactics of entryism designed to erode social groupings from within. These are aspects of the nature of Neptunian influence, which is like the alchemical universal solvent which dissolves all boundaries and barriers. As Uranus had previously given a fatal shock to the Western states, Neptune arrived to dissolve the dying corpse of the old feudal and aristocratic traditions of power and social control. What was rising in the mid nineteenth century was the influence of a mercantile trading and business class, materialistic and aspirational, and an oppressed proletariat and working class, consequences of the recent industrial changes in society. Marxist communism also took advantage of a disillusionment with the role of the Church in maintaining elitist traditions, trying to stimulate a violent uprising of the masses by evoking an anti-religious sense of despair, with Marx describing religion as the opiate of the masses.

What was really stirring during this phase was the birth of a spirit of socialism, of a collective social group with dreams and visions of that ideal society and another impulse supporting the Uranian political visions, only this time more focused on the heart level of human life and relationship. Neptune represents the collective's need for aspiration, the hope of the perfect life, and these early politically founded ideals are the initial reaction of man to these transpersonal planetary influences affecting the collective mind and heart. Romanticism was emerging as another response, focused by such groups as the Pre-Raphaelite Brotherhood of artists, and the seeds of the century's culture began to break through the ground into the light of day.

Socialism itself began to emerge during the next Saturn–Neptune conjunction around 1882, to be followed by the Russian Revolution in 1917 immediately after another conjunction. The conjunction in Capricorn in 1989 is expected to signify another crucial step for humanity, and this is likely to be involved with Neptune dissolving traditional Saturnine thinking and attitudes related to exploiting Earth; it will be an ecological realisation that will begin to reshape man's future thinking, an awareness of our global reality and interdependence on living on One World.

Paralleling these early and socially transformative political responses to the influence of Neptune are two others, closely connected and representing two levels of human reaction to the visionary dreamer qualities of this planet. These are the emergence of a heart response to the suffering of others, as for example in the development of altruistic humanitarianism, Christian Socialism, the International Red Cross movement, human rights; and in the sudden original integration of a new spirituality in society, imported from the Wisdom teachings of the East.

From the early 1840s, Neptunian interests began to dominate man's awareness of the intangible influences within life, a counterbalance to the powerful prevailing materialistic attitude that was rapidly spreading and which the existing Church seemed unable to resist. Anaesthetics were introduced into surgical practice, making operations more bearable for the patient, and through the increased use of and attention to mesmerism and hypnosis (the name introduced in 1843), a greater fascination with the complexity of the human mind was born in society, a trend that would result in the birth of the psychoanalytic movement with Sigmund Freud.

Other dimensions of life were discovered through spiritualism, which became extremely popular and signified an attempt to dissolve those imprisoning boundaries of body consciousness and life by contacting the 'dead' and invisible guides talking through mediums, another Neptunian tendency. In 1848, the Fox sisters episode in America became a *cause célèbre*, and the public interest in table rapping, ectoplasmic projections and messages from deceased loved ones laid the foundations for an explosion of the Ageless Wisdom into the stagnating spiritual life of the Western nations. Of passing interest is the observation that, one hundred years on from the Fox sisters, UFOs were first sighted in 1948. Another form of 'message from the beyond' in a more contemporary appearance and context?

America became a seeding ground for several of these impulses, with Spiritualism, the Christian Science of Mary Baker Eddy, and Blavatsky's Theosophical Society forming with the assistance of Olcott and Judge in 1875. Blavatsky initially used the interest in spiritualism to become a public figure, and gained recognition by her use of psychic powers and reputed materialisations of the later Mahatma letters. In 1877, *Isis Unveiled* was published, causing a sensation and was later followed by *The Secret Doctrine*, seminal books for several generations of esoteric enquirers. For a society formed under a Neptunian influence, the theosophists were to experience periodic scandals of various kinds — over Blavatsky's 'genuine materialisations', Leadbeatter's homosexual tendencies and masturbation activities with young boys, and Krishnamurti's denial of his role as the new Messiah, Maitreya.

In addition to the theosophical espousal of the wisdom of the East, and the recognition of the non-uniqueness of Christian teachings amongst many other themes, this period in the late nineteenth century saw the first flow of Eastern holy men across to America and Europe, a flow that has since become a flood. Instead of perceiving the Orient as a less evolved and developed culture, the realisation began to dawn that spiritually they had much to offer the West; and of course, there was the appeal of a fascinating, colourful and glamorous culture to add some spice to life. Teachers like Vivekananda of the Ramakrishna Vedanta Movement and the Buddhist Angarika Dhammaphala were early emissaries, sowing seeds that have ripened into powerful trees bearing fruits today.

Prior to this absorption of Eastern mysticism into Western society, there was a parallel movement to original communism started in the Middle East that took the concepts of collective human behaviour and purpose and gave them a spiritual foundation, as though the overshadowing Neptune influence had anchored itself in both a political and religious context, where the visionary ideal was a world society characterised by universal brotherhood. This was the Baha'i faith which in several ways has acted as a forerunner to many of the ideas now circulating in respect of a new planetary politics for the twenty-first century and the dawning of the Aquarian Age.

In May 1844, the Persian Prophet, the Bab, declared that the Islamic era was coming to an end, and, like John the Baptist, declared that the advent of the Coming One was near. In 1863, a prisoner incarcerated in a Turkish prison with no contact with Western society declared that he, Baha'u'llah, was the expected one and issued his vision to the world. What Baha'u'llah declared was a proclamation for a new global society, the essential principles of a new world order. He was a founder of a detailed system of world social organisation, giving distinct practical directives for others to follow – and this from a cell! Transpersonal channels can manifest themselves anywhere, and often appear in the most unlikely of places.

The Baha'i movement still exists and is rooted within a socially orientated religious framework, yet it is of great interest to consider how this vision of Baha'u'llah is still being worked towards in the modern New Age and progressive thinking. It possesses a coherent concept of social unity and integration, and is a religious attempt to unify mankind by means of an inclusive and impersonal love and the power of faith and spiritual awareness. Amongst the essential principles of the movement are: the oneness of mankind; an independent investigation of truth without distorting prejudices; an acknowledgement that the roots of all religions are one; a belief that religion should be a cause of unity not dissension; an awareness that religion, science and reason should co-exist in unanimity, all indicating the same underlying reality; that all types of prejudice need to be transcended; that an objective for humanity is universal peace; that a universal education needs to be developed; that a spiritual solution of world economic problems needs to be achieved through interdependence; that a universal language is needed for mutual understanding and comprehension; and a universal legal tribunal should be established for dealing with individual grievances and international disputes. In addition to these aims, followers of Baha'u'llah were amongst the early advocates of liberation for women, seeing them as equal participants in all social and religious affairs, allowed no priesthood to serve as intermediaries between God and man, and believed that the absence of racial discrimination and colour prejudice was essential for world unity between races.

This was an imposing agenda, and still to be achieved by humanity, yet it is an indication of the type of Neptunian vision that was entering the collective mind at that time. The Baha'i movement is still being persecuted as heretical by Islamic fundamentalists today; yet the Baha'i vision still shines as bright as ever, because it is a holistic one and in accord with the evolutionary plan.

The effects of the Neptunian influence have been considerable over the last 150 years, and this book seeks to explore some of the themes and characteristics in greater depth, so that we can begin to grasp several of both the positive and negative tendencies of Neptune that affect ourselves and society. The influence of Neptune on images, fashions and art has been profound, especially with the development of television, photography and cinematography, and with design and appearance becoming the key to attracting consumer spending in modern society. The lure of images and the collective fashion of mimicking generates social trends and projections of assumed aspirations, ideals and fantasies which are instantly communicated to others through the medium of clothes and appearance. Image dominates society, often serving as a guiding embodiment of collective dreams and obsessions. Through film and popular music are transmitted those unconscious archetypes of humanity; and in a true Neptunian sense, our culture becomes increasingly fascinated by other worlds, and alternate realities. Escapist films like *Star Wars*, *Close Encounters*, *E.T.* and the plethora of fantasy, science fiction and horror films, novels and comics all attest to a collective need for imaginative worlds to explore.

Imagination dissolves false barriers and restrictive limitations by saying 'Why not think this . . . ?' Liberating the human imagination is one of the major keys to transforming the global life. By starting with personal dreams for betterment, moving onwards to visions of global unity and abundance, we may become effective and transformative visionary dreamers.

CHAPTER 1

The Neptune Myths

HE EMERGES THROUGH the ocean waves, towering over the frenzied seas, seaweed and water sliding off his gigantic body, droplets glistening in his wild long hair and beard as the majestic presence surveys his realm. Eyes tainted by divine madness and divine inspiration, he looks to see if any are drawing near to him, those brave sailors on the astral seas who are entranced by the trumpet sounds of the sea conches blown by his beautiful sea nymphs. When they arrive and see his glorious divinity, some will be driven mad and some will be spiritually inspired; it depends upon what mood he is in, and on the sailor's ability to withstand his presence. His trident gleams in the sunlight, like a beacon of hope, or source of glamorous despair; illuminated by the light or blinded by the light. His role is to make the light available; dispassionately he feels unresponsible for how mere mortals react to that shattering encounter of the realisation that awakens the heart.

This is Poseidon of the Greek world, Neptune in the Roman pantheon of gods. It is within the older Greek myths that the stories of this god are to be found, mainly because the Romans tended to absorb the Greek legends into their own gods with the result that initially Neptune was only a minor sea god of relative insignificance until the Romans became a seafaring nation. Once the seas became important to them, the power and importance of Poseidon was grafted onto Neptune so that due propitiation could be made to ensure safe sea journeys, although in Roman times no large cult developed around Poseidon–Neptune.

In the earliest Greek sources, Poseidon was originally more of an earthy god, known as the Consort of Da – which was the pre-Hellenic name of the powerful Earth goddess Da or Demeter – indicating the more dominant role of a matriarchal consciousness. As the early Greeks began to explore marine travel, Poseidon was transferred to become ruler of the seas, so that on land they could invoke the protection and favours of their familiar Earth Mother, and on sea invoke her Consort. The relative importance of Poseidon is indicated in his title 'the Husband of the Mother'.

In several ways, the Poseidon myths parallel those of Uranus, although on a lower turn of the involutionary spiral. Uranus was known as the First Father and was the 'husband' of the primal Earth Mother Gaia; he was the source of the divine ideation of the universe (see *Revolutionary Spirit: Exploring the Astrological Uranus* for more details). With Uranus and Gaia, the elements of Air and Earth united Mind and Body, and with Poseidon and Da it was Water and Earth or Emotions and Body that were fused, thus creating a threefold division of man. Also, as Uranus was overthrown by his progeny, so was Poseidon to be involved with his brother Zeus in overthrowing his father, Kronos, the son of Uranus. It seems that these ancient cosmological and evolutionary theories that were developed in the early phases of the Hellenic period, depended on the actual experience of the Greeks. When land-locked, they saw only the physical earth and skies, and so imbued them with exalted meaning, forming the concepts of as-sociated gods and goddesses of earth and sky; when they became intrepid sailors, the seas became part of their experience and so gods of the water needed to be similarly created or realised as existing.

Due to the early association of Poseidon with the land, there continued to be attributes of Earth powers still linked with him. He was known as the Lord of Earthquakes, Fertility and Vegeta-tion, the 'EarthShaker', although these correspondences have faded in relation to the oceanic imagery that now surrounds him. He was one of the Olympians born to Rhea and Kronos, and was subjected to the tendency of Kronos to swallow his children to pre-empt any possibility of his power being usurped in a similar way to his castrating of Uranus. Rhea became weary of producing so many children only for Kronos to reabsorb them again, so she hid Poseidon amongst a grazing flock of sheep and gave Kronos a foal to swallow as a substitute. As Kronos often took the form of a horse himself, he was not surprised at having fathered a foal, and so ate the substitute without any questions. By such means, Rhea succeeded in saving Poseidon and Zeus from Kronos, and eventually the rebellion occurred, as the two brothers poisoned Kronos and overthrew him and the Titans.

There is a further parallel to the overthrowing of the old gods by the new gods, in that Poseidon and Zeus banished Kronos and the Titans to Tartarus, securing their imprisonment by huge bronze doors fashioned by the skills of Poseidon. Previously in an earlier cycle, Kronos had been incarcerated in Tartarus by his father Uranus, and now the same cycle was repeated.

The most powerful of the three Olympian brothers drew lots to divide the domains of the world. Zeus chose the heavenly skies, Hades preferred the underworld, and Poseidon was granted the immense seas. Both the Earth and Olympus, the realm of the gods, were jointly owned, although Zeus was acknowledged as the King of the Gods, a decision that often rankled with Poseidon and which led to periodic disputes and either favouring or vindictiveness against certain humans, depending on their affinities to their patron gods.

Poseidon was often not content enough to be 'the holder of the Earth' and the god of the deep waters, and so he had a tendency to break his discontent by becoming involved in the lives of men, especially through seducing their women, or by contesting the rulership of the gods with his brother Zeus. Sometimes he varied this pattern by competing with his fellow gods and goddesses to be recognised as the patron deity of particular regions, and to have temples and prayers dedicated to him. Gods always desire attention; when people turn away from them, their power wanes and fades away.

The Greeks had a legend that Poseidon had been given an island continent which had a huge mountain at the physical heart of the land, where Evenor and his wife Leucipe lived with their daughter Cleito. Poseidon became infatuated with the beautiful Cleito, seduced her and fathered ten sons, one of whom was Atlas, who eventually became ruler of the land which was then named Atlantis in his honour. Reputedly, one of the major cities to exist on Atlantis was named Poseidonis, and dedicated to the god of the oceans. The myths of the destruction of Atlantis imply a Poseidon rage, as EarthShaker and Lord of the Seas; the water deluge flooded the continent, which descended under the waves, perhaps as a consequence of the impiety of the Atlanteans and their failure to control the results of their astral magic.

Poseidon was married to Amphitrite, who originally was a personification of the sea, but this role was taken over by Poseidon, who then proceeded to transform the seas into a more volatile nature. Amphitrite was a more gentle and placid goddess, who resignedly tolerated the many promiscuous affairs of her consort. One of their sons was Triton, another sea god in the form of a mer-man.

However, Poseidon was notorious for his ability as a shape-shifter, a seductive lover who appeared in a variety of different guises, similar to the general shape-changing abilities of many of the Greek gods. These usually took the forms of animals, and continued the theme of divinities being clothed or symbolised by animal images, a religious pattern that was probably ancient even by the Greek period. The Egyptian gods are represented by animal heads, and the Sphinx statue joined a lion's body with a human head. Even today, most magical and astrological approaches to the gods and planets are mediated through the use of associative images, the use of god forms and archetypes rather than any attempt to approach the inner mysteries directly without the trans-forming and stepping-down quality of filters. As in the Old Testament, there is the warning not to look directly at God, and the fears of physical or spiritual blinding.

The animal forms that Poseidon favoured were stallions, white horses, giant bulls, rams, dolphins and, less frequently, birds and other humans. He was usually impressive, and gained the favours of many women who fell under his seductive spell. He fathered many children and strange mixed offspring of animal and human intercourse. With Theophane, who he approached as a ram, the result was the glowing ram of the famous golden fleece, which became the glittering goal of the Argonauts in the famous legends of seafaring adventure. Poseidon was also responsible for father-ing several of the crew of the Argo, as well as the hero Theseus. In addition to his female conquests, possibly reflecting Greek tastes, he was not immune to the attractive charms of beautiful young men, and often maintained a few male favourites as well.

It was Poseidon who sent a beautiful white bull to King Minos of Crete as an offering of sacrifice to the gods of Olympus. Poseidon was also known as the 'Lord of the Bulls', and Minos was foolish enough to choose to keep this bull and to substitute another as the sacrificial victim. The gods were angry at this action, and chose to punish Minos by bewitching his wife Pasiphae to fall in love with a common herd bull. The result of their union was the Minotaurus, the creature with a man's body and a bull's head. There are echoes of the Age of Taurus in this myth, possibly indicating a time 6000 years ago, rather as the Egyptian Sphinx may reflect the Age of Leo even further back in time. Minos was ashamed of the consequences of his action, and hid the Minotaurus in a labyrinth of caves near his capital Knossos, feeding it young youths and maidens who had been sent to Crete as a tribute from the state of Athens. Eventually Theseus was sent as a sacrifice to Crete, and on arriving at the king's palace was seen by Minos's daughter, Ariadne, who fell in love with this special young man. She helped Theseus to escape from the cave labyrinth by providing him with a thread which he followed to discover the way out after slaying the Minotaurus by a sword which she had secretly given him. Theseus became a hero, and married Ariadne, although a later legend suggests that they did not live happily ever after, but that Theseus deserted her on the island of Naxos, where eventually she was found and became the wife of Dionysus, who also has Poseidon–Neptune associations.

Eventually there developed the Dionysian cults, those ecstatic cults of fertility, nature and wine, which were often associated with the mysteries and enchantments of music and poetry, and the inspired or possessed creative spirit. Dionysus has been described as the god image of 'creative madness' or the 'irrational ground of the world', and in the Roman guise is Bacchus, the Lord of Bacchanalia, whose drunken feasts and orgies were so beloved by the degenerating Roman nobility.

Dionysus is associated with the concept of instinctual unity and the participation mystique with nature and the animal kingdom which led to an experience of ecstasy, often through the inebriating effects of drugs and wine, which apparently opened psychic doors to release heightened and exalted feelings. In effect, the experience was of contacting the collective feeling life, where the need to transcend the separate identity was fulfilled by merging with the whole. The inspiration for the initial spiritualised Dionysian cult (before a later degeneration) was that of cleansing and redeeming the psyche through total immersion in the oceanic unconscious mind, an experience that was felt as a religious conversion, and would later re-emerge in the form of the Christian and Essenic Rite of Baptism as one of the most ancient mystery rituals.

Poseidon had a strained relationship with the goddess Athene, who was a daughter of Zeus, and associated with wisdom, war and industry, and whose symbol was the owl. Once, Poseidon had joined with Athene and Hera (wife and sister of Zeus) in a conspiracy to wrest control of Olympus and the rulership of the gods, but this had dismally failed. Sometimes Poseidon clashed with Athene over being chosen by states and cities as their patron deities; losing to her threw Poseidon into violent rages, who aggressively drove his two-horse sea chariot across the waves, causing great storms and tempests, and tossing vulnerable ships to their doom. Inland states tended to choose Athene, as they had little need of a sea god's patronage, whereas the coastal towns sensibly chose the goodwill and support of Poseidon.

There is an infamous incident in the legends where Poseidon's seductive prowess was not always beneficial to the poor women who responded to him. This is the story of Medusa, immortalised as the Gorgon, the evil and ugly woman with writhing snakes as her hair, and who turned anyone who looked at her into stone. Poseidon seduced the young, innocent and beautiful woman in the Temple of Athene, and the goddess, infuriated by his presumption of taking the temple priestess, transformed Medusa into the Gorgon, a baleful harridan with an evil eye. Another variation of this 'seduction' is that Poseidon raped Medusa, and that the terrifying visage that became frozen on her face was an expression of horror and outrage at Poseidon's act. This is reminiscent of the abduction and rape of Persephone by Hades–Pluto (see *Phoenix Rising: Exploring the Astrological Pluto* for more details).

The mating of Poseidon and Medusa resulted in the offspring of the magical winged horse Pegasus, although birth was denied due to Medusa's hatred of Poseidon until the hero Perseus succeeded in killing Medusa by reflecting her own basilisk gaze back to her through his mirror-like shield. Pegasus then sprang fully grown out of her dismembered body, and as a winged horse symbolised the creation of a bridge across the opposites, whereby the creatures of Earth were now allowed to ascend into the spiritual worlds.

In the legends associated with the initiatory cycle of the Hercules myths, Poseidon helped the hero by giving him a gift of powerful horses. The image of horses and chariot also reoccur in the Tarot trump VII, where the king's chariot is drawn by his control over the horses. In Alice Bailey's book *The Labours of Hercules*, which traces the initiatory path of the spiritual aspirant and disciple through the signs of the zodiac, both horses and Poseidon–Neptune as the deity of the watery, fluid, emotional and astral depths symbolise the human tendency to become lost and uncontrolled by an obsessive line of thought or by the passions of emotional reactions. The positive aspect of this tendency – symbolised by the king controlling the horses – is that a rightly used and subordinated fluidic emotional nature offers the enriching power of feeling and sensitivity, and that under the guiding influence of the inner soul is one of man's greatest potential assets, as well as being a major source of his multiple problems in the unintegrated individual. It is through emotional sensitivity that we can be in empathy and *en rapport* with our world and fellow man. Poseidon's gift to Hercules was an extremely valuable one, although obviously Hercules had to first learn how to safely control the horses through purifying his own volatile emotional level.

Poseidon's power symbol and seal of office is the trident, and the glyph of the astrological symbol for Neptune is the trident pictograph. This symbol includes the semi-circle of soul or the mind and evolving human spirit, which is pierced by the cross of matter, resulting in a three-pronged fork. This fork symbolises the three levels of the human being which require purification by Neptune's divine waters: the physical body and senses, the astral–emotional–desire nature, and the lower mental and separate egoic centre. A successful achievement of this involves the ideal of the crescent of soul breaking free of the crucifixion of matter, as the formless rises high above the world of form, and crystallised matter is dissolved and liberated as a consequence of a successful completion of an evolutionary task which leads to the transcendence of the physical plane, and the walking of the path of transpersonal development.

This trident symbol also reoccurs with the Hindu Shiva and the British Britannia figure, as well as being a weapon in the debased form of Roman gladiatorial contests. In Hinduism, the attributes of Poseidon are reflected in three gods: Idapati is described as the Master of the Waters; Narayana as the Mover on the Waters; and Varuna as Lord of the Oceans. These are also considered to be aspects of Vishnu, who has been identified with the principle of Zeus–Jupiter. In fact, prior to the discovery of Neptune, Jupiter was thought to be the ruler of horses through Sagittarius and ruler too of Pisces in the older traditional rulerships; now, Pisces is co-ruled by Jupiter and Neptune. All three of the transpersonal planets of Uranus, Neptune and Pluto were physically unknown to the ancients, but in their mystery temples the powers and principles of these hidden planets were recognised and intuited, and so they became anchored through myth and legends.

Whilst Poseidon and Neptune are portrayed as male deities, powerful gods in cult and myth, currently Neptune is perceived as essentially a planet that embodies recognisable feminine principles. Obviously these planetary gods and archetypes are asexual, androgynous or hermaphrodite at best, and essentially beyond our conceptual and physical sexual dualism; but it can still be valuable to conceive and approach them through a 'sexual filter'. We are enabled to grasp the hem of their complex natures, which, with the transpersonal planets, tend to flow and merge together as a trinity of gods whose function is to stimulate humanity to follow the unitive and transpersonal path. Establishing distinct boundaries between Uranus, Neptune and Pluto is virtually impossible, although indicating their different ways and levels of functioning and their impact on man is more revealing. Contacting these levels brings one into realms of paradox and contradiction; with one hand they give a holy and divine blessing, with the other they shatter lives and societies; with one face, the individual perceives the radiance of 'God'; turning the other face, one can see the malevolent smile of the 'Devil'. Certainly they are beyond our poor conceptions of good and evil, beyond all of our dualistic thought patterns. Only by approaching them from a unified consciousness can we truly have a glimpse of their nature.

Retreating back into personifying Neptune as a feminine planetary principle, we see that it is often connected with archetypal images of woman, sometimes a martyr, sometimes a sacrificial quality, or a victim, but invariably involving impressions of vulnerability and suffering. The image of the Virgin Mary is one such mediatrix to which many respond deeply. In this are the aspects of positive feminine qualities – receptive, exalted and self-sacrificial love. This highly developed and selfless nature of love reaches its apotheosis in the romanticism and spiritual ideal of the Holy Grail mythos. Neptune is identified with inspiring the path of mystical devotion, and embodies the heart and love aspect of the Grail. Uranus, on the other hand, reflects the mind and light level, and Pluto the physical anchoring in the service of the Grail Knight towards the spiritual revitalising of the wasteland of earthly life.

Within each one of us, the deep oceanic waters of Poseidon's realm stir in perpetual motion. Diving deep into these depths in search of the god's undersea palace is a quest that can attract many, artists as well as mystics, but in which many can regrettably drown when out of their depth, especially if they persist in retaining the old personality patterns. In Poseidon's temple, standing before him seated on his throne, and requesting that pearl of great price, all that you can do is to surrender to his watery realm; and water has the power of gradual erosion, of earth and rock. In that temple, you have no alternative but to accept the transforming impact of dissolution. Poseidon's seduction is total, but so is the gift that he offers.

CHAPTER 2

Images of the Astrological Neptune

NEPTUNE HAS THE MOST subtle and elusive impact of the transpersonal planets, yet despite what may seem a gentle touch – a mild sea breeze invigorating the senses – its effects are extremely powerful and transformatory. Whenever Neptune is activated, there are no resistant barriers that can be erected which can successfully defend against its eroding potency. If the waters of the physical plane can re-create continents over time, by eroding the coastal shore line, by flooding land, or by denuding a fertile area of sustenance through drought, then how can we evade the influence of the Cosmic Waters of Life?

As the Koran states: 'From water all life comes'; and in the Bible one of the first divine commands was that water should cover the face of the Earth. In this we see indications that primordial life was associated with oceanic depths, and that the mystery of life with its beginnings and possible ends emerges from out of that undersea realm. Contemporary science tends to support this conception – that life was somehow formed out of ancient seas – speculating that chemical reactions occurred which created the bio-chemical building blocks for later physical life.

The oceanic and sea imagery that has coalesced around the astrological Neptune is very apt, and in modern astrology is associated with Jungian theories of the collective unconscious. Here, there are images of vast inner seas and realms of paradox and ambiguity, a psychological world that is unknown and unexplored, where dragons lie as in the old maps, with areas marked symbolising violent storms and the lurking dangers of Scylla the devouring sea monster and Charybdis the whirlpool, those challenges facing intrepid sailors attempting to navigate the narrow straits.

The world seas also symbolise the female womb, the physical

source of life, and the image of the maternal woman or the divine feminine, the gateway for life to pass from another world/level into this. And so, whilst Neptune is portrayed as a dominating male in the Greek patriarchic culture – as a water deity – the symbolism is primarily feminine, and water has been correspondingly associated with the realms of emotions, feelings, love, imagination and artistic creation.

The difficulty in entering Neptune's world is that of learning how to survive; swimming in waters of confusion is only possible when staying on the surface, and even peering down only reveals a fraction of his kingdom, enough to fascinate but not sufficient to illuminate and inspire. It is like placing a straight stick into water: you know that it is straight yet the impression you receive from the part under the water is that it isn't – the issue of illusion and reality. The only way to really begin to understand the complexity of Neptune is to drown through undergoing the ancient rites of baptism in water (see Chapter 7), where the waters will disintegrate the limiting personality and cleanse and purify. The intellect and separate self will drown in the inner oceanic depths prior to the resurrection of the holistic self.

NEPTUNE'S FUNCTION

Neptune has the power of dissolution, and performs the function of breaking down antiquated life forms and structures on the physical, emotional and mental levels. This is achieved by a transcendence of inhibiting boundaries through dissolving spurious limitations and entering a broader sphere of universality and expansion in order to liberate and release the imprisoned self and spirit, so that a more suitable form can be created to embody the next step in development. What Neptune does is to erode the definitions and restrictions imposed by the Saturnian thresholds, those patterns of thought, belief or identification which Saturn establishes as consensus reality and collective living. Neptune seeks to transform these – at the appropriate time when a previously progressive step has become reactionary and crystallised – into more inclusive, holistic and universal systems.

Neptune symbolises and represents the urge for transcendence, the moving-beyond that is so ingrained in the human spirit and which is a reflection of the programmed evolutionary impulse.

It is a search for greater freedom from the limitation of the personal and separated self and the material environment, a response to the inner evocatory call of the undines (water spirits) to return into the consciousness of oneness and to merge again with the whole. It is a principle of repolarisation, where the purpose is that of self-redemption and the means is through a transformed relationship of self and society.

Neptune integrates through a process of disintegration by slowly dissolving barriers and psychological patterns of behaviour. Uranus tends to trigger an integrative process by shocking and cracking structures, perhaps by a sudden experience that changes a static lifestyle; and Pluto subverts through deep undermining leading to an eventual transformative subsidence and rebirth. Essentially, Neptune seeks to dissolve form itself, and on touching form reduces it again to its formless origins, reflecting the alchemical *solve et coagula*. The eternal message of Neptune is to look beyond the physical experiences within the worlds of matter and psychological structures, to discern that subtle and invisible foundational world of the higher spirit and universal self, and to exalt the personal emotions and nervous system to such a pitch that sensitivity, attunement and intuition can occur. From that point, inspiration can be transmitted into the world.

As part of this process, the personal imagination is aligned with the archetypal dimension, especially in the context of collective feeling and emotional levels – the World Heart – and the contact is then released in creative artistic expression. If inspired, this is demonstrated in the level of shared emotional empathic affinity, as in music, literature, art, theatre and dance, which resonate deeply in the realms of collective common experience, where the emotions expressed are familiar and evocatory, or collective imagery is employed to generate a predictable response. There is a price exacted for this internal contact, however, and this involves the transformation or sacrifice of the separate ego as the individual becomes more universalised in his effect and awareness; the recognition is of what he shares with all life, rather than any illusions concerning his separate elevation and achievement. He perceives that he is a creative channel rather than a creator, and acknowledges the pre-eminence of the Eternal Artist.

It appears that these inner channels are opened through the right hemisphere of the brain, and that each of the transpersonal planets – Uranus, Neptune and Pluto – is contacted through activating that part of the brain. This results in the dissolution of the individual Saturn patterns which are associated mainly with left-brain activity and characteristics. Once the transpersonal influences are awakened in the individual (through artistic or spiritual aspirations), there can be a gradual bridging across the hemispheres, bringing them into synchronisation; in Norse myth, this has been termed *Bifrost, the Rainbow Bridge*. Eventually the channel of inspiration and communication becomes established and the mid brain co-ordinates the holistic perception. A more extended discussion of this can be found in my *Revolutionary Spirit: Exploring the Astrological Uranus*.

NEPTUNE: THE UNIVERSAL SOLVENT

This intrinsic quality of Neptune becomes increasingly active in situations where there is a longstanding inhibition or repression within the personal or collective psyche. It is as if once a certain degree of crystallisation has occurred then the process of dissolution is automatically activated. In astrology, this is often indicated by transits into new houses, transiting aspects or progressions, and several life cycles of various planetary influences.

Each personality contains an Achilles' heel in some area, where the seeds of personal dissolution lie latent, where a fog of glamour or illusion may prohibit clarity of self-perception, or where personal characteristics may – if unconsciously followed – lead eventually to a traumative confrontation. It is often through this blind spot that the Neptunian demand for sacrifice for the benefit of the collective may be made.

There is a psychological belief that there is a death urge latent in most people (Freud termed this *thanatos*), which is primarily an impulse for the disintegration of the individual consciousness. It is the Saturn barriers of the ego that support the urge of self-preservation, and thoughts and threats of possible dissolution are responded to with fear and inner shaking, associating them with final physical death and seeking to repress them into the unconscious mind. Neptune and Saturn function as two polarities, an eternal conflict between them as Neptune seeks to discover freedom in unity and universalisation, with Kronos–Saturn still trying to prevent this from happening by swallowing the first signs of independent life in Poseidon–Neptune.

The egoic Saturnine walls may be cracked by an Uranian impact, some type of turning point in the life reached, and following on from that, the Neptunian influence continues the process. As Neptune is associated as a planet of metaphysical thinking, involving ambiguity, paradox, contradiction, non-linear thought sequences, imagery and symbols, one effect of its activation on the human mind is to dissolve those ordering patterns of consciousness and the rational mind.

The universal solvent is an alchemical phrase which conceives of a powerful 'acid' which can disintegrate the cohesiveness of repressive barriers and boundaries, and when applied is irreversible in effect. Slowly an inner change begins to seep into the conscious mind of a collapsing deep foundation, where internal worlds begin to intersect and overlap, where life securities fade away as an unknown world dawns on the awareness. Self-preoccupation and introspection dominate, and often the consciousness is turned towards a dreamy and astral sensitivity, a little other-worldly, possibly mystically attuned, but often exhibiting signs of timelessness, being spaced-out, unreal as the separate self slowly sinks under the waves and becomes less conscious of the demands of the external world. An interiorisation occurs, a withdrawal in some respect.

What happens within the individual when this process happens? The Neptune influence can take place through transit, or through the position of the natal house, using those channels established by natal planetary aspects. Confusion, disorientation, lack of focus, indecision, diminution of self-assurance and psychological certainties are all common effects, and the sense is of entering an internal state of fluidity where the familiar patterns of life have been swept away by some unseen tide. There is a psychological trembling, a state of fear as supports are eroded in that limbo-transition phase and old motivational patterns of behaviour often lose their spark of life. With such inner activity occurring, there can be a loss of interest and involvement with the external world, a lack of meaning and purpose can ensue. A psychological isolation is common, where personal awareness remains and is acute, yet the sense of self is extremely diffused and apparently lacks a defined centre.

What can you do when you feel as if you are drowning, when the waters of the universal solvent are dissolving every support that you try to cling to, and the waters are slowly rising over your head? Many panic, and make the situation worse by acting in ignorance of what is actually occurring. Many nervous and psychological illnesses are stimulated by the activity of the trans-personal planets operating in personalities that have no suppor-tive conceptual framework which can create a context for the experience. Neptune is often linked to hysteria and hallucinatory experiences, and to types of mental illness. Many sensitive souls have been submerged in the experience of opening to the seas of collective feeling, through the transcendent irrational shock of a realm where there are no boundaries and no measurable depths; it is more than the personality structure can bear. The individual is sacrificed to identify with the unity of the whole in a paroxysm of universalised emotional empathy, and as a separate personality ceases to emerge from the experience intact. Such an act of attemp-ted self-redemption can be deliberate, as in the mystical path, or one which apparently occurs unwanted and unasked for; for the mystic it can prove to be a liberating experience; for the unpre-pared, it can devastate life.

It is the initial passage through this phase of the experience that is crucial, and it must be pointed out that degrees of the Neptune experience vary considerably; it is certainly not inevitable that the experience will be so profound. But certain common experiences are likely, and these are repetitive patterns of human reaction to this energy.

The worst period of inner confusion and disorientation occurs at the earliest phase, especially when you realise that something unsettling has happened without you really noticing it; Neptune is a master of disguise, and often quietly comes up behind you, touches with that dissolving effect and disappears again. You only realise that something has happened when you go to nod your head and your head falls off. It is a period when transition is happening, and you are in a state of inner flux, lacking sufficient anchors to keep you safe by the familiar shoreline. A lack of grounding earth is common, and you still persist in trying to categorise this new experience in terms of the old patterned order, by repeating the old established attitudes, thoughts, values and behaviour. It doesn't work, and this failure may have to be experi-enced before you realise that this is indeed the case.

Resistance is inevitable in most people, but that inner struggle to restore the old ways becomes a futile task as the life is just draining away from them. It is almost like attempting to dam the dyke wall with your finger; the pressure still builds up and further fissures begin to leak the pent-up waters, and in any case, you can't do that forever! It is the struggle between two polarised tendencies; the issue is how to contain that boundless energy within those limiting Saturn structures, how to stop the Saturn walls from collapsing, and you will eventually understand that they are not strong enough and that Neptunian change is inevitable.

THE SATURN–NEPTUNE POLARITY

This involves the direct challenge of two main alternative routes in life; one is to repress those inner promptings, striving to ignore those intensifying inner stresses and tensions, denying the need for change and struggling to maintain those established patterns in the psyche, possibly resorting to forms of addiction as a way to evade awareness of a meaningless state; the other is to find a way forward into a more holistic and unifying state of being and self-perception. It is necessary to discover a route of positive and constructive transformation.

The friction and stress between an activated Neptune and resis-tant Saturn result in several consequences. There is likely to be a decrease in physical vitality and motivation, where the demands of everyday life loom larger and more insistent, at a time when you feel less able to successfully cope with them. Self-confidence diminishes, and you may begin to indulge in a more active fantasy and day-dreaming life, trying to fulfil those inner yearnings and desires through dreams or by planning impractical schemes that it is beyond your ability to implement. Moodiness may become common, especially emotional swings, as if you are being tossed around on a pendulum between Neptune and Saturn; anxiety, discontent and disillusionment are regular companions. En-thusiasms wax and wane, making persistence difficult and aims hard to achieve.

A lack of satisfaction in the natal house of Neptune or in a transiting house is usual, or in a house where aspects may be made by transiting Neptune to a personal planet. That area of life will be agitated, and yet it may prove difficult to identify the actual nature of the inner problem to be resolved; Neptune is slippery, and as you approach near to a partial resolution, seeks to divert your attention in order to escape from your grasp, until a more complete transformation is close to being achieved. Often, you'll feel creatively blocked or you'll struggle to clarify your objectives and purposes, unable to make firm decisions due to excessive fluctuations in that diffused self.

Many prefer to withdraw into their own nature, trying to minimise discomfort by reducing life involvement, or responding to the call of the inner depths magnetically pulling them inward. In this internalised state, many negative psychological patterns emerge, based on the partial death of the Saturn ego and emerging as self-doubts, inertia, passivity, feelings of paranoia and threat, a refusal of relationships, possibly attitudes and feelings associated with martyrdom, sacrifice, victim abuse and dependency. The complexity of reality becomes too much, and a partial temporary 'shutdown' can happen, both as an inner healing process or as a process of denial and rejection through asserting the supremacy of the Saturn structures, which can result in nervous breakdowns. The lifestyle can begin to fall apart as a consequence of dissatisfaction and discontent. A loss of direction occurs, yet the old has been dissolved and the lack of connection to it brings considerable anguish and a yearning for those familiar, once meaningful contacts. Going through the motions is common, and is a likely response to this phase, because until a new light begins to shine what else can be done? The physical-plane lifestyle may display signs of stress, and financial control often lapses as energies are apparently withdrawn back into the unconscious self. Emptiness is the main experience, an internal vacuum that seems to be filled by nothing as life loses vitality and colour, and all the channels of old fulfilment seem blocked or denuded of energy.

NEPTUNE–SATURN: A POSITIVE INTEGRATION APPROACH

Dealing with the Neptune–Saturn polarity within yourself can be difficult and challenging, as both these energies seem to be pulling you in contrary directions, with the result that you experience this as a stressful reaction. It is necessary to determine the natural tendencies of each of these planets, and then to try to decide how a natural balance can be created in your life so that a creative polarity can emerge, and not one where splits occur as you temporarily side with one planet in favour of the other; otherwise, over time, Neptune will probably be relegated back into the unconscious mind. In effect, you should try to use the qualities of Saturn to liberate the positive characteristics of Neptune, or vice versa.

It is crucial at this point to begin a process of reorganisation and self re-evaluation by taking a new look at everything you have established in the past, including your whole sense of identity, and try to discover why it is 'hat it now fails to satisfy or work. You have become a wasteland, and need the fructifying, invigorating and revitalising Neptunian waters to flow through you in order for the resurrection to happen. Having lost that sense of meaning and value, you now need to discover a more integrated replacement, where more inclusive structures are erected which are suitable for the next stage.

This process may require a determined look at how you are evaluating your current situation. Answers are often dependent on the nature of the questions that are asked, and it may be that you need greater clarity in order to determine what the issues requiring resolution actually are. Such inner questioning may take several forms, and there are many techniques of stimulating inner guidance and support which should be considered as means of help in moving through this phase. The following questions are suggested as a guideline for this enquiry, and are applicable to the experiencing of the universal solvent, the Saturn–Neptune polarity and Neptune transits.

Do you know what you want in life? Look at your physical, emotional and mental needs and desires and identify what you believe you want.

Are these really lacking in your life, or are your deeper needs unrecognised and unrealised? Reconsider, and see if you are identifying any discontent with the wrong causes; perhaps looking again at your life through a new perspective could rejuvenate your spirits by greater appreciation of what you have.

Consider these needs on each level of your being; physical needs, emotional and feeling needs, mind and intellectual needs, and those deeper spiritual needs. See how they may differ and contradict, and where you can take easy steps to fulfil each one of them.

Determine what is uniquely and personally meaningful to you; what makes you feel good with yourself and life, what makes you more loving and content. And then decide to change your life in order to experience these more. Follow the paths of your enjoyment.

See how and in which ways you feel confused. Which are the key areas affected? Why do you choose to maintain this confusion? What can you do to consciously dissipate it? Are you avoiding making decisions by pleading inner confusion to yourself? Is it a delaying tactic? Are you willing to transform this confusion and become dynamic and decisive? Is that dilemma just a means of avoiding change?

What is it that stops you changing? Is it fear, insecurity, lack of confidence in your abilities?

If someone gave you the key to achieve your secret ideal dream, would you take it and turn the lock? Or would you create a thousand and one reasons for evading the challenge? Look at the self-chosen ways in which you attempt to stop yourself from achieving your dreams. See those unconscious beliefs, attitudes and personality characteristics that inhibit your success. And then ask yourself, why should they? And then decide to move forward irrespective of their influence, and affirm that success and satisfaction is yours for the asking.

What do you gain from remaining in your present situation? Especially when it fails to provide meaning, purpose and enjoyment in your life.

Are you looking for the essence of life, a quality both of living experience and of yourself that fulfils? What part of you stands in your own way of experiencing a richer life? Are you prepared to let it stand there until you die?

Become more clear in your life intentions. Make plans to achieve them and at least walk on the right road to that destination. What may need to be left at the roadside to lighten your load, so that those dreams can be safely attained? Are you willing to sacrifice for that? How much are your dreams worth to you?

Are you willing to move beyond your familiar ground? To explore new lands? Ask yourself, why not change?

And believe in the fact that positive change will happen, affirm this and visualise the way that your ideal dream will be realised and make you content on every level of your life. Evoke the Neptunian faith that it will be so.

Yet we need to acknowledge the necessary role of Saturn in the process of allowing the Neptunian energies greater freedom in our lives. Saturn shows us our temporary limitations; rapidly expanding beyond our natural capabilities is not often wise, and can create additional problems, so a more gradual development is safer, and Saturn will provide us with the brakes when necessary. Additionally, the form- and structure-making tendency of Saturn will force us to reassess our Neptunian dreams and fantasies, sifting them for their hidden potential and encouraging us to turn them into an active reality through living out those ideals and spiritual visions. It is Saturn that gives us the discipline to serve the needs of the planetary consciousness of Gaia, the urge to manifest spirituality on Earth, whereas Neptune tends to transcend the demands and restrictions of form life. Neptune gives us a rekindling inspiration, an energy to transform life and patterns of inertia through imagining attractive alternative dreams as pointers to new potential directions. Fusing both Saturn and Neptune together as a working partnership can create a powerful platform to work from, a point of centre where the needs of both idealism and practical application are recognised, and from where a clarified purpose can be attained.

Following such a process transforms the situation from one of being merely passive to one of co-operating with the higher Neptunian impulse, and of taking the personal life into your own hands instead of being a victim of the god's capricious whims. Neptune is not really content with remaining locked in your unconscious mind; he wants to shine through into your world and be acknowledged as the creative and inspirational power that he is.

Essentially, you have to decide to direct this transformation so that its positive intention is revealed in the constructive changes that come about in your inner state and lifestyle. Self-acceptance is vital, as is an acknowledgement of this transition that faces you; a new direction and purpose may need to be established so that the energies can flow easily into a new pattern of expression, one which succeeds in fusing both personal and social needs together, so that beneficial consequences for the whole can occur. Looking back towards old redundant inner patterns is futile now; the way onwards is to build your new future. Many who enter this phase of transitional transformation become attracted towards spiritual and holistic teachings (which appear in many guises), and are especially attracted towards more unconventional teachings which relate to experiences of inner dissolution and rebirth. Slowly, a new world and perception comes into being, and like the sun rising over the horizon of a new day, casts its dawn light and so begins to heal and integrate that shaken internal state. Meaning reappears in life, confusion lifts, and life seems to become reassembled as the time of chaos passes; yet, whilst chaos can be a painful state to endure, it marks the inner burning ground of moving between an inhibiting pattern and one which offers progression and opportunity, and in that sense, chaos should be welcomed and acknowledged as a liberator.

NEPTUNE AND SOCIAL RESPONSIBILITY

The superficial effects of Neptune in society are displayed in the transiency of fashion and glamorous trends, where creativity is devoted to generating consumer interest and business profit, or within the sphere of leisure activity or mass entertainment as in popular music styles. These changing externalised patterns of expression are symbolic of the underlying emotional desires of the collective, and one of the most revealing modern movements has been the rapid growth over the last thirty years of the international youth culture.

As Neptune passes through the signs, indications are displayed of the prime images of social fantasies, ideals and aspirations within the collective unconscious, and obvious signs of these are through the culture's images expressed by film, music, theatre, art and literature. The transiency of social fashion mimics the changing swirling nature of flowing waters, although – unlike the statement of Heraclitus that you cannot step into the same water twice – modern fashion tends to undergo periodic recycling of previous styles. For many, being a dedicated follower of fashion reveals their innate urge to follow the path of a collective image, a form of group involvement.

Whilst Neptune rules self-image and projected images, what seems to become essential to many is a form of social obligation and responsibility. This has many similarities with the mystical impulse, although perhaps expressed in a less religious context, and may just emerge as a natural response to that sense of human solidarity and community rather than as an impulse to dissolve in an other-worldly spirituality. This can be demonstrated too as surrendering to a creative energy, one which uses the individual as a means to creatively express an emotionally resonating collective group image.

What appears to be a common reaction to Neptune are personal feelings of social obligation, guilt, conscience and civic or spiritual duties. If the individual has been influenced by religious teachings, then these are likely to be the route by which these feelings announce their presence; equally the route may be through political conditioning and political ideologies. Christian religious symbolism is rife with the sacrificial image, one which attracts and repels in equal measure, and to which many only give lip-service in the actual performance of their lives.

Part of this inner anxiety arises from a need for deeper social and collective integration. This should not be a reversal towards an unconscious group identification and a diminution of personal identity, but should be a positive move to a higher identification with the oneness of all life. It is a feeling tone of unity, redeemed from that imprisonment in the social unconscious that is manifest in the social tendency of repressing and inhibiting the feeling function of people. Such inhibition, under the inevitable pressures of life, erupts into distorted and often violent types of expression against social peace and harmony.

This sense of social responsibility which is stimulated by Neptune's activity can pose various problems for the individual. Often the source of internal disquiet is not recognised or identified; it just gnaws away, prodding the person to look in certain directions. Sometimes it reveals its presence by a sense of ennui, of existential angst, where life seems to lack something vital. A transformation of inner focus and self-perspective is required, where the dualism between self and other is sequentially broken down by the emergence of a compassionate spirit.

Sensitivity to the needs and suffering of others is intensified, especially with respect to those in the world whose life options and choices are constrained by social circumstances and lack of caring. Whilst there may be a personal element of mitigating guilt or conscience related to caring about others' suffering, positive results can be achieved in the broader society. Many become highly motivated by realising that they can make a difference and help compensate for social chaos if the will and commitment to do so is present and active within them. The development of this trend in human development is expanded in Chapter 8.

Many people adopt a self-sacrificial persona, devoted to using their lives in an attempt to fulfil an inner impulse of social obligation; this is often through a highly developed religious ideal, such as through the work of Mother Teresa in India, who exemplifies a Christian image of selfless service in the impoverished and destitute slum areas. For the sacrifice to a collective need, some aspect of the personal life needs to be relinquished, and this is ultimately a reflection of the psyche which is willing to transcend individual desires in order to bring about a benefit for the larger group. In furthering the needs of the whole, the part is often relatively dispensable. Neptune symbolises the aspect of mass emotional response, and the unity and integration that Neptune represents is that of emotional identification and empathy, especially with those figures who appear to have been victimised by the circumstances of life.

In modern societies, despite the advances made in Western cultures in the role and status of women, many women are expected to perform a lifelong sacrifice to male dominance in terms of their more menial tasks in life, in bearing and raising children, and in a general subservience to men. Such roles are often validated by religious scriptures and social conditioning, and severely restrict the opportunities for self-development and the option to follow a personal path through life. For many women, personal needs and desires are sacrificed to the good of the family unit. Neptune is considered to be essentially a 'feminine planet', connected to the archetypal image of the *mediatrix*, which is often associated with the concept of the suffering woman who becomes open to the suffering of the world.

NEPTUNE AND THE INDIVIDUAL RESPONSE

For most individuals, Neptune operates in an unconscious manner, and indeed, seems to activate extremely deep-seated patterns in the unconscious mind which are often tainted by personal glamours and illusions which makes clear perception extremely difficult. This is partly because the ego will turn a blind eye towards a presence in the psyche which seeks to undermine the temporary reality of the ego's structural foundations by attempting denial, ignoring that energy, or by surrounding it with taboo-like injunctions and dangers.

A lack of integrating Neptune is common, and one sign of this occurring in the individual is the tendency of *projection*, where experiences and events in life have been unconsciously attracted so that Neptune can find a route through into the life. What happens is that the individual unconsciously makes certain choices and decisions that lead him inexorably towards the destination where

Neptune is waiting. Before he fully realises what is happening, his blindness has propelled him into an extremely vulnerable situation, where his power is stripped away from him and he is defenceless; the only way out of the situation is to sacrifice something that had previously been of great importance, and his old foundations crumble and dissolve as Neptune's purpose has been achieved. Often part of the realisation that emerges as a consequence of this experience is that of a sense of fate, the unknown manipulative hand against which he is powerless; when touched by that presence, his emotions and feelings rise in awe and fear. Neptune was called the EarthShaker, and the ground of ego truly trembles at his approach.

As feelings and emotions come flooding to the surface of the conscious mind, this tidal wave feels as if an inner dam wall has burst. Relationships are a source for contacting the Neptune energy, as it is one of the transmitters of *anima–animus* power projections (even more powerful in nature than when either the Moon or Venus is activated). The Neptune aspect of *anima–animus* seeks to lose itself in a merging with the other, a breaking of separation, whereas both the personal planets of the Moon and Venus reinforce identity by reflection and giving and receiving. Neptune is often considered to be the higher octave of Venus, to be universal as opposed to personal love, but this can leave the individual extremely vulnerable to being used by others less scrupulous and caring.

Romantic deception is a cliché, yet it is an experience of many who have been taken advantage of, and tendencies for this can be noted through Neptune aspects in charts. For instance, challenging aspects made to Mars can indicate difficulties in relationships of women to men, through a loving open temperament and a liability to the wiles of the seductive lover. As the woman may be uncertain as to what she really needs whilst under the influence of heightened emotions, she can be fooled and manipulated. Neptune aspects to Venus can imply an excessively romantic nature, with images of ideal lovers and perfection being sought. For men, Venus and Moon aspects to Neptune can indicate that tendency to seek the ideal woman, a quest that can forever only find disillusionment and dissatisfaction in life unless the man is extremely fortunate or succeeds in bringing reality into his dreams.

There is a sub-personality that can be associated with the Neptunian impulse to universal love, and this is the Love type. This type can be identified by that urgent need to be loved and belong through relationships, and the need for this is a dominating pattern in the life direction. Empathic and environmental sensitivity is common, and often the focus of identity has been projected externally for approval and acknowledgement, so that the well-being of the ego structure is connected to what others think and say, and allied to a need to establish personal boundaries which are expanded to include relationships; the ego can be very vulnerable if rejection occurs. In a chart, it is either the 4th, 7th, 12th or Water houses that are emphasised.

Coming to terms with these powerful private emotions is a task that faces all of us. The ego hates feeling vulnerable and open, and is often uncomfortable when inner feelings flow from that whirlpool of emotions. Relationship rejections and failed love affairs often throw us into emotional trauma and paranoid delusions as if the whole world has rejected us. Romantic heartache is inevitable for the majority, and emotional integration is a vital step for everyone who is seriously attempting to integrate the Neptune vibration into their conscious lives. Failure and refusal to do this may eventually bring feelings of discontent and psychological disturbance, especially in those who have a distinctly Neptunian emphasis to their natal chart. This can create a feeling of low energy, states of confusion and loss of direction, where the old contacts between self and others seem to lack vitality, and life seems coloured by a lack of certainty as the old ways fail to be satisfactory.

Rejecting the need for integration can lead to a seeping away of meaning, purpose and direction, and yet as this happens, there can be a simultaneous reliance on the need for compensatory fantasies, those dreams of the ideal job, marriage, lifestyle which are clung to as substitutes. The circle of escapism intensifies, and as these unrealistic dreams grow stronger, the needs which are represented by them move ever further away from possible satisfaction as the perception of the world and people becomes more distorted. Running away from inner pain can take many forms of evasion, yet almost contradictorily, the way through this phase is to turn inwards and discover a new way of dealing with painful issues. Sometimes an activated Neptune can signify a period of introversion, partial seclusion and withdrawal from the activities of life and social involvement. Inner unconscious patterns rise into awareness, and personal illusions, dreams, phobias and neuroses can be exposed to a clarifying light. If the challenge is taken, this time can become very productive and personally beneficial, as the inner fogs are dispersed and the higher creative and visionary aspects of Neptune shine through. Whilst unintegrated emotions can be very painful, emotions can also serve to heal past wounds, dissolve patterns of constriction and so liberate blocked energies into new life.

Those inner *mélusines* of the ocean depths can pull people through two different channels; one where people drown in the depths, created by a personal refusal to change and too deep an immersion in the darkness of personal misery; the other towards mystical death and transformation, the route that Neptune is attempting to encourage people towards. Whilst Neptune may incline the individual towards fanciful dreams in the areas of life that he can particularly influence, it is often in these same areas that radical solutions can also be found. Through search, the individual who chooses to discover a way out from disillusionment can discover that ideals need to be personally lived in order to make them real. The disruption caused by the outer planets is a spur to make idealism and inspiration real, to encourage us to anchor that awareness on the physical level through manifestation in daily life.

Individual attitudes will determine the nature of the Neptune influence through our personal value structures and in how easily we can allow those winds from unknown lands to penetrate our lives. Do we welcome that touch of the mysterious, or do we deny it access, pretending that we are in full control and understand life, and in so doing reject the open hand of Neptune? Yet welcoming that god can take us to the world of spirit, to levels of archetypal realities and to the inspiration of imagination attuned to the inclusive mind. Some grasp this opportunity, warmly acknowledging this intervention in their lives and allow the anointing by the trident, experiencing this as a descent of grace and a deep spiritual mystery as, through drowning, the rebirth is achieved. As Dane Rudhyar states, Neptune is 'at every level, the healing and sustaining power of the wholeness of the whole'.

WORKING WITH NEPTUNE

The location of Neptune in a chart tends to indicate a source of idealism and possible creative vision. Neptune's value is to signify an inner awareness of a personal utopia, and this can vary according to its position and individual needs and dreams.

A contemplative approach to life is often suitable to co-operating with the Neptune energy, where life is lived in accord with the element of water, unresisting, free-flowing, non-judgemental and inherently surrendered to the higher life. Philosophies like Taoism reflect such an attitude and world view of self and the world, where a deep egoic relaxation occurs, and a more inclusive perception of universal realities adds a sense of proportion. This involves an acting from a new centre, a point of stillness entered by an inner silence and freedom from personality chatter. Only the present exists here, the past has faded away and the future does not yet exist to be concerned about; attention is focused only within the present moment and the whole being is opened to that experience. The surrender has been made to that hidden self, and not to the vagaries of outer life.

From such a stance, a meditative lifestyle can develop, where, in the stillness, integration and mystical atonement can happen and alpha brain waves can attune themselves to the spiritual and psychic dimensions. Dream life may become more active, and Neptune often chooses to work through evocative and repetitious dreams to convey messages or future premonitions. For instance, throughout my childhood I had a regular and repetitive dream which always disturbed me, and was always the same, but I didn't understand what it meant. This continued for years, until in early adult life, a real situation happened which was the exact correspondence and duplication of the dream, although the crucial heart and meaning of the dream had always been veiled by waking; time had eventually caught up with the timeless knowledge of what apparently was destined to be.

Through fantasy, creative visualisation, day dreaming, imagery and symbology, Neptune can be evoked and awakened. Journeying and pathworking are powerful tools to stimulate activity in the transpersonal planets, and these approaches can be successfully used to channel their energies into practical results and creative artistic inspiration. Meditating on the Sabian symbols associated with a personal natal chart can often be highly valuable and, when taking the Cross of Life image (Ascendent, Descendent, MidHeaven/Zenith, Nadir), can provide workable symbolic images for the pattern of your life. Rudhyar's book *An Astrological Mandala* is the best source for the 360 images.

Trying to grasp and define Neptune is an impossible task. Eventually the realisation is that there is no limited Neptune, he is formless and resides deep within the essence of everyone and everything, the guarantee that no form or structure is eternal, but arises and then passes in the infinite creativity of the Divine Visionary Dreamer. We can symbolise Neptune as the Master of Dance, where the dancer merges deep into the underlying rhythms of the music and sound, like the great Nijinsky, lost in the universal note of the celestial musician. He is the Master of our Dreams, the Master of Disguise, hiding within matter and inspiring us to transcend our limitations.

Neptune and the Physical Body

The Neptune vibration has several correspondences in the physical human structure with which it has been associated, although Neptune is traditionally considered to transmit the most subtle and refined energies which the human instrument is capable of receiving.

Neptune is the ruler of the pineal gland (Uranus has also been associated with influencing this gland) and those parts of the nervous system that are particularly receptive to less tangible and subtle psychic influences. The pineal gland is the approximate location of the traditional 'third eye' which is awakened by spiritual development and which opens to look upon the hidden inner world beyond the material appearance. This is also connected to the yogic ajna centre from where spiritual energies are directed outwards into the world. Because of Neptune's affinity with the etheric and astral realms, Neptune is often considered to be highly influential in the changeable human aura and chakra system (energy centres), and where effective functioning is either activated or impaired by the degree of integration of the Neptune vibration in the personal life.

In addition, there are physiological correspondences with the spinal canal of the nervous system which receive and transmit the processes of physical, emotional, and mental nervous activity endemic in life, and with the part of the brain known as the thalamus. The thalamus is within the interior brain where several important sensory nerves originate, especially the optic and hearing nerves, and from where nervous connections are also made to the pituitary gland. The pituitary gland is vitally important for the conducting and co-ordination of the chemical secretions of the endocrine system which are related to the rhythms of human growth and physical unfoldment. In botany, thalamus means the receptacle of a flower, which has a resemblance to the Neptune astrological symbol, and the word was derived from the Greek *thalamos* which indicated an inner or secret chamber, or from *thalasic*, meaning of the sea.

In certain esoteric teachings, it is believed that the level of spiritual development of the individual can be gauged by an analysis of glandular activity and by the secretion of certain chemicals into the bloodstream and in brain activity. The science of the importance of the major human glands is still relatively new, and yet it is in the right balance of the glandular system that many keys to human evolution and good health lie.

From an astrological perspective, individuals with a powerful Neptune influence in their charts are generally advised to be cautious in consuming drugs, alcohol, sedatives or anything addictive, as they can be especially responsive to the chemical effects. Neptune is considered to be the ruler of intoxicant plants, such as mushrooms, psilocybin, peyote, cannibis sativa, opium poppy, as well as tobacco, coffee and tea, and, with the Moon, is ruler of those medicinal herbal plants which are beneficial to the human body. In recent years, the West has seen a greatly renewed social interest in the effects of plant use on the human consciousness and body.

Sometimes an afflicted Neptune can be noted in charts where the individual suffers from repeated ill health, illnesses that are difficult to diagnose, a lack of general vitality, a diminishing of a zest for life, or inner emotional and mental disturbances associated with passivity and a lack of self-confidence; in extreme cases, there can be a tendency to lapse into permanent mental illness, and paranoid or neurotic behaviour patterns.

CHAPTER 3

From Illusion to Reality?

Two of the major themes of Neptune's influence on the individual are the impulse for creative expression – the path of the artist – and the impulse for self-transcendence – the path of the mystic. Both the artist and mystic are preoccupied with the issue of perception, interpreting the experience of life in a manner which reveals an underlying and interpenetrating 'other dimension' beyond the purely earthbound consciousness; both seek to reveal and expose the hidden numinosity within form.

The artist responds to an inner impulse to create, and in so doing illuminates a unique window of perception on life, sharing with others a glimpse of something that has proven to be inspirational to him or her and that has stimulated the artistic process. Artistic creativity can, of course, take many forms, and can be imbued with a wide variety of personal needs and compulsions within the nature of creation, yet it is also one of the unique characteristics of humanity – in distinction to the rest of the animal kingdom – and is a consequence of a more evolved species, one which has become self-reflective, and uses this natural gift as a means towards development and understanding. Music, painting, sculpture, literature, drama, dance, film and photography are all forms of artistic expression that are associated with Neptune, and these are often the basis for a social, creative and cultural unfolding.

In the contemporary Western world, there are many opportunities for individual creative expression to be achieved, often due to the increase in money and leisure time which allows artistic pursuits to become an integral part of the lives of many. Mass media offer a wide availability of films, literature, music, theatre, art galleries and museums which serve as cultural repositories for those who are interested, and represent a progression that has never before been so accessible for virtually the whole literate population, and previously had only been available to the upper classes of society.

This is, in fact, a major development of civilisation, one that we often take for granted and whose importance we often fail to recognise. Today, we have virtually unlimited access to the total human knowledge from all cultures in the world, plus considerable knowledge of ancient societies that have now disappeared. The range of potential 'windows' on the perception of life is vast, and constitutes an expansion of consciousness in its own right. As the growth of personal computers increases, there is the likelihood that each home will eventually be linked into a global encyclopaedic data base, where information on any subject can be obtained at the touch of a computer keyboard. The possible mental stimulation for a creative individual through even the current information access is extremely high, as cultural perceptions cross-fertilise and generate new hybrids, new thinking and new styles of artistic expression.

For the individual who attempts to walk the path of personal artistic creativity, one consequence is the opening of corresponding channels in their psyche. Some feel that they have to be artistic in some way, responding to an inner need to channel their energies out into the world. Wherever Neptune is found in the chart lies a likely field for personal creativity to flourish within, and often planetary aspects with Neptune indicate artistic potential. Creativity is transformative, opening the mind to greater dimensions of subtlety, meaning and direction, and becoming a way of life.

Society has an ambivalent attitude towards the artist, musician and writer; there is both respect and some deference given, yet some distancing made too, possibly due to a sense of there being 'something other' in the creative spirit. In more authoritarian and totalitarian societies, the artistic spirit is one of the first victims of the state, where imposed censorship and state penalisation soon emerge to restrain that social voice. This is because the creative individual is more adept at communication and is often acute in his social commentary and perception, asserting the freedom of human rights and tolerance of free thought; an authoritarian state cannot allow such a person to become a social agitator, and so any dissent is soon removed.

This 'something other' in the persona of the creative person is the presence of the Muse. In Greek mythology, there were Nine

Muses who served as the goddesses of arts and science, and these were highly inspirational inner *daemons*, supernatural beings who acted as intermediaries between the higher gods and man. Whilst stimulating sparks of creative genius in many, such a higher vibration also stimulated the unintegrated personality of many individuals attempting to walk the creative path. Latent compulsions and obsessions often dictated the form of artistic expression as personal eccentricity grew more powerful, as for instance with Salvador Dali, and many, such as Van Gogh and Friedrich Nietzsche, slipped deeper into types of madness even as their artistic light burned brighter.

This aspect of the creative muse cannot be denied. Possession by the artistic vision, ideas, symbols, characters, light, colour is commonplace, due to the fact that the creator has to become absorbed within the nature of the creation if it is to succeed and be true to the original conception. The difficulty lies in maintaining the personality structure under the pressures of the artistic labour process and of 'giving birth' successfully. In the search for enhanced sanity and clarity of perception, some enter a phase where things become too clear and, as insight floods through, protective barriers dissolve and – like Nietzsche – they become a victim of their own success and lack of personality integration. In cases like Nietzsche, the precarious balance between personal identity and receiving the power of intense imagery from the collective and unconscious mind led to the descent into mental breakdown.

Sexuality is often a major obsession in creative lives, partly because of the vitalised energies that course through such people and which require release, and because excess energies can be channelled in that activity. Also, for many, it can be a relatively unintegrated part of their nature, and so the energy is attracted towards a 'weak spot' in their body-psyche. Creators like Picasso, Rodin and Gill have a satyric nature, whereas Dali was more interested in voyeurism and sexual deviancy, conceptual sex rather than a physical activity.

Creative individuals act as a focusing channel for the collective; their social role is to give voice to collective undercurrents, needs, desires, aspirations, as well as revealing their own private vision of life and sharing their own window of perception to illuminate alternative ways of looking at and experiencing the phenomenal world. The strange power of creative works of art flows from their ability to focus aspects of the collective psyche into an objective form. Popular musicians succeed in evoking common collective experiences through their love songs, lyrics which – for many of today's young – serve to be inspirational, supportive and illuminating of the complexities of emotions and feelings; in hearing lyrics of affinity, the love-torn person realises that they are not alone in their anguish, and this can be extremely beneficial in the eventual healing of vulnerable emotions.

The world of human creativity is immense, and can only be briefly indicated. It is a realm of human expression that will become more important as time passes, essentially playing a vital role in the unfolding and development of the individual. There are many examples that could be taken to display the Neptunian influence in artistic endeavours, but the two that have been chosen are also bridges between the artist and the mystic, and include a distinct social awareness too. These are the works of the Pre-Raphaelite Brotherhood, and Kahlil Gibran.

THE PRE-RAPHAELITE BROTHERHOOD

Two years after the discovery of Neptune, the Pre-Raphaelite Brotherhood was formed in 1848 by Dante Gabriel Rossetti, William Holman Hunt and John Everett Millais.

This was probably the first artistic movement that was influenced by the spirit of Neptune (emerging in the year of European social revolutions) and was the response of a group of rebellious young English artists barely aged twenty. They created an entirely new school of painting, one which deliberately chose to look back to the romance of medieval chivalry, and which also documented the contemporary Victorian social themes and conflicts with a technique of painting which required an intense attention to naturalistic details.

One of the earlier small groups that had inspired them was known as the 'Nazarenes', German artists who had been living in Rome since 1810, and which had been formed as a semi-religious order dedicated to the revitalisation and renewal of religious art.

The Pre-Raphaelite Brotherhood was conceived as a close affinity group, a secret society of artists who were devoted to the pursuit of the highest ideals of art and its role in social culture and development. Inspired by the energy and fervour of young spirits, the Brotherhood saw itself as rebels, wanting to turn the minds of men to see that which is highest and ideal in life, through creating noble and serious paintings. They imagined themselves in the garb of crusaders for a forgotten level of quality art, intending to produce inspirational, uplifting and ennobling masterpieces to benefit society.

In addition to their artistic visions, the small group also possessed a corresponding social awareness and concern. They saw the inequalities and social injustices of their time, and were highly sensitive to the political undercurrent of tension and stress that was overshadowing the European states a generation after the turmoil of the Napoleonic Wars. Whilst coming from reasonably favoured homes, they were not immune to the needs of the masses in Victorian Britain, and their formative teenage years developed under the social threats of the 'hungry forties'; this turbulent and disruptive social period reached an apotheosis in the huge Chartist demonstration of 1848, the high point of the endeavours of this political pressure group dedicated to the furtherance of workers' rights and political change as embodied in the *People's Charter*. Both Millais and Holman Hunt had been witnesses to that event, and the potential power of a collective movement had been inspirational to them. Transferring this stimulus into what they perceived as a stagnant and moribund world of art proved to be irresistible.

The Brotherhood's conception of a good picture was one which succeeded in conveying several important ideas to the viewer; the picture was not just a pretty composition to momentarily attract the eye, but one which carried a 'message' which the spectator would carry away with him for further contemplation. In that way the Brotherhood's influence would spread across society. The paintings were thus didactic in essence, a teaching device and a means of communication of a perspective and vision of life and society. As art, they contained a high moral dimension, extremely romantic and deliberately socially revolutionary. Their underlying vision was one of social advancement and change, where the ideas and ideals they included in their art would become ingrained in the quality of society, so serving to uplift the oppressed masses. Neptune is often associated with the collective and with political theories, and in this desire of the Brotherhood they were quite in harmony with the prevailing revolutionary social trend in Europe.

As the Pre-Raphaelite Brotherhood became more prominent in

the artistic and cultural world, they became increasingly controversial. They possessed an ambivalence that both reflected establishment attitudes and Christian beliefs, and yet through subtle
differences transformed this into an entirely renewed social direction, a modernistic trend that presaged future developments over
the next century. The Brotherhood were visionary dreamers,
reflecting romantic idealism, socially moralistic concerns and a
scientific rationalism, all tied up within the sphere of artistic
creativity as being one of the highest expressions of the human
being.

Several themes became prominent in their art: the social position
of women in Victorian society, as in *The Awakening Conscience* on
the theme of prostitution (Hunt), biblical topics, and the Arthurian
legends. The *Morte d'Arthur* of Malory was a favourite source of
inspiration and thematic content, and the Pre-Raphaelite paintings
helped to re-evoke that archetypal legend within the European
psyche, restoring the symbol of the Grail almost at the same time
as Neptune was discovered, and stimulating that consequent
emergence of human compassion that began during the Victorian
age. Concepts of romantic and tragic love fascinated them, echoing
the sometimes complex personal relationships that the members
of the Brotherhood became involved with; one popular image of
the Pre-Raphaelites is that of 'the Love School', especially centred
around Rossetti's more Bohemian type of lifestyle, dedicated to
the artistic and poetic muses.

The Brotherhood's lovers often appeared in the paintings, used
as models for their conceptions of unearthly womanhood, often
garbed in disguises of ancient sorceresses or as characters from
legends. Such women reflected *anima* personas for the male artists,
and were almost deified into extremely virtuous, beautiful embodiments of the female gender, given elevated ideal characteristics,
or were perceived as casting spells which mere man could not resist,
as in *The Beguiling of Merlin*. They were *femmes fatales* or *les belles
dames sans merci*, fascinating and hauntingly bewitching, through
whom the muses communicated their inspirational whispers to the
artists. In these paintings, the Neptunian themes of sacrifice, martyr,
victim and saviour reappear in an idealistic context.

Rossetti, in particular, shared such perceptions of women, and
his paintings and poetry are suffused with an obsessive sensuality
and heightened sense of vital colour and feeling. He was a wor-
shipper of the aesthetic grace and lines of female beauty, striving

always to make it more mysterious and evocative through his paintings, whose women offer depths of experience that few living women can achieve, and who seem to beckon the viewer into almost another dimension of experience. For any men who have an awakened Neptunian sensitivity, several of the Brotherhood's paintings which focus on women are powerfully evocative of stirrings beyond the purely physical; they activate *anima–animus* images in men and in women who respond to the chivalric ideals and who have an inner image of themselves-performing those roles in daily life – at least in their private fantasies!

Rossetti's *Beata Beatrix* is, from one chosen perspective, an image of a woman in mystical raptures, and conjures speculation from the viewer as to just what it was that stimulated such a feeling. *Proserpine* and *Astarte Syriaca* are great paintings in this portrayal of the feminine mystery, and a poem by Rossetti to complete *Astarte* ends with the lines:

> That face, of Love's all penetrative spell
> Amulet, talisman and oracle –
> Betwixt the sun and moon a mystery.

In 1856, Rossetti met William Morris and Edward Burne-Jones, and the work of the Pre-Raphaelite Brotherhood entered a second phase. This included a cross-fertilisation of the Brotherhood's ideals with those of the Aesthetic and the Arts and Crafts Movement, and represented a new sense of direction where the limitations of painting were broken through an absorption of the Brotherhood's ideals into every aspect of contemporary Victorian society. Morris spearheaded this approach, which was imbued with socialist principles, and it spread into furniture, design, decorative arts, illustration, literature, interior decoration and architecture. Morris had a dictum which he applied to the creation of his 'Palace of Art' at the Red House in Bexley, Kent, where together with Burne-Jones they designed everything from carpets, wallpapers, tapestries, stained glass, metalwork and furniture: 'Have nothing in your house that you do not know to be useful or believe to be beautiful.' The Pre-Raphaelite Brotherhood has been described as 'an expression of the final rich flowering of the late Victorian civilisation'.

Henry James spoke of the Brotherhood and Edward Burne-Jones in this way:

It is the art of culture, of reflection, of intellect, luxury, of aesthetic refinement, of people who look at the world and at life not directly, as it were, and in all its accidental reality, but in the reflection and ornamental portrait of it furnished by literature, by poetry, by history, by erudition.

Burne-Jones was born in 1833, and it is often his paintings which capture the Neptunian spirit in its more chivalric and glamorous nature. He found that inspiration from romantic poetry and legendary myth was the ideal subject matter for his vision of art; the two intermeshed perfectly. Whether it was Homer and Greek myths, Shakespeare or Arthurian legend, that mixture of the semi-divine that enriched human life suited his intent to revivify a more exalted spirit in the depths of nineteenth-century Victorian materialism and social division. He wanted to stop the pernicious spread of social injustice, and was often responsive to this type of missionary fervour based on a high moral attitude devoted to improving the quality of life for his fellow men, leaving the world a better place than he had found it.

His conception of the role and function of art was idealistic. The artist was a favoured child of the gods, whose duty was to inspire and uplift, responding to the lofty, noble calling of the Muses. Initially, he believed that the most noble style of life was that of the religious man. He nearly joined the Church, but eventually transferred his religious ideals into art. The search to create beauty in life obsessed him; beauty was a revealer of truth and everything that was good and holy. His inner goddess took the form of Beauty, and he strove to be her amanuensis through his paintings and designs. Beauty became his Holy Grail: 'Only this is true, that beauty is very beautiful, and softens, and comforts, and inspires, and rouses, and lifts up, and never fails.'

He was probably the member of the Brotherhood most inspired by the Arthurian legends, and many of his paintings include shining knights, lovely damsels in distress, and a sense of an otherworldly land: 'I mean by a picture a beautiful romantic dream of something that never was, never will be – in light better than any light that ever shone – in a land no-one can define, or remember, only desire . . . ' Malory's *Morte d'Arthur* became his guiding light, where the legends of the Round Table and the glamours of chivalric knighthood fascinated his need for romanticism. The never ending struggle between good and evil, light and darkness, and sin and salvation were constant themes. At one time, Burne-Jones even considered forming an Order devoted to the service of Sir Galahad, one of the perfect knights of Camelot: 'Lord, how that San Graal story is ever in my mind and thoughts . . . was ever anything in the world beautiful as that is beautiful?' For Burne-Jones, the answer was no. It embodied his dreams, visions and aspirations. The Pre-Raphaelite Brotherhood was an artist's Round Table, dedicated to sublime artistry.

His final and unfinished painting was *The Last Sleep of Arthur in Avalon*, a fitting epitaph for a modern Grail Knight. Towards the end of his life, in 1898, Burne-Jones began to realise that his artistic attempts had failed to ignite Victorian society against rampant materialism. He began to withdraw more into his own private dream world, creating paintings of inner dreams and visions like *The Golden Stairs* and *Depths of the Sea*, and was described as giving 'the sense of a highly cultured, refined spirit, living a sheltered life'. Perhaps the image of *The Soul Attains* of a man kneeling to hold the hand of an idealised nude female figure is apt for an artist attuned to his inner *daemon*.

Few major members of the Pre-Raphaelite Brotherhood lived long lives, most seemed burnt out from the intensity of their inner states, love lives and artistic endeavours at a relatively early age. Rossetti died at sixty-four, Morris at sixty-two, Burne-Jones at sixty-five. The spark of their creativity burned brightly, inspiring many talented followers to adopt and adapt their ideals. Certainly to gain a sense of Neptunian images, ideals and glamours, wrapped in the guise of artistic and mystically orientated creativity, the work of the Pre-Raphaelite Brotherhood is one of the most revealing and explicit.

KAHLIL GIBRAN

Kahlil Gibran was born in the Lebanon in 1883, and only lived to the age of forty-eight, dying in 1931. For a modern generation, he became known again through the re-publication of his most famous book *The Prophet* during the sixties and seventies.

He was a writer, poet, artist and mystic and lived a very Neptunian type of life. His father had been a farmer in Lebanon, strong, vigorous, with little education. He was a quarrelsome, aggressive drunk who regularly abused and beat his wife and

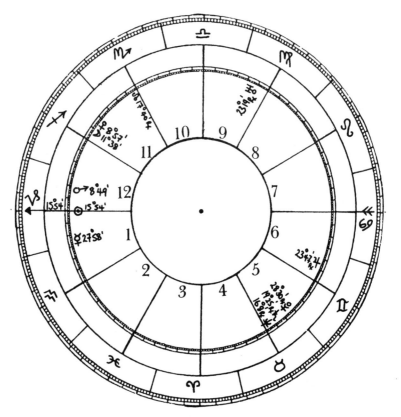

KAHLIL GIBRAN
Solar Noon Chart Born 6.1.1883 B'Sheri Lebanon

children, especially Kahlil whenever he tried to draw. The family
suffered from perpetual anxiety, lack of food and poverty, and
lived in an atmosphere of tension and bitterness, with a mother
who tried to do her best despite her despair and sacrifices, a
victim and martyr figure.

In 1894 he moved away to America, where he eventually settled
into an artistic lifestyle. He called his small studio *The Hermitage*,
where most of his focus and energy was poured into creativity and
reflections of his artistic sensitivities. There was an other-worldly
atmosphere about him, and his personality and presence have been
described as 'all electricity and velvet, as mobile as a flame, as silent
as a tree, wonderful responsive face full of stars'. This reflects his
major astrological aspects of Neptune and Uranus in particular.

He was a visionary, highly nervously strung, whose 'days were filled with burning ideas, and nights with strange dreams, who lived in ecstasy, floated in rapture'. He considered that his dream life was extremely significant, containing important visionary indications. As a result of his creative spirit enflaming him from within, he suffered from poor health for most of his life; part of this may have been psychosomatic in nature, or derived from the stresses of artistic endeavours and being a channel for higher wisdom. His own personal integration may not have been sufficient to withstand the quality of vibrations that he laboured under. As Gibran states, 'The difference between a prophet and a poet is that the prophet lives what he teaches – and the poet does not. He may write wonderfully of love, and yet not be loving.' The Muses can work through any available channel.

Gibran recognised the need for self-understanding: 'If one will accept himself he hinders himself no longer. As soon as a person accepts being unlovable, he becomes very lovable indeed. Nobody can love me if I'm not myself . . .' The illnesses that he suffered from included the grippe, (an ailment with periodic influenza-like symptoms), heart palpitations, stomach ailments, bad teeth, and a mysterious unknown affliction prior to his early death.

Amongst his books are *The Forerunner, The Madman, Jesus The Son of Man,* and his most famous one, *The Prophet,* which is certainly one example of teachings channelled through an artistic medium. Of this book Gibran commented that 'The Prophet . . . he dominates me now. I must yield myself to possession by that spirit until I have finished it'; a situation which summarises many an artistic creation where possession by the inner genius is part of the personal sacrifice required in order to create. Gibran's books are inspirational and evocative, and can be considered to be an example of the higher Neptunian possession through an artistically talented person, where personal sacrifice was demanded for the work.

THE MYSTICAL PATH

One of the main characteristics of Neptune in the natal chart is to indicate an interest and attraction towards the paths of self-transcendence, including psychism, extra-sensory perception, religion, mysticism and occultism. Part of this attraction arises from a heightened degree of sensitivity to people and the environment, where more subtle messages are received beyond the level of superficial contact and appearance, and the affinity to receive impressions from the unconscious mind tends to make the attention turn inwards, through introverted self-investigation.

Since 1846, it is the Neptune influence that has intensified the development of channelled 'spiritual teachings', commencing with the days of the early spiritualist movement, through numerous mediums and psychics, contacts from UFOs and space brothers, to the modern emphasis on received teachings from discarnate inner masters. Anyone who has examined the content and quality of teachings over the last century would surely agree that the nature of the communications and the transmitting receivers is extremely variable; many hoaxes have been perpetrated, and yet amongst the painted tarnished 'gold' lies some real nuggets, but discrimination is vitally needed in threading a path through such realms.

This is one of the peculiarities of the spiritual path, its contradictory and often paradoxical nature, where truth, reality, illusion and glamour are so intertwined that it is hard to attain a clear individual interpretation. Where Neptune is involved, there is the glimpse of 'reality', yet to arrive there requires the passing through of worlds of mists and fogs, dense pea-soupers like the old images of the London fogs, entering inner mindscapes where all is not necessarily as it appears to be. The plasticity and mutability of what has been termed the *'astral plane'* is a strange land, formed by thought, emotions and desires, individually and collectively. In Chapter 7, I look more closely at the spiritual task related to this level of existence.

It is one of the disconcerting facts about our modern knowledge concerning recent embodiments of spiritual teachings that often the lifestyles and actions of the teacher do not match common perceptions of what a 'holy man' should be. For every disciple's book about the glories of their teacher, there is another book being written as an exposé. One man's reality is another man's illusion, or so it seems from a detached perspective. Certainly we need greater understanding of what the transpersonal and spiritual life actually involves, and of how it is expressed individually and collectively. And indeed, should the ways in which the Spirit expresses itself be limited by our puny conceptions of how an individual channel should act? Perhaps it is through ignorance of the real spiritual life that we even presume to be able to judge and understand what is really going on.

Many of the more acknowledged and famous guru-teachers of modern times have been extremely controversial personalities. In none of these is the reputed 'ego-death' obvious, and all are powerful and charismatic individuals, whose presence and teachings elicit polarised opinions and attitudes from others. Blavatsky, Gurdjieff, Crowley, Rajneesh, Da Free John, all come into this category, and, as Alan Watts has affectionately termed them, such characters are 'rascal gurus', reflecting the 'trickster' archetype in several respects, with swirlings of glamour and illusion surrounding them, especially in the perceptions of their followers.

Perhaps it should be clearly stated that individuals who walk the transformative path and become inwardly opened to transpersonal energies are not necessarily what many people would consider 'suitable' for such employment. There is an antagonistic and uneasy relationship between such characters and mainstream society. They do not fit the general conception of a mediating priesthood that is so rooted in most religions; instead they assert the potential for personal *gnosis* and offer techniques to achieve such an exalted state. There is an aspect in Eastern religions which pays homage to such types of teacher, especially in the Tibetan, Zen and Taoist traditions. Rascal gurus are probably symptomatic of the Western emphasis on individuality, and so have to perform a type of media star role in order to attract attention to themselves and what they conceive to be their destined mission. It is of value to study the lives of such teachers as well as their teachings, because it helps to dissolve a variety of glamours and illusions, and demonstrates that in the case of transpersonal channels the message can be separated from the individual. There is a saying that can illuminate: 'Wherever the greatest light is found, there is the greatest darkness.'

The path of the mystic is traditionally the approach of the heart towards beauty. Nature mysticism is common, often expressed in terms of poetic insight, and probably was the initial source which conceived the nature of ancient elemental gods. Religious mysticism is the heart love for a spiritual teacher, the love for Christ, Krishna, and the way of the Bhakti-Yogi. The mystic is ever aware of the nature of duality, that he is separated from his beloved, and is torn apart by the strength of his emotions for

what seems to be an unattainable love. He is a seeker in search
of his beloved, soul or light, chasing a vision that has fascinated
him, like the vision of the Grail which destroyed the Brotherhood
of the Round Table as the knights left to travel the wild ways in
search of the Holy Chalice. He demands recognition from his
beloved, a sign to show him that he is not forgotten or spurned.
He becomes the ideal devotee, seeing no evil in his beloved, only
the possible ecstatic joys of dreams of union where the separative
gap between him and the other is finally dissolved. What is really
attracting him is his own self, like an irresistible magnet, appearing
in a disguise which is totally evocative of the mystic's deepest
desires. The life of Ramakrishna is a fine example of this path: he
fell in love with the Divine Feminine and followed each major
religious path to the peak, where he experienced the vision of the
Divine Mother garbed in many disguises – as the Virgin Mary,
as Kali, as Radha and as several more feminine spiritual images.

The mystical path is that of the heart, attempting to transcend
the use of mind to reach the hidden inner self, whilst the occult
path involves a use and development of the mind to penetrate
through the veils of form and appearance in order to discover the
self. Most on the spiritual path develop a way which combines
these two distinct approaches, where one ideal is to integrate both
the paths of head and heart together, ensuring that a viable balance
is achieved.

The way of the Neptunian mystic is inevitably the path of self-
renunciation and sacrifice; the ideal is the love for the collective
that demands no external rewards for the expression of humanitarian service. It is a feeling of oneness with life, and reflects the
role of ancient Western kings in becoming *one with the Land*, which
was a sacrificial performance of their collective duty. The failure
of a king to perform this act is seen in the imagery of the Wasteland
in the Grail Legends. As the Saturn boundaries of self are dissolved
by the Neptune energies seeping through the personality barriers,
the mystic begins to surrender to the higher force and, through
merging and dissolution, he partakes of the spiritual mystery.

There are dangers to this process, and most involve the stimulation of glamours and illusions. The contact with collective reality
can often release patterns associated with self-appointed divine
missions (the messiah complex) which may have an element of
truth in function, but are often just an attempt to hold together
a fragmented ego. Inflation is common, where the egoic sense is

expanded without being transformed, and this can degenerate into an unquestioning assertion of being right, a symptom that has resulted in religious fanaticism, intolerance and violence against heretics and unbelievers, as in the Inquisition and witch trials of Christian nations.

GLAMOUR AND ILLUSION

One face of Neptune is glamour and illusion; the other face is reality, truth and beauty. The first problem may be in deciding which road is the right one to take; the second is deciding how you can be sure which face you are actually seeing . . .

Both mystics and occultists, and anyone walking a transpersonal path, face common challenges centred around the difficulty of discriminating between the false and the real. The fact is that at best we can only experience and understand a fraction of 'the real'; most is beyond our comprehension and capacity, but in a spiritual context some things are more real than others, some insights are more accurate than others. The Gautama Buddha's disciples believed that he had revealed universal truth and reality in his teachings, but Gautama knew otherwise. He bent and picked up a handful of leaves, and said 'This much have I revealed to you'; in a forest full of trees and fallen leaves, he was indicating that only a miniscule fragment had been transmitted through his transpersonal channel. Christ promised his followers that 'greater things than this shall ye do', knowing that in time greater expressions of Wisdom would walk again on Earth. We have difficulty in even understanding and following the handful of leaves available to us so far.

Neptune is the planet of glamours, and these arise through separatist emotional and personality activity, which casts a mist or fog in which the individual wanders without recognition, and which has the effect of distorting all perceptions, preventing him from seeing himself or life with any clarity, and so immersing him in a state of isolated separation of consciousness. It is a sobering event to consider the nature of common glamours that afflict individuals, and which also exist on a collective level too, distorting all types of relationships from the family to international dimensions. Spiritual groups are quite prone to suffer from glamours and illusions, and it is an inevitable corollary at this time. Few are free from such influences.

Glamour floods the astral plane, and is a consequence of the ancient heresy of separativeness and dualism. The Buddha proposed one way to become more free of glamours with the technique of the Middle Way, where in the individual movement between the pairs of dualistic opposites, confusion and distortion arise like those mists and fogs, causing powerful mood changes from deep depressions to ecstatic bliss, leaving us prey to our emotional reactions which colour, bias and prejudice our perceptions of self and life.

Whilst we persist in our separative perceptions and our egocentric image of self and selfish emotional reactions, we continue to generate glamours and illusions. If we can begin to transcend personal feelings and move to re-centre ourselves on the level of the illumined mind, then the power of glamour will dissipate. How this occurs is through spiritual development, and by serving as a channel for the transpersonal energies to work through an open personality. Meditation is often the key to initiate this process, where, by holding the mind steady in the light, greater clarity can be achieved. This has been called soul contact and alignment, and in that channel to our inner self the increase in light entering the brain and mind disperses the fogs and mists, enabling the individual to see more clearly and to follow their own lighted way onwards. In Chapter 7, this process is described in the Esoteric Neptune.

Transformation occurs as a result of experiencing the inner battlefield. And it is not easy. A simple listing of common glamours (from the works of Alice Bailey) can be uncomfortable reading, but as learning to look dispassionately and clearly at the facts is crucial to transcend our distortions, it is essential to associate these with the tendencies of the astrological Neptune, as the two walk hand in hand. In addition, they illumine the challenges of working with Neptune, and the inner realm that can be opened up for the individual. The truth is that most of us fail to recognise the glamours that we labour under, and instead often deify them as positive assets and characteristics of our personality, for thus is our perception warped!

Glamours include: aspiration, destiny, self-assurance in being 'right', duty, devotion, desire, personal ambitions, suspicion, mind, self-pity, criticism, pride, separativeness, fatigue, disappointment, authority, materialism, idealism, environmental conditions restricting through frustration, futility and impotence.

The real name of the collective glamours is Legion. They can be extremely subtle, often inhabiting a world of half-truths, where, for instance, an individual may have a spiritual destiny to perform. But is it as he conceives it and lives it, or have his own needs beglamoured him in certain respects? Glamours often masquerade as truth. Their way into consciousness is often via unconscious tendencies in the mind, or through those repetitive habit patterns of thought, emotion and action that are rarely re-evaluated due to their automatic behavour patterns. Behind those emotional and separative miasmas, truth is hidden and veiled.

Idealism is one major source which attracts glamours. Whilst idealism offers a sense of purpose and direction, it can easily become a source of fanaticism, where the ideal eventually restricts freedom of thought and personal independence by allegiance to an obsessing ideal. Spurious senses of pride and individual or national separatism are often generated by idealism, as the attitudes become exclusive and antagonistic to others who do not agree or support that way of thinking. The result can be wars between conflicting ideologies, as in the ongoing struggle and Cold War between Communism and Democracy. Ideals can separate more than they serve as bridges between people and nations, inhibiting mutal understanding and a sense of being one of the human family. For ideals, we threaten to blow up half of the world; if that isn't a crazy attitude, then what is? Ideals tainted by glamours create a crystallised situation in the mind; it freezes, oblivious to other world views and shades of opinion, tending towards impracticality and aggression in defence of itself. This is the consequence of glamours attached to ideals. Ideals can be extremely high and representative of formulations made by the human mind, and in many ways are to be encouraged as vehicles for progressive visions. Yet at present, due to the strength of the collective glamours, they are certain to be distorted and will probably end in opposing their own ruling principles. Becoming free of idealistic glamours is difficult, but we should always remain aware of their existence, allowing space for greater tolerance and understanding in our exchanges with others.

A list of the glamours associated with the Rays' correspondences to the transpersonal outer planets is also like a list of the planetary characteristics!

Neptune–Ray 6: devotion, adherence to forms/persons, idealism, loyalties, creeds, emotional responses, sentimentality, interference, dualistic opposites, saviours/teachers, narrow vision, fanaticism.

Uranus–Ray 7: magical work, relation of opposites, subterranean powers, physical body, mystery, secrets, sex magic, the power that brings together.

Pluto–Ray 1: physical strength, personal magnetism, self-centredness, personal potency, one at the centre, selfish ambition, rulership, dictator, control, manipulation, political messiah, selfish destiny, destruction, isolation, aloofness, superimposition of will.

Looking at the theme of illusion can be even more disheartening. Illusion exists on the level of mind, rather than emanating from the emotional level of selfish desires. Briefly described, illusion is a misunderstanding of ideas, misinterpreting thought-forms that exist on the collective mental level. Illusion builds a wall between the individual and the light, a wall that appears translucent, yet like a prism distorts and divides the light into several rays of colour. Through limited perception and understanding, 'truth' is incorrectly registered and received. Often the mind is lost in the surrounding thought-forms about truth and does not look at 'truth', in the same way that many have ideas about what enlightenment may be rather than having any personal experience of the state. Thought-forms become more real and apparently powerful than the truth which they are veiling.

Illusions can occur as a consequence of: wrong perception of an idea, incorrect interpretation, incorrect appropriation of an idea not meant for you to develop, wrong direction for an idea, lack of integration of an idea, incorrect embodiment of an idea, and a failure in applying the idea in the material world.

The visions of Neptune are contaminated by glamours and illusions; they can be beautiful and even inspiring, in the way that the Pre-Raphaelite paintings evoke an age and glory that never was in order to act as an inspiration in the contemporary world. But be wary of the bewitching smile and spell that is so cleverly cast in Neptune's domain; always try to determine which face is turned towards you now, and don't blink or else a switch may have occurred. It can be a perpetual fascination with Neptune, and it is certainly the strangest influence and vibration of all the planetary gods.

CHAPTER 4

Neptune and Planetary Aspects

THE NATAL ASPECTS of Neptune need to be carefully analysed, as they hold essential information concerning the more obvious ways that Neptune will operate and reveal its activity through the natal chart.

They become intrinsic patterns of personality expression, and because of their impulse to expand beyond known boundaries should generally be quite recognisable even if not personally acknowledged or acceptable. It can be an interesting exercise to study your own major Neptune aspects, and see how strongly you are conditioned by their influence. A basic overview of the nature of the five major aspects may be useful at this point.

CONJUNCTION

The conjunction, or close proximity of at least two planets, is usually considered to be the most potent aspect. This involves a merging of the undiluted energies and characteristics of the planets which are in conjunction, and can be seen as a channel through which the functions of these planets can be more easily expressed via the personality. Often, these combined tendencies are asserted with considerable vigour by the individual, who may consciously recognise that they are expressions of personal power and individuality in social situations, yet this assertiveness is often achieved with a less than conscious awareness of its impact upon others.

There is an ambiguity about the influence of the conjunction, often derived from the nature of this inner tension and the challenge of blending energies which may well be uncomplementary or even antagonistic in nature. This often reveals itself in life as creating certain difficulties in relationships with others, especially in those situations where you may need to consciously moderate or control your initial forms of response in order to prevent avoidable friction occurring. Such a 'lifeskill' may need to be learnt for social living, but should never be over-used so that you develop a pattern of inhibition of your thoughts and feelings when in company; it is a form of sensitivity by the fact that in certain situations it may be wiser and more harmonious to remain quiet. Certainly this blended energy almost insists on its need to be expressed, and channels for this are consciously looked for in the relevant spheres of life.

Much depends upon the relative affinity of the planets in conjunction as to the ease and efficacy with which a person can apply these energies in daily life. They can flow almost 'magically' together, enabling certain talents and qualities to emerge spontaneously and miraculously into effective creative channels once a focused attempt at drawing them through has been made. The right use of personal resources is then achieved for the benefit of the individual and ideally for others too. If the planets are lacking affinity or ease of collaboration, then utilising the energy will be more difficult, and an inner struggle is likely to create inner adjustments to enable the energies to work better with each other. A conjunction is a point of concentrated power in the natal chart if it can be properly released through the appropriate area of life signified by its natal house position.

SEXTILE ASPECT (60 DEGREE ASPECT)

The sextile indicates a natural energy relationship between the planets involved, and has a particular association with the mental level. According to which planets are involved, indications are given as to the nature of the person's mind and the likely natural content of his thought patterns. It facilitates the ability to absorb information, to collate and connect fragments of knowledge into a synthesising comprehension, and is an integrative function of the mind, being then revealed through the person's actions and his ability to communicate to others. It is often associated with a talent for creative expression, especially using words, and helps to build a catholic mental outlook on life built on the ability to grasp the intellectual knowledge and cultural developments of man.

There is an openness about the influence of the sextile that aids harmony, as it is not closed-minded in its inner effect, and this is conducive to the development of curiosity, space for new/other perceptions, and an ease in the wider social environment and in group co-operation.

TRINE ASPECT (120 DEGREE ASPECT)

The trine is a positive reconciliatory aspect, capable of uniting in a working manner two apparently opposing energies, hence its symbol being like a triangle. A trine is suitable for resolving areas of difficulty that may be experienced by other hard or challenging aspects which are made to either of the planets. As the symbol of the triangle is associated with understanding and resolving dualism, the trine aspects involving Neptune and any other planet are likely to hold a key to processes of personal integration, healing and transformation, and should be carefully considered in this light.

SQUARE ASPECT (90 DEGREE ASPECT)

The square aspect between planets indicates an energy relationship of tension and challenge which cannot be resolved without some form of internal adaptation being achieved. Potentially, the results of working with the square can lead to greater inner harmony, but this is likely to occur only after prolonged effort and psychological frustration, and through such refining fires the character becomes reborn in some essential way. It often seems to indicate barriers in the individual psyche, which repeatedly block a chosen route.

There are 'lessons and challenges' that the square represents that cannot be avoided, inevitable crises that will require confronting as stages along the path of life. Squares are frustrating, a source of inner conflict which, unless the nettle of challenge is grasped, will have a negative effect upon the inner life and thwart many a desire and intention. If the square is 'overcome', then it serves as a point of release for power and energy which can be applied to achieve personal aims. The square is associated with internal psychological problem areas, and an attempt to restructure the inner life, mind or emotions is vitally necessary.

OPPOSITION ASPECT (180 DEGREE ASPECT)

The opposition is often more concerned with the outer objective world and with relationships with others, but unless the personal focus is entirely orientated towards achievement in the outer world it is likely to prove less of a constant personal struggle than the inner square. Where the square is more of a unique private personal challenge, the opposition tends to be projected outwards (similar to the Shadow) on to others, thus creating an eventual context where they can be realised, observed and worked with as psychological projections. There can be signs of compulsive behaviour, demands made upon others, expressions of the power of focused will and self-absorption, which often have an interfering effect within close life relationships, coupled with attempts to manipulate others and situations for personal gain.

Creative and harmonious relationships can be a help to resolve the conflict between the opposition of planetary energies; also, any trines or sextiles which are made to either opposition planet can help to resolve the problems.

THE NATURE OF NEPTUNE ASPECTS

Any Neptune aspects made to other planets should be carefully considered to determine the probable impact that this planet will have on the personality. The planets that are aspected reveal those areas of life that will become highly sensitised and activated by stirrings in the unconscious mind. These constituent parts of the personal psyche (as symbolised by the specific planets) will often strive to open to new horizons, creating a sense of individual discontent in those areas of life.

Neptune will sensitise each aspected planet, forming an alignment to those formative yet hidden intangible forces of life, and one sign of this is the need to become free from all limitations and restrictions; ultimately this is the impulse to transcend the barriers of ego, intellect and the separate identity. This will involve the need to feel that universal oneness, melting and merging with the whole that characterises the effect of affinity with the transpersonal Neptune vibration.

For individuals with close Neptune planetary aspects, or a strong Neptunian attunement – with the personal planets, any planet in Pisces, Pisces Ascendant, or Neptune in the 1st house of identity – there is the potential of achieving a realisation of the reality of the transpersonal spirit and universal unity. Often, signs of this potential are manifested through more subtle levels of perception, with clairsentient abilities, and with inner guides or astral teachers, although this can equally be another symptom of Neptunian delusion if a realistic and perceptive discrimination is not applied. Some, when initially contacting such realms of existence, misunderstand what is happening to them, and their ego distorts the situation and begins to inflate. The end product can be self-delusion, where they close their minds only to see what fits their preconceptions and personal beliefs, eventually circling in their own private reality. Personal imagination has become too dominant for the more subtle spiritual dimension to be clearly registered. One problem of the tendency of Neptunian mediumship is that of sealing the aura, where oversensitivity and relative refinement can lead to a diminution of vital energy and increasing gullibility to astral messages as the repeated mediumistic opening can create a defenceless over-trusting mind.

A sense of personal discontent will be found with most Neptune aspects to any personal planet or Ascendant, especially the conjunction, square and opposition, and this can be experienced as a feeling of being trapped or imprisoned in the restrictive material world, perhaps by family, marriage, employment and social situation. Neptune starts to look for the escape door, a situation that creates many individual and social problems, rather than a decision to acknowledge responsibility and obligations, and then determine a conscious path to transform the lifestyle into a more favourable one. Yet it is these same types of aspect that are often found in charts of people attracted to the transpersonal path as a possible release from such deep-seated feelings. The trine and sextile are often more associated with imagination and creativity expressions, rather than a need for transpersonal contacts, as in the case of a Neptune trine, which may stimulate an intellectual curiosity yet falters at the demands to actually walk the transforming path.

What commonly happens with an opening to the Neptunian energies is the dream-vision of new potential and an ideal world waiting to be entered, which simultaneously co-exists with an awareness that there is a gap between the current personal situation and achieving those aims. As the actualisation of this dream-vision requires change and movement in the individual, this stimulates both feelings of discontent and confusion as the old pattern rapidly loses its vitality and no longer sustains life. The old world is dying and the new world is not yet born. The intervening limbo is the transformative ground that needs to be passed. Decision making becomes difficult, and whilst the vision may burn ever brighter, the sensation can be that you are stuck, treading water rather than actually swimming anywhere.

This confused state often reflects deep meaningful yearnings within the individual, but where a lack of understanding of these feelings creates a situation in which ways of dealing with them cannot easily be found. Personal attention is still directed towards the old world, and patterns related to expecting fulfilment from the external world still dominate. People look for supports – other people, money, ideals – instead of recognising the need to turn within and discover real self-responsibility. Dissatisfaction and disillusionment intensify as the outer search for answers and support disintegrates into fragments. Neptune indicates an inner path, and until this is commenced, only failure in judgement and action will be discovered.

It is a difficult stage, where glamours and self-deceptions run rampant; dissipation of energies, confusion and evasion are the usual reactions. Neptunian sensitising of contacted planets increases such a susceptibility in those associated areas of life, and it is here that disillusionment will be experienced. For instance, challenging Neptune aspects to the Sun may indicate deceptive projections on to the image of the father, distorting the actual reality of the parent until experiences later in life shatter this image and create disillusionment. Later, the actual reality and humanity of the father may be reintegrated and loved again, but in many cases, an unbridgeable gap has been formed. Similar experiences can occur with the Moon–mother image. Neptune–Venus contacts can imply a shattering disillusionment in the sphere of personal and intimate love, associated with *anima–animus* projections. There are many types of disillusionment possible.

The ideal way to work with a stage of Neptunian change is to understand that this energy needs to be contained and redirected in some way, that definition and commitment are necessary so that through disciplined application a way forward can be found. For many, this requires the clarity of a way towards devotion to an ideal, perhaps self-development and a spiritual or creative path. These are the signposts that Neptune tends to point people towards, and it is unlikely that real progress can be achieved and the life re-created unless the individual follows a path of Neptunian affinity.

This is a refining and cleansing process, where values and attitudes are to be redefined, and the accretions of the material world are to be shed like a snake-skin so that the new physical structure can be revealed to the world, one which has discovered more inclusive and realistic spiritual values and perspectives.

The challenging, hard or stressful aspects often hold a key to progress, and these often result in potentially more creatively beneficial and productive results in the individual than the trine or sextile, where sometimes the impulse to act is dissipated. The astrological implication of challenging aspects is that there is a misunderstanding, misapplication and lack of integration of those forces and energies which are symbolised by the planets involved. Some type of confrontation with these contentious areas is necessary, so that a greater understanding is attained which then leads to a redirection of the blocked and distorted energies towards positive channels of expression; in this way, by building a new inner structure, the Neptunian energies can become constructively and practically applied. The key is often realised once the individual recognises that the outer world will ultimately fail to satisfy and liberate, and that the only alternative direction is to move within and strive to demonstrate the viability of our own deepest ideals and dreams.

In many ways, the challenging aspects hold the keys to personal transformation as energy is generated by such pressures, and this can stimulate the individual to actually make those essential changes by confronting him with the consequences if he fails to do so. Dealing with Neptune in a person's chart often displays the area of life and consciousness where he is the least rational, as in sign and house position and aspects, and it is here that the influences of the unconscious mind are more easily discernible. Still, rationality has its limits, and Neptune loves to transcend them. Whoever said that the universe is ultimately rational anyway? It is always important to remember that the transpersonal planets of Uranus, Neptune and Pluto influence us through activating their contacts and channels of the other planets, houses and signs in the ways symbolised by astrological representations. These are the gateways from the unconscious and transpersonal levels into our conscious minds, where gods and humans interpenetrate.

SUN–NEPTUNE CONJUNCTION

Any Neptune aspect to the Sun is likely to have a distinct impact on the individual expression of personal power, identity and life direction, so it becomes important to create a positive approach to the Neptunian energy and especially so with the more influential aspects like the conjunction, square and opposition. The difficulty with an unintegrated or repressed Neptune is that its influence often appears to be negative, and with this conjunction aspect it is imperative to discover a personal way of joining this energy to the natural form of expression that the Sun sign indicates.

You will probably experience an ongoing challenge of self-confidence and of establishing a suitable and satisfying style of purpose and life direction. The nebulous influence of Neptune's sea mists tend to confuse you, dissolving many of your intentions away, and making your sense of a strong individual identity almost transparent at times as that personality centre seems to ebb and flow in tune with an inner tidal rhythm. Because of an inner experience associated with insubstantiality, you can lack the strength of a firm and fixed ego structure, and this has the effect of diminishing confidence regarding your actual capabilities and your will to achieve any objectives. You can find it hard to persevere and be consistent through self-discipline and application for long periods of time. Your identity can appear to be periodically submerged by the powerful Neptune energy, dissolving plans and ambitions, and then leaving you washed ashore in another inner place wondering what to do next, even before you have completed the last project.

That ethereal Neptunian music will invade your conscious mind, acting as a diverting distraction, and in some cases can influence the listener to become lost in the swirlings of his own hyperactive imagination – the path to self-delusion. Confronting the stark realities of life is not always easy with a prominent Neptune. There is a tendency to build a private reality, one which excludes the dark sides of self and the world, establishing a veiled and limiting perspective of life which only generates activity by additional repression into the unconscious mind. Personal responsibility is avoided if possible, and all experiences are filtered through this restrictive veil, a state that, if prolonged, leads to alienation from the self and others.

Often these forms of self-delusion emanate from personal

desires, emotions and sensitive feelings, as Neptune is associated with the plastic and pliable astral level, and there can develop unusual desires and needs which are subtle, intangible yet peculiarly insistent, and you may feel inwardly driven to experience or actualise them in some way. For many, such hard-to-define feelings and yearnings create more personal confusion and self-deception, especially when attached to idealistic images of perfection and unrealistic expectations which can only bring disillusionment and disappointment in their wake. For the few, Neptune may bring genuine inspiration, although even in such cases, this may become mixed with desires of self-elevation and ambitions.

One of the hardest lessons facing anyone with a close Neptune aspect is the facing of the realities of life. Neptune finds such confrontations almost inimical to its sensitivities, preferring to slide away instead of looking. You may have noticed such evasiveness in your own life, manifesting itself in a variety of disguises through the years; the evasion of problems (the ostrich syndrome), the evasion of decision making, the evasion of self-assertion and the evasion of the effort to unfold your inner potential. The disguises are legion, but their cumulative effect is considerable, gradually creating an unsatisfactory lifestyle and the diminution of direction, meaning and purpose as the real inner self is lost under veils of escapism. We are all prone to this tendency, and it is this that keeps us spiritually asleep. 'Wake up' is the cry of the spirit, a waking up that gives us the experience of a direct unfiltered confrontation with life, a light which exposes all those shadowy corners, revealing both the simplicity and complexity of the cosmic mind in manifestation. Facing the higher aspect of Neptune is not a self-deluding experience, but a sobering one. An unintegrated Neptune may offer delusions and glamour, but integrating Neptune is a path towards fusing the individual emotional level with the universal life, in a way similar to that of integrating Uranus fusing the mind through intuition with the universal mind.

Recognising the negative expression of Neptune is the first step; the next is to choose to integrate this power into the personal life so that the positive dimension opens. There have undoubtedly been times when you have felt in full control, confident in your self and your direction, confident in your ability to achieve ambitions, only to pass into another phase when this confidence seeps away, dissolving as quickly as you try to hold on to it. This occurs where Neptune and the Sun are at odds with each other, where a fusion has not yet happened. Whilst this aspect can become a gateway to an inward turning, an entering of the inner worlds and mystical devotion, it is more useful to consider how external expression of the energy can stimulate greater integration.

What Neptune can offer is a variety of gifts that can be applied as a means of personal expression, gifts which emanate from the inner seas and which are simultaneously a channel or path back into conscious contact with Neptune's realm. These include art, music, poetry, drama, literature, psychism, mysticism. The potential is for inspiration to be revealed through such channels for the benefit of all who are capable of receiving the transmission. Unlocking inner doors so that creativity flows is extremely enriching, and shifts the level of consciousness; there can be dangers in unlocking the flood gates, as so many creative individuals have discovered, but in many ways it is a sacred task to reveal the numinosity behind the appearance.

Adding or developing a creative and artistic dimension to your life will be a means of integrating this Neptunian energy, as it will begin to flow into those particular channels that you have opened; allied to this it will begin to display its positive face, as greater meaning, purpose and life direction have more cohesiveness and substance, instead of periodically dissolving. Even if such creativity is purely personal and for your own satisfaction, enjoyment and need to self-express, over time you will become aware of the benefits that it has brought to you. Such talents may need deliberate training and development, but time spent in this way will be rewarding. Moving into such a direction may require you to reconsider your whole lifestyle, as its influence will be profound. Your type of employment may stand revealed as deeply unfulfilling and unsatisfactory, being a restriction on you rather than a positive factor, and this can pose the problem of an economic restructuring of your life. Finding a way of living that can satisfy those creative abilities may be difficult, but the alternative is even more damaging if you choose to turn your back on the seductive music of Neptune. Personal creativity or craftsmanship is the route that Neptune is indicating, or alternatively, working with people in ways designed to be of social benefit is a way of community service. Perhaps through teaching, medicine or social work you can contribute to others' welfare. This is a heart response to the music, equally significant and satisfying to that desire to

be positive in the world. Find a way which offers you more freedom than more traditional work structures tend to offer, a way
that encourages creativity or service to flow. In so doing, you
unravel the path to travel along, and those times of confusion
and indecision are relegated to memories. The potential of working
with Neptune is considerable; the god can transform you if you
are open to his promptings and messages. If he is rejected, then
his waters will slowly erode away your dreams and desires, leaving you with an unfulfilled life; it is wiser to acknowledge his
inner promptings and try to change into accord with them. The
gods do not take kindly to being mocked through being ignored,
and they make their presence felt.

SUN–NEPTUNE SEXTILE

Unlike the conjunction aspect, which poses the problem of dealing
with both the positive and negative influences of Neptune on the
individual life, the sextile is an easier aspect to live with.

Once again the themes of creativity through art, music, crafts,
writing and drama are highlighted as ways of co-operating with
the Neptunian impulse, as are the inner paths of mysticism and
psychic senses. You are likely to be aware of your own creative
potential, and be inclined to allow this natural expression. One
ability that you may possess is that of being able to create vivid
inner mental images, which through the process of creative visualisation you can use either in the building of your own future
path, or by offering these for the stimulation and enjoyment of
others through music, art and literature. Manifesting these evocative images into a tangible form is a very important gift, and can
be applied in a variety of ways, both for self-aggrandisement and
the accumulation of wealth or power and to help benefit the lives
of others. This issue of self versus selfless actions is one which
may confront you, influencing your decisions and motivations.
The art of visualisation is a powerful merging of mind–will–
imagination, and is the source of creation.

Your sensitivity to others and the pain in the world will be
strong, and there is likely to be a reasonably well developed awareness of social responsibility, where by empathic feelings you believe that you should and could aid in the alleviation of suffering
by others. Yet this psychic absorption of pain can also make you

turn away from actually doing anything about this social awareness, where you register and acknowledge its existence yet attempt to deny your role in healing. It is unlikely that you will be
capable of dealing with the causes of suffering, but may prefer
to hold a soothing and healing balm to the symptoms of the pain.
You hope that others who are stronger and perhaps less sensitive
than yourself will deal with the negative causes in society.

One area where you could be of value to others is that of communicating inspiration, perhaps through public-orientated writing or though any of the communication media. Linking your
grasp of social responsibility with a good dramatic expression
could bring to the attention of others those areas in society that
need transforming; crusading journalism and TV documentaries
are prime examples of such expression. This is an asset that you
could apply, and certainly if you choose to develop this, then
your natural imagination and inspiration will be re-kindled. This
need to maintain a channel of relationship with people which
also involves a broader social sphere than that of just friendship
is a route which Neptune will work through, especially as you
are able to use those inner imaginative visions to build external
tangible forms.

With most people, you experience a *laissez-faire* relationship,
where tolerance and human empathy dominate, and interpersonal
pressures are not imposed. Whilst your sensitivity is ever present,
you are not overly demanding or tied to impossible expectations
of others, although you do prefer self-confident companions who
by association force you to firm up any tendency towards Neptunian nebulousness and indecision. If anything, you have a
humanitarian spirit, relating freely and easily to a wide range of
human types, seeing value in all and not just in those who are
'successful' in terms of social evaluation.

There is an element of the chameleon nature about you though,
a malleability enabling you to fit into a variety of situations and
social scenes, an inner flexibility whereby your attitudes and expressions mould themselves to their specific environments, taking
over from any deeper personal preferences. This is a Neptunian
water quality in your personality, where you 'take the shape of any
container'. This can be advantageous, yet also can lead to the loss
of a distinct personal identity due to repeated chameleon transfor-
mations, so this may need to be carefully monitored or guarded
against if your personality begins to fragment and dissolve.

However, if you are following a mystical path, dissolving into the 'ocean' is your aim, where the droplet of the separate self loses all boundaries and disappears into the ocean of life.

SUN–NEPTUNE TRINE

With the trine, there is the potential for a successful reconciling and resolving of the energies of Neptune and the Sun, leading to a powerful positive blending of the planetary natures – of the egoic Sun and the transpersonal outer planet and god operating through the superconscious level of the unconscious mind.

The potential may be present, but there may be question marks against your incentive, motivation and application in exploiting your latent talents. This is the hurdle that can face you, especially the one where you are confronted with the nature of choice and decision over the direction to travel towards. Some can be multi-talented in a variety of artistic and creative ways – music, art, literature, dance, drama – yet find it hard to be focused and sufficiently disciplined to become a master and not a jack of all trades. Ideas spring forth easily and naturally, followed by an enthusiastic grasping of them, only for them to be put aside quickly when replaced by the next set of shooting-star ideas. Commitment and perseverance may be lacking, and the propulsion of directed energy is fragmented by turning in too many directions at the same time.

Associated with a perceptive mind, which is capable of good assimilation and understanding, should be an intuitive quality too, which you can use as a source of insight and knowledge. This intuitive or psychic faculty will mainly operate through the emotional nature as empathic identification, in distinction to the Uranian intuition which is more mental and impersonal in nature. This intuition often gives you insights into the nature and motivation of others around you, and environmental atmospheres can influence your state of mind and well-being.

There can be an ambivalence towards social involvement and responsibility. Much depends on the nature of your expression; if it is within the creative and artistic spheres, then most of your energy is absorbed within that, and your focus of attention is displaced into a personal creative vision. It isn't that you are unresponsive to social concerns, but you feel that being a creative channel is your contribution to society. Others reacting to the Neptunian vibration respond by opening their hearts wider, feeling themselves to be a channel for 'universal love' supporting and uplifting others. Their path is one of service to the community of human beings, and medicine can be a favourite expression, or similar forms of physical, emotional and mental therapy and healing.

Becoming clear as to that direction is the challenge; once that has been clarified, then you should be able to pour your energies and talents into achieving those aims. You do have the capabilities to achieve your objectives, once definition and focus is made. There may be a need to be more practical, perhaps modified by a strong Saturn or Mercury ensuring that material results occur, or you could waste those talents and end as a negative visionary dreamer, chasing your imagination but never containing it within objective form.

In personal relationships, emotional freedom and trust are highly valued as natural components of ideal romantic love. You tend to be emotionally faithful and give priority to the virtues of a close and loving family environment. Your empathic nature adds to those feelings of closeness with family and friends, and you are very sympathetic.

SUN–NEPTUNE SQUARE

The tendencies associated with the square aspect often indicate psychologically based inhibitions, restrictions and frustrations which pose considerable challenges that need overcoming before the more positive characteristics of Neptune can emerge.

You tend to lack real confidence in your personal identity and your ability to achieve your ambitions in life. Part of this may have been derived from your relationship with your parents, especially your father, as your developing nature may have experienced conflict through lack of understanding or perceived love; it may have been that in asserting your own individuality you clashed with the stronger parental will. The results are that your self-confidence has fragmented, that your application of will is less focused and effective, that you have developed inhibiting forms of psychological defence against others, and that you do not face up to personal failure.

This is displayed in attempts towards escapism and in the avoidance of responsibilities and the needs of self-discipline, unless a powerful Saturn in your chart rebalances this tendency. Preferring to run away from confronting reality leads both to distorted perceptions, which makes careful evaluation of opinions difficult, and to the fear of making decisions which may prove to be unwise. At its worst, this can create inertia through fear of deliberate action. These inner images of failure tend to create external failures, and so emphasise a vicious circle repeated over time. Yet by wrapping this pattern of failure within aims and ambitions that are probably beyond your current capabilities to achieve, you also succeed in evading the realisation that you are self-creating failures in your life. This is exacerbated by the dreams of the unintegrated and unfilfilled Neptune, who may be noticed as a thread of guilt related to your lack of achievement, and as an ongoing sensation of discontent.

These challenges can be mitigated by a conscious decision to make sufficient effort to connect to your hidden centre, to move beyond those superimposed images of guilt, failure and inferiority that have developed as a defensive response to emotional pain. Such a reorientation may not be easy to make, as you will be opposing established patterns of behaviour, yet the gains that can be made are likely to positively transform your life.

The first step is to accept your own nature. Do not condemn yourself or make judgements. Feel confident that change can occur, if you really want it to happen. You have sufficient inner creativity, imagination and potential waiting to be released from imprisonment, although finding appropriate channels of expression may still take a little longer. However, you need to clarify any ambitions within a more realistic perspective than previously. Possibly some form of counselling may be effective in helping you to gain more clarity regarding your self and potential, or you may use workshops in self-assertion and decision making or goal setting. In effect, you are being asked to see yourself as a young child, ready to enter adulthood, and you are expected to re-create yourself into a new and more suitable identity. Take smaller and easily achievable steps in this process of re-creation; acknowledge that occasional failures are inevitable, but try not to turn them into traumatic dramas, and realise that success will not happen without the parallel risk of failure side by side; acknowledge too that everybody is a failure at something, and that it isn't an excuse to condemn yourself again. As your self-confidence grows, your life will begin to take a more positive shape. It will not happen overnight, as long-established behaviour patterns cannot be changed that quickly, but persevere and changes can happen. Perhaps the use of techniques such as creative visualisation and affirmations, or subliminal programming on self-development cassette tapes, could strengthen this process. The essential point to accept and have faith in is that change is possible, and that you can achieve this in your own way; in hope lies the fountainhead of the waters of potential and transformation.

Such improvements can also benefit your intimate relationships too, as well as enhance your own self-image, self-confidence and decision-making abilities. Generally you are emotionally vulnerable, possibly exploited or abused by others, deceived or manipulated in various ways; but if these tendencies exist, then they are reflections of those dominating patterns within you. There can be unusual emotional needs and desires, linked with romantic idealism, that are expressed in physical sexuality which may require healing and cleansing in some way. But the proposed transformation and refinement that is implied by resolving the conflict of the Sun and Neptune would simultaneously deal with that level too.

There can be an attraction towards occultism and mysticism and, if followed in the pre-transformation stage, this can lead to self-exaltation as an antidote for that inferiority complex; you are deluded into regarding your own voice as being that of God or the Masters. However, if the transformation has been made, then you could actually function in such a way as a purer channel. But some degree of caution and restraint may be needed if you do explore such dimensions of life, as there can be an unconscious desire for self-aggrandisement operating and motivating your actions. As the imagination aspect of Neptune is so strong, this can create inflated egotism and self-delusion; instead of being found in the light, you then become lost in the lights of glamour and illusion.

SUN–NEPTUNE OPPOSITION

The opposition between Neptune and the Sun will stimulate a distorted and self-deluding perspective of reality, which tends to create additional problems and obstacles in your life and decision making. You may find it difficult to correctly analyse and evaluate your options and choices, often focusing on self-created and imaginary issues rather than actual problems. Sometimes these can take the forms of voluntary suffering arising from inner guilt patterns associated with deep-lying desires, an expiation or atonement of 'sins', actual or imaginary. This can manifest itself as the sacrificial martyr attitude, and is often quite unnecessary, yet in a strange way provides a foundation to the inner life. A sacrifice may well be required – that of your imagined illusions – but this is often misunderstood and misapplied in daily life.

You tend to strongly react against any imposition of domination by others, yet can submit easily if under the influence of a misplaced sacrificial trip. Your relationships can be characterised by degrees of confusion and misunderstandings, and through powerful emotions you are liable to overlay the nature of your intimate relationships with fantasies and wishful thinking, forming a deceiving miasma which affects all involved. There can be a pattern operating through you that subverts clear, honest and direct communication, even though you may not fully accept or realise this. As you tend to be personally insecure and defensive in relationship attitudes, tensions can be generated by your style of expression, which rarely accepts being wrong or any responsibility, yet does so in a manner which attempts to lay any blame on the shoulders of others; it is a form of expression that confuses rather than clarifies, and which over time creates considerable friction. This nebulousness dominates your personality, turning you into a 'psychological chameleon', changing appearances and attitudes as your distorted perceptions and personal biases intrude into reality.

Commitment is often avoided, and you may avoid really entering into emotional involvements through a fear of being trapped or dominated, which allied to a suspicious nature does not augur well for stable relationships. As you are liable to fall under the negative Neptunian glamours regarding love and romance, this tendency may have developed from previous shattering disappointments, but if it becomes a repetitive pattern in your life, then the cause is probably within yourself, and it is through an inward journey and exploration that you can discover a solution.

Coming to terms with such influential patterns concerning your own identity and relationships with others requires considerable honesty and commitment. Beneficial change can be stimulated, but only if you really want it and are willing to put in the effort. The main problem with inner glamours and illusions is that they are so difficult to correctly identify, and obviously such distorting mirrors make it hard to perceive clearly and correctly. The real effects of spiritual transformation shatter these mirrors. Being able to recognise and acknowledge that such problems exist is the first and most important step, followed by consistent action to discover the appropriate remedy.

Through insecurity, you are liable to doubt your own capabilities and potential, fearing challenges as exposing your failings and weaknesses. Retreat or defensive mechanisms may have been established as forms of protection. Essentially, you need to strip down your patterns of perceiving others and yourself, so that the reality of situations can shine through more objectively. Facing the reality of avoidance patterns and observing the influence of your emotional biases and defensive mechanisms can be very revealing, as can noting how you distort communications within your relationships. Do all this without condemnation or judgement of yourself. In looking are hidden the seeds of transformation.

Refinding your own centre and self beyond these ephemeral influences is the journey, and establishing a personal strength in your own identity and resources rather than any unhealthy reliance on others will demonstrate a developing maturity. Becoming clearer regarding your aims in life, perhaps developing a programme towards achieving some of them, can give a directional focus to work with. This can allow you to be independent and to express that blocked and frustrated creative potential that has been inhibited for so long. Taking such steps can renew yourself and relationships, and protect you from being negatively influenced by surrounding psychic environmental influences entering your psyche. Once the changes are made, you can have much to offer people; your sacrificial tendencies can be beneficial. Working with styles of meditation which deglamorise and strip away illusory veils of personality, or with relationship therapies, can be suitable approaches to take.

MOON–NEPTUNE CONJUNCTION

This conjunction emphasises emotional sensitivity and vulnerability to others, especially through an impressionable, sympathetic psychic empathy. The nature of your environment will be highly influential in affecting your inner balance and well-being, so ideally you need to live and work within suitable places and with suitable people, or else you may discover that your spirit and vitality begin to wane through absorbing what are negative influences on your sensitivity.

As your heart is so open to experience life, it is equally likely to experience suffering, anguish and disappointments. Evolving ways of self-protection or essential filters to this sensitivity may be necessary over time, otherwise life could become too painful for you. Through your innate understanding and sympathetic attitudes, you are likely to become a listener and confidante to others' problems; yet a degree of detached impersonal objectivity needs to be developed or else you will take their problems and pain away with yourself. This is not a sacrifice that needs to be made, even though you are rightly willing to offer aid and assistance to those in need. It may be that you are attracted towards employment in the spheres of social welfare and care, where you can serve deprived people and encourage them to take steps of advancement. Certainly that compassionate heart will be a main motivating factor in your life, and it is probably through such a route that you can most easily display your natural qualities and abilities. Your influence can have a beneficial and catalytic effect on others, stimulating them towards either personal growth or resolving problems. Employment which fixes you into a repetitive mundane work pattern will not be satisfying, and will ultimately be a denial of your talents and abilities. It is easy to recognise when you are stuck in the wrong place: you are beset by the intensification of wishful thinking and daydreaming, of desires to escape, and of a lack of interest in application.

You have a powerful imagination which does not like to be inhibited or denied and is constantly looking for ways to be expressed; there will be considerable artistic and cultural appreciation as well as creative gifts within you waiting to be released. Suitable channels are art, music, poetry, design, ways that preferably evoke an emotional-feeling response in yourself and others. You could develop into being visionary and inspirational if this area was especially focused and all your energies were committed to such a task. Your psychic sensitivities could play a role in this, offering the awareness of more subtle currents in life and the power inherent in symbols and images, or even your dream life with a prophetic quality could be influential. It is probably best to use any such psychic or mediumistic talents only as a support to artistic creation, because you may find that they can be too unreliable or too shrouded in Neptunian sea mists and make clear perception difficult. These tendencies can develop towards religious or spiritual interests, such as the exaltation of the mystic's emotions and heart devotions.

In your personal life and intimate relationships, you may need to be wary of a tendency to be excessively romantic, preoccupied with dreams of the ideal lover, always searched for and never found. In real life there are real people, and disillusionment is never far away from the *anima–animus* projected obsessions which create self-delusions and the experience of being shocked by the reality of your 'dream lover'. Turning men or women into gods or goddesses is a dangerous game; they always fall off the pedestal that you have placed them on. Like Humpty Dumpty, the fall shatters the illusion which can never be put together again around that person. Yet falling in love again with the real person is often much more rewarding and enriching.

There can be tendencies to evade the impingement of harsh reality at times. That isn't the way, but making adjustments to your own attitudes may be the key to deal with this challenge. Accepting reality is a process that we have to continually confront in life, although this doesn't necessarily imply a surrender to the inevitable; it can be the initial action required to determine how to transform an unsatisfactory situation. Sometimes the influence of Neptune dominates the Moon, and the result is a retreat towards private worlds, hiding within defensive shells, unable to face the real world, and living within the glamour of those castles in the air of your imagination, lost in dreaming worlds.

Additionally, Moon aspects indicate an association with the Mother image, symbol and real parent. The conjunction implies a close bonding with your mother or an important influence over your development, but as with your romantic relationships, illusions can be present which may need cleansing or releasing if they are negatively affecting your adult relationships.

MOON–NEPTUNE SEXTILE

The sextile aspect poses less ambiguous problems than the conjunction, and you should find that this aspect is more comfortable and allows the releasing of your potential more easily. There will be the qualities of imagination, psychic and empathic sensitivity which are present in Moon–Neptune contacts, but these are clearer with the sextile and less liable to distortion through personal and outer perceptions.

You will be very responsive to the dimension of social relationships, obligations and service, and this could form the key foundation in your life, both in providing a sphere of employment and as one which allows your intrinsic talents and qualities to emerge. You have a heart response to negative social conditions, whether in terms of individuals, alienated minority groupings or global undifferentiated sympathies. This may attract you towards employment which involves you in dealing with social-problem areas, or at least towards associating with pressure groups concerned with areas of social deprivation and negativity. You can become quite passionate in denouncing man's lack of humanity and care for others, and feel concerned enough to add your support to more positive and beneficial causes.

You tend to be externally focused rather than inwardly preoccupied, and this can lead you to become a spokesperson for your social objections, attempting to wake the public up to those dangers or lack of care that so offend you as causing people to suffer unnecessarily. This search to promote social remedies can help you to express your creative spirit through evocative writing, through the dissemination of relevant information as an educational aid; some may feel drawn to crusading journalism designed to awaken the sleeping social conscience. Having high social ideals implies that one important role that you could perform is as a mediator and enunciator of proposed social progress and development. Working with the burdens of social welfare in some respect would give deep satisfaction, as through your heart response you create alternative suggestions for improvement transmitted via your inspired intellect.

You are less prone to illusions and pedestal building in your intimate relationships, as you should have a more realistic appraisal of the fallibility of human nature, and your tolerance and understanding should lead you to less disappointment in this area. Provided that you create the right channels for external activity, then both your domestic and social life should fulfil. Try not to forget that the Moon will anchor you in deep family ties, both to your parents and to any current family, and that these are probably more important to you than you may realise, especially if you become extremely involved in social action.

As you will be liable to be sensitive to the subtle psychic influences around people and environments, you may need to periodically retreat into isolation and quiet in order to inwardly cleanse and renew your energies. Your inner life and imagination can often indicate suitable directions for you to travel in, or even themes for social action, and probably many of your decisions are taken by acting on your more unconscious impulses. If such actions are taken and result in failures, then you may need to investigate your own attitudes and motivations more so that unredeemed unconscious tendencies are brought into the light, thus diminishing their power to lead you into cul-de-sacs and self-created failure.

MOON–NEPTUNE TRINE

Both the sextile and trine aspects of Neptune to the Moon are often found in the charts of artistic and creative people, especially those with a personal interest in increasing the amount of beauty and goodness in the environment of social life. This can manifest itself in a variety of ways, from improving someone's living conditions, through more aesthetic cultural appreciations, to enjoying a well-made film or admiring an evocative painting of harmony and beauty.

The trine indicates the potential for a successful resolution of these two planetary energies, so that the inner imaginative and sensitive life is integrated with a suitable form of outer expression. As there is a tendency towards environmental hypersensitivity, you need to discover a way of response that allows you to use this perception in creative ways, through revealing to others this more subtle and perhaps hidden invisible dimension of life, so that they too can appreciate and contact the vitalising, uplifting and inspirational quality of the inner realms. This is why this aspect can often be found in those who are dedicated to film, dance and the arts as revealers of enriched perceptions of life, and where the Neptunian muse works through into the world.

You are likely to possess such innate talent, and provided that you make the effort to manifest your inner imaginative dreams –

perhaps associated with your Venus – then you can be productive. If, however, you have a weak or badly aspected Mercury, Saturn or Mars, then you may have certain obstacles to overcome first before your dreams can turn into reality. Otherwise, you may be able to offer rich dramatic artistic creations for the stimulation and enjoyment of others.

Generally, you are a beneficent spirit, warm and compassionate to others and aware of the social dimension to life. Yet you may be more attuned to applying your energies in a distinctly creative manner than to being preoccupied with more direct social action, believing that creativity is the best way for you to contribute towards the advancement of society. Your interest is usually in the unfolding of individual potential, and you can place much effort into encouraging this in others, especially your family and younger people. Sometimes, though, you may be a little self-centred in attitude – especially when under the influence of an artistic muse – and prefer to be freer from social or family obligations in order to concentrate on releasing your creative spirit.

In relationships you prefer a partner to have independent interests and the ability to be more self-reliant and not excessively dependent on you. Partners should have a corresponding artistic appreciation and sensitivity, culturally developed so that mutual understanding is present.

It may be that your creative spirit is fully satisfied by the creation of projects which can have a direct benefit for others, which contribute to improving social conditions in some way. From these you too would benefit as the quality of the social environment improves, and so diminishes the level of negative impact that it can make on you.

There can be a prophetic element in your creativity; intuition, related to people and directions, can play a vital role in your life, and art can give direction or voice to underlying social needs too. This is the psychic dimension operating; it requires attention.

MOON–NEPTUNE SQUARE

The main challenge facing you with the square aspect is that of discrimination between reality and unreality, between fact and fiction, and the consequences of confusion when these are not correctly perceived and established within consciousness. Volatile and tidal emotions and feelings are often intertwined with your imagination so that your perceptions are clouded by personal bias and fantasies. There is a tendency to change experiences in your own mind so that they fit more acceptable emotional patterns, yet through distorting real experiences and re-creating your memories illusion spreads until your accounts of the past and reality are at odds with those of others. Attempts to warp realities, especially those concerning others, are never welcomed and are a source of conflict within relationships. Insisting that you are right – even against the recall of several others – will eventually generate antagonism, as no one enjoys having their reality and memory threatened by others, even if they are family members. Alternatively, you may resort to imaginatively building inner landscapes to escape into that are populated by personally satisfying fantasies; the dangers here lie in their intrusion into everyday reality.

You often feel uncomfortable with your feelings and emotions as they are not easily assimilated and integrated by you, and being liable to moods you find it difficult to feel centred in any stable emotional pattern of responses to people and life. There may have been some emotionally based difficulties in your parental relationships, especially to your mother, where emotional needs were not satisfied or where you imagine failings to have occurred. You tend to resist accepting responsibility, and can display anti-social behaviour, perhaps being contrary as a knee-jerk reaction to those inner feelings of pain and disappointment regarding social expectations, deliberately refusing to express any potential at all, acting just to assert a hurt negativity. Possibly your earlier home life was one of change, tension, stress and confusion, maybe a broken home or an unsatisfactory parental marriage whose psychic impression has been left on you. In many ways you often feel that you are holding back the floodgates from bursting open, and these can be stresses emanating from your unconscious mind caused by unresolved and blocked powerful emotions which are seeking a cathartic release. Fear can result from this, a fear which manifests itself in a variety of ways, for example that of over-stretching yourself or that of allowing yourself to be vulnerable within relationships. To diminish these pressures, some allow themselves to fall into the grip of addictions, drugs, alcohol, forms of sexual and emotional indulgences, searching for those brief periods of blankness from reality.

Yet none of this is inevitable or essential to experience. Changes can be successfully made by working with those intrinsic assets which you may have blocked so far, or whose presence you may have denied, rather than acknowledging them as gifts. Imagination is present; this can be used in positive ways. What you need to do is to build positive images of a 'new you' who has less of a chip on your heart, and who is prepared to change into a more creative and loving person.

Understanding your own nature is the first step towards being tolerant of others' weaknesses and strengths, so some form of inner psychological enquiry is required. Releasing pent-up emotional tension is essential, and should be carefully done, probably with the aid of trained counsellors or psychotherapists, because too great and sudden an emotional explosion of pressures may be more damaging than healing. Types of body work, manipulation and massage could possibly be additionally beneficial too. Acknowledging the hurt or anger in your emotions is necessary, but do not be self-condemnatory about this; accept that it is there and resolve to release it in order to allow healing to happen. Be more open and honest in relationships concerning any feelings of confusion; try not to let them fester inside. Organise your life more consciously, determine suitable directions and aims, although ensure that they are realistic and that you can persevere in any commitment needed to achieve them, perhaps starting with easier short-term objectives. Take things steadily during this period of re-creation, for change rarely happens overnight and always needs a thorough integration into the personality. Be cautious, and begin to relate more consciously with the material level, allowing those inevitable limitations to become a necessary structure for you to grow safely within. Work with others, so that you realise that all need support and guidance at times in their lives from others who may be perceptive on a clearer level. Believe in your own potential, and determine to allow it access into your life.

In so doing, the negative aspects of the square can be transformed into positive assets. Preferably work with more down-to-earth schools of therapy, which can then ground you better, rather than following a natural tendency towards more imaginative escapism, which can result in involvement with any religious/mystical cults which aim to fly in holy skies of grandeur and hallucinations rather than experience real life. Try to keep away from attempts to develop psychic or mediumistic abilities, as these can throw you back into that confusion of reality–unreality.

MOON–NEPTUNE OPPOSITION

There are several similarities between the opposition's effects and those of the square aspect between Neptune and the Moon, although with the opposition the inner tension and stress is more projected outwards into the world so that it is reflected back by other people and the environment.

You tend to look for the solutions to your problems in the outer world, often by forms of dependency on others, or by misidentification with people, places or material possessions which seem to offer some sense of security and respite from those inner pressures of emotional confusion. By doing this you are liable to fragment an already fragile emotional nature, and by displacing your centre suffer a loss of motivational and directional cohesiveness to your life.

As is common with these planetary contacts, there is an over-imaginative production of illusions, where the boundaries of truth and fiction become blurred at the edges. It is within your more personal and intimate relationships that these illusions are probably most active and observable, especially as they tend to create distortions, disorder and confusion in communication. There can be friction in your home life, partly as a consequence of your projections of unresolved illusions and stresses on to others, and this is likely to continue until you withdraw these projections back into yourself and resolve them.

At times you may feel trapped within your lifestyle, aching to become free of any situations that you feel are oppressing you. You often respond to such feelings by attempts at escapism, tending to prefer 'running away' from problems rather than confronting them in an effort to resolve them. In some cases this leads to the common Neptunian addictions towards drugs and alcohol as easily available 'remedies', which of course they are not, just crutches that only add to your existing difficulties.

This psychic emotional sensitivity and empathy to people and environments tends to be very influential, and you tend to absorb all impressions without any protection or discrimination. These add to your emotional insecurity and instability, as well as to that tendency to allow yourself to be used by others for their own advantage. These inner conflicts reflect the Neptunian tendencies towards being a victim, rather than a voluntary sacrifice, and you may find that the inner tensions become reflected externally in your physical body through a psychosomatic reaction.

Yet if such a situation is afflicting your life, then it need not remain this way; it can be improved through conscious change. Underlying the emotional vulnerability and lack of confidence is a reservoir of creative talent that can be used; the difficulty lies in being able to clear a path for it to flow through into manifestation, and to do so requires the transformation of inhibiting emotional patterns. If you seriously choose to apply your energy, then perhaps through disciplined training and tuition you could unlock the closed doors to this inner imaginative talent and release that frustrated energy.

You need to learn how to stand firmly within your own light, to be powerful and centred in your own being, rather than relying on others or by displacing your centre into the external world. Your challenge is to be yourself, not to compare your abilities with others, bemoan your fate and feel envy regarding the successes of friends. You will have enough struggle to reorientate your own established patterns of behaviour, but the effort will certainly be worthwhile and dissolve all those restrictive emotionally based festering inner poisons; the task is that of re-creation and renewal, a second birth. Self-confidence will improve as each small step is taken and you begin to observe the improvements that are happening, and slowly you'll believe that you can exploit that reservoir of hidden potential that is so deeply located within you. You'll start to reclarify your aims and intentions in life, piecing together a new direction to travel, forging a lifestyle that fits you and which does not generate friction through inner frustration and conflict. You'll feel strong enough to follow your own counsel, trusting in the validity of those inner promptings, and finally being able to take advantage of your acute sensitivity, appreciating the perception that it offers of an enriched life, and of how it can be used positively for the benefit and support of others instead of being a source of emotional anguish in an unbalanced and confused psyche. Relationships will improve as clarity deepens through more realistic appraisals and understanding, plus the awareness to make essential compromises and adjustments to live harmoniously with a partner. The joys of a stable domestic life will be revealed, instead of the traps and limitations that you have previously experienced, and your old ideals of perfection will be recognised as illusions that are dissipating in the wind, so that you are not chasing rainbows in the sky but accepting and loving real human nature, that of your partner and yourself. Your projections lose their force and are reabsorbed within yourself to be broken down to liberate that blocked energy. These are the potentials that are yours to grasp within this aspect; living with its negative impact and an unintegrated Neptune is the other alternative if you choose not to make the transformation that is indicated.

MERCURY–NEPTUNE CONJUNCTION

With the Mercury–Neptune contacts, it is the mind level that is primarily sensitised and activated, so that the imaginative quality is emphasised and the main focus of life appreciation is through mental receptivity. The conjunction indicates a channel between the conscious mind and the unconscious mind, and both the energy and information flowing through this conduit need to be carefully integrated if a variety of imbalances and distortions is not to be created.

The faculty of imagination will be highly stimulated and developed, and this will certainly require appropriate channels to be focused on so that other problems of perception are not created. The issue of mental realities is one which can make you unsettled, especially as you can tend to make mistakes in judgement based on misinterpreting facts and suggestive information. You have a mental process that can attempt to re-create experiences into more acceptable forms for personal absorption, a style of selective manipulation which excludes aspects of reality that you refuse to acknowledge. If this process becomes a regular pattern of mental behaviour, then you are liable to create a distinctly personal reality that is a fusion of the real and unreal which can pose additional challenges when it comes to disentangling them. This is often amplified by a tendency to be mentally escapist, avoiding the possibility of any painful experiences and situations by refusing to become involved in things.

Relationships are likely to be characterised by over-idealism of lovers, either through having the mental illusion of a perfect lover that is unlikely to exist, and comparing everyone to this perfect lover and so ensuring that they fail to match up, or by wrapping lovers in over-glamorised ideals, elevating them to a mental pedestal and so ensuring that at some time they will inevitably topple off. Your mental images will be shattered, yet this does not deny the real experiences of disappointment and disillusionment that you will suffer . . . and continue to suffer unless you become more realistic in your evaluations within intimate relationships. Part of this process can arise from the sense of personal inadequacy that you feel and which you try to alleviate by imitation of others you respect or sometimes through attempts to bask in the glow of reflected glamour by associating with publicly famous people, which allows inner fantasies to develop. Certainly you are often easily influenced by others, and this may need to be guarded against.

You are likely to have some creative and artistic talent, and your cultural appreciation will be developed. Your ideal type of employment will offer channels for such forms of personal expression, and it may be that you do develop towards writing, arts, photography or film as you have a gift for visual imagination which also has some inner content. Your approach will be intellectual and mentally resonant, rather than more emotionally evocative as with the Moon contacts. Training may be necessary to help draw out these talents, and your main talent may be related to giving an intellectual substance and context to artistic creations, as a critic does, although there you may need to be careful regarding a degree of intolerance in your attitudes.

Another area of life that could be very attractive to you is that of a mental fascination with mystery, romantic illusions, the worlds of psychics, mystics and psychology: the realms of the mind. Because of that close channel between the unconscious and conscious mind, you may experience serving as a conscious channel between the two, with information, such as personal examples of telepathic communication or prophetic dreams or visions, being transmitted to the rational mind. If you have properly come to terms with reforging reality into acceptable patterns and have broken free of that impulse, and have a real understanding of how your own psyche functions by integrating the transpersonal planets into a functioning unified consciousness, then moving towards less tangible realms of the mind may be safe for you. However, if those initial steps have not been made, then following your own fascinations into the inner worlds may not be so wise owing to that uncontrolled active imagination, and you could retreat inward to inhabit a nebulous dream world of your own making. So ensure that you carefully evaluate any ideas, impulses and motivations that enter your mind to clarify whether or not they are self-delusory or actual inner guidance. Such discrimination can be difficult to achieve, but it is essential to avoid becoming lost on the inner pathless path.

MERCURY-NEPTUNE SEXTILE

The sextile offers a more fluent and easily flowing contact between Neptune and Mercury, one which can be better expressed in daily life and where the faculty of imagination can be beneficial both to yourself and to others. Neptune adds an emotionally vitalising quality to your mental creations, and where an intuitive insight can sometimes offer surprising solutions to personal dilemmas. There is less evidence of the illusions which are often associated with Neptune contacts, and you help to dispel the build-up of any by having a fairly discursive and evaluative mind which carefully sifts through experience and information and attempts to transform it into usable knowledge. There is likely to be an inherent curiosity at work, able to explore behind appearances and not being susceptible to accepting ideas or people at face value.

This aspect is often found in the charts of successful writers, creative individuals or those involved in media communications, those who have an ability to perceive clearly and broadly, to represent a variety of opinions, attitudes and beliefs, and who have a wide and tolerant perspective on life. The spheres that the creative potential of this aspect can attract you towards include journalism, education, media, art, social programmes and welfare. As there is a natural intelligence, this often implies the pursuit of more advanced knowledge or skills through college/university education. This can tend to lead to associations with others who have an intellectual bias, and those with a developed sense of social responsibility. There are idealistic tendencies within you, but less glamoured than most, and you should ensure that you succeed in maintaining a realistic perspective with your social optimism. Your fertile imagination and keen perception can lead to contributing towards expressions of social change, of alerting the general public to possible or existing social dangers.

Within relationships you are able to maintain a close and loving partnership and family, and friendships are similarly rich and rewarding, as you are relatively easy to get on with and good company. You have the potential of inspirational qualities, and if these are developed, then you may become a leader or spokesperson for some affinity group, representing it ably. There can be a subtlety to your thinking and strategic planning that some may find surprising, yet it can be carefully evolved to avoid direct confrontational opposition, especially with more powerful social adversaries. The only points that you may need to be wary of are being distracted by others and losing your momentum by following side tracks. If this happens, it is partly your own fault as you are obviously not clear enough regarding what you intend to do, and you may need to clarify your intentions and aims sufficiently so that such false routes are rarely taken again. Otherwise, you have a lot of scope in taking personal advantage of what this aspect can offer to you.

MERCURY–NEPTUNE TRINE

The trine aspect offers a quite favourable potential, where the energies of Neptune and Mercury work together well, each helping to define and focus the positive and constructive attributes of the other. Similar to the sextile, this aspect is often found within the charts of successful and creative individuals. Making use of the trine's energy will stimulate the unfolding of considerable creativity. The essence of your creative spirit will be evocative imagery, often including meaningful depths and at times an inspirational quality. The way in which you succeed in expressing this could be through art, music, vivid literary creations, poetry, film or photography. Your creativity should possess substance and context, rather than any superficiality.

Communication to others is important to you. You are potentially very effective in transmitting your ideas and intentions, and skilled in the forms in which you clothe your messages. There can be a taste for dramatic presentations, but this is also effective as it ensures that anything you create is noticed by others, and that by grasping their attention you create a situation where some response is evoked. You have a talent for influencing people's minds by subtle manipulation and perhaps through clever handling of communication media, as you have a natural understanding of the essential motivation patterns of others. This can be amplified by using the Neptunian vibration to emphasise an intuitive or telepathic ability, which sometimes also manifests itself in the guise of prophesy. It may be best not to overdevelop any such tendencies, or to openly publicise them, but to use them quietly and with little fuss in daily life, especially if through your empathic awareness you are able to support and aid others.

There is the potential to have extremely powerful visualisation abilities, that inner picture-making faculty where within the mind you can create images in detail and colour, 'seeing them in the mind's eye'. In a variety of modern spiritual approaches such an ability is highly valued and, rightly used, can be a major tool in stimulating lasting spiritual development. Through creative visualisation you can direct or re-create your life and personality in many ways, and this is a skill and technique that you should explore; through pathworking and exploring inner mindscapes, perhaps through archetypal figures and mystical symbolism, such as the Arthurian and Grail legends, or the myths of the Greek gods. Pathworking offers the potential to unlock inner doors – even into astrological archetypes – and these are the realms that are ruled by Neptune.

There should be a developed social conscience and awareness, and work in this broad area may appeal, although your sensitivity may not be suitable for a direct involvement with impoverished and problem families. Your contribution may be that of support, or by using your talents to highlight social iniquity. Others recognise your abilities, and you should find that several avenues of expression are available to explore over time. Holding positive and optimistic attitudes helps others to transcend cynicism and lack of application, and so make their own steps of development. Your perspective on life is likely to be balanced, so that trivial and unimportant aspects of life are not invested with excessive reverence, and this works too in your relationships, where the transiency of moods and friction is not over-exaggerated and only the positive is emphasised. This does not ignore spheres of disharmony, but is always founded on a recognition of the strengths and important values of the relationship, which can then be used to shed a transforming light on any passing difficulties.

There can be a degree of self-sufficiency in you, as you are centred and generally inwardly balanced. Appreciating the richness of your inner life is vital to you, and you tend to need time and space to do that, as well as to manifest that creative ability. One area that you may be effective within is that of public speaking, where you can be very persuasive and your genuine qualities are at least recognised by others even if on occasion they may disagree with your opinions.

MERCURY–NEPTUNE SQUARE

This aspect indicates a difficulty with an overactive imagination interfering with rational and logical processes of thought; this can result in self-deception and the construction of a private version of truth and reality. There can be a preference for mental avoidance and for escaping from directly confronting aspects of life that you find unpleasant, such as personal truths and social problems. Sometimes your logic is very circuitous, too personal or abstracted for easy communication to either yourself or others, and as it often absorbs an imaginative influence, it can veil the truth from sight. You can shy away from accepting responsibilities, domestic, family and marriage ones especially, as you can feel uneasy with your emotions, and this results in you often becoming unreliable with others. There may have been factors in your earlier life that have helped bring this about – childhood or parental relationships which have exacerbated this innate tendency of escapism – but one result has been distorted images on the mental level of your own identity and mind activity, as well as a diminution of personal confidence.

There are steps that you can take to improve matters. The first involves the willingness to face the actual realities of yourself and the world, so that a clarified perspective can be established. A greater integration of Neptunian sensitivity is essential, but in a way that absorbs it into a renewed life rather than as another excuse for escapist tendencies. Following that development, additional progress can be made in reorganising your mind to work down more productive channels of expression. As your self-confidence grows, through constructive self-evaluation and an acknowledgement of the dormant talents associated with the repressed Neptunian energy, it will lead to a sequential release of that blocked energy into your life; you should observe that previous restrictions and limitations are dissolving. Do not re-establish them again, but learn how to take advantage of your assets. Creating a new disciplined structure for your mind may take time and effort, but attempts at training and reprogramming it will draw benefits if persevered with, and may lead towards creative or socially orientated directions. However, to take these later steps may require you to become more clear regarding your aims, and to apply yourself to achieve them one by one. As part of this proposed transformation in you – and of resolving the inner tensions of the square – you may find it more helpful to look towards forms of external expression that have a social dimension and may offer some solution to social problems. In serving others you may discover that your own problems become surprisingly resolved, especially as the personal obsessions of self-preoccupation are dissipated through a redirection of your energy flow.

Whilst you may often have insight into the motivations of others, you need greater clarity in your own nature. Relationships may remain problematical for you until some degree of personal change has been achieved, and you may be advised to be cautious within your emotional commitments. This is basically because of elements of illusion that can afflict you, and that tendency to avoid facing facts that you do not want to see, such as the fundamental one that a relationship is not mutually satisfying if you need it to continue. Those dreams of the ideal lover and partner will be present, and it is always difficult not to project these on to others, or use them as comparison markers. Some may take emotional advantage of you, and you may experience that victim syndrome of the Neptunian vibration by falling prey to your own tendencies and the selfish desires of others. Yet as you change, your potential for better and more fulfilling relationships increases as clarity intensifies. As always, the decision to change is yours to take.

MERCURY–NEPTUNE OPPOSITION

Similar to the square aspect, there are indications of an inability to distinguish clearly between the real and the unreal, and of a blockage of the creative and imaginative faculty. The key to resolving these issues appears to lie in your relationships with others, and especially in those projections from your own psyche that you are overlaying on to the world and thus distorting your own perception and insight.

It is often your own sensitivity and impressionability to environmental influences that causes inner insecurity and fears of over stretching yourself. There may be an unconscious telepathic ability which transmits to you others' thoughts and motivations, and this can lead to confusion in your relationships, such as at times when they may be saying one thing and you are 'receiving' an entirely contradictory set of impressions on a more subtle level, which you register as a feeling of unease, disquiet and a lack of trust in them. In that context, you find it hard to believe the evidence of your own senses, and this has a direct impact on how you communicate to others. When reality becomes confused and distorted, some respond by imagining conspiracies and enter a paranoid state, and this is a reaction to such intangible senses operated and being distorted by an unintegrated Neptunian imagination.

You are often socially 'touchy', strongly reacting against real or imagined social slights, and this acts as a weak spot in your personality, especially as you lack a strengthening inner confidence. Competition is not your style, although that does not make you immune to the influences of other competitive spirits in your environment, such as those at work who can easily ride roughshod over you in their scramble to reach the top. Sometimes you act as a victim, drawing out such tendencies from others, and then begin to bemoan your fate as they succeed and leave you only with disappointments. Linking your rising star to working closely in employment dog fights may not be advisable. Your own gifts may flower more effectively once you have withdrawn from a social rat race. Perhaps exploiting latent creative talents may be the key, or entering some form of employment where co-operation is the underlying dynamic may offer you more satisfaction; but as human nature intrudes even there, the only answer may be a detached and independent self-employment.

Cleansing yourself of deceptive influences is essential, not just those outer influences affecting you, but also that pattern of creating them in your own perception and evaluation. Unrealistic daydreams which are unachievable or never manifested are symptomatic of deception. For example, you create imaginatively high aspirations which because of their 'perfect nature' soar beyond everyone's grasp, yet glitter in their pristine purity. Ultimately there is no real value in self-deception. It is a waste of valuable time and never leads to satisfaction. Perhaps it helps to avoid facing an empty, aching inner void, but that can more profitably be filled by something real, achievable and personally meaningful. Effort is needed. Anyone can dream, millions do, but trying to achieve those dreams at least offers a direction to focus along. False naivety needs to be dropped, as do the fictitious aspects of your life and your approach to self-evaluation. A more straightforward type of communication, inner and outer, will reap benefits and break the stranglehold of illusory deceptions, leading to a greater understanding of your own and others' natures, so that in your own life you move from illusion to reality and increase the quantity of light in the world. Personal 'redemption' is always positive within a larger social context.

VENUS–NEPTUNE CONJUNCTION

This conjunction of Neptune and Venus indicates that there is likely to be a high degree of idealisation in the spheres of romantic relationships, images of 'perfect lovers and partners' emanating from an overshadowing by either the *anima* (if male) or the *animus* (if female) inner patterns arising from the unconscious mind. When evoked by powerful emotions of love, lust, passion and attraction to another person, these images of perfection are projected on to the loved one forming a glamour which is quite bewitching – until frail human nature eventually reasserts its presence and the image collapses through a phase of disillusionment, when the lovers fail to conform to that pattern of perfection which has been superimposed upon them.

Essentially, you'll have a simple trusting attitude, which can become unwisely gullible at times, resulting in consequences of deception and exploitation. This emotional sensitivity makes you extremely vulnerable, and is often the source of difficulties in your personal and intimate relationships. You hate confrontation, tending to be more passive and giving, and will shy away from any emotional aggression and insensitivity shown by anyone. Part of your ideal relationship includes refined culture, art, music and literature as common interests or personal talents, and where the concepts and environments of harmony and beauty predominate in a peaceful and tranquil lifestyle. You have an appreciation of the more subtle delights of life, with a sensitive and perceptive aesthetic sense, and your standards of partner and lifestyle will be quite high and demanding.

There will be an active and vivid imagination at play, looking to see or create harmony and beauty, perhaps reflecting in an artistic manner contemporary fashions in art, music, literature, fashion and culture. Your heart will be soft and tender, and often that sensitivity will be unsuitable for many of the more jarring and discordant environments of the modern world; you will hate having to rush around jostling in large groups of people. You prefer those sophisticated cultural scenes, with perhaps a small grouping of successful and intelligent people. Being delicate in the modern world which is swept by powerful collective changes can be a disturbing sensitivity. This is why you often wear those rose-coloured glasses, so that the stark reality and grim harshness of certain aspects is not clearly perceived or is kept at a distance. You can't avoid the wholeness of the world, and such abrasive experiences often stimulate disturbances in your life, as if trying to force you to look at them without distortion. This tendency continues into evaluating others in a realistic manner, especially when projections are evoked; often you are disappointed when their true natures are revealed.

You can be too impressionable at times, especially through that emotional empathy with others, and can resort back into being an impractical idealistic and ineffectual dreamer if clarity and focus are lacking. You may need to learn to stand on your own feet, and be less reliant on others. Some can succeed in expressing degrees of universal love, healing through their spiritual understanding and acceptance of others; but in treading this path, there is also the crucifixion of the heart, and a willingness to share in the world's suffering.

VENUS–NEPTUNE SEXTILE

With the sextile, the sensitivity is still present although not felt so intensely, and there is more of a mental orientation towards the external world and an ability to work effectively with people for social harmony. Creativity and communication are enhanced with the sextile, and these gifts are used to create meaningful and evocative objective forms which many others find resonant and inspiring, such as those in art, music or literature. The imagination is active and fertile, and the channels are present through which the images can flow easily and naturally; this creative talent can greatly enrich your life once it is properly released. You prefer to emphasise the positive and beneficial aspects of life and human nature, and are basically optimistic, although there should still be a realistic streak within you which adds a shade of balance.

Whilst your emotions are too general and diffuse to be restricted to any one person, your basic outlook is that of a universal compassion linked to an understanding and acceptance of human nature, and you may find that you become a confidante to others and perform a role whereby you offer counsel and support to others in difficulty. The love aspects as represented by Venus and Neptune (individual and universal) flow well together, and the emotion expressed through the heart and mind is very comforting and soothing to others, often possessing healing qualities. This could be more formally expressed through medicine or psychotherapy situations, and you can be an adept resolver of conflicts through restoring harmony in confrontationary tensions between people. Social or community work could be attractive to you in some form, if you choose to work in the outer world. Some prefer to work in the inner realms, and choose to apply their talents through music, art and literature to express similar qualities to the world.

Privately you are likely to hold romantic ideals, often entering alliances with similar-thinking and -feeling individuals, especially those of a mystical and sensitive disposition. Ideal love relationships are probably sought, and this can leave you quite vulnerable to emotional pain and disappointment, especially through others failing to live up to your probably unreasonable expectations. You tend to elevate your love affairs to sublime realms, using them as a mystical stepladder to reach those subtle spiritual lands that are your private dreamscapes of paradise. Often your emotions are associated with a mystical and religious importance, and the sextile and trine have been described as 'lovers of the universe'. Relationships may be an area of sacrifice for you, a sphere of transformation, as well as an area where you may be forced to come to terms with the real world through compromise with others and by realising that for harmony to exist difficult inner emotional battles may need to be fought and adjustments made. Sometimes, when under pressure, you may retreat into that inner ideal world, and lapse into a rejected state of apathy and inertia whilst your sensitivity is renewed and made ready to face the world again. Your natural gifts and talents could be used to restore more beauty and harmony to people and the world, to make it more like your ideal dream of a perfect universe, so look to that direction to express your creativity.

VENUS–NEPTUNE TRINE

There are several similarities between the trine and the sextile, based on the fluid sensitivity and creative imagination that is the potential of this aspect. The trine has a reconciling function between planets, and with both Neptune and Venus there is an essential fusion of affinitive qualities and characteristics. The challenge here may be actually applying your innate potential, as there may be relatively little inner pressure to resolve personal conflicts through releasing the energy in creative expressions. There should be artistic cultural appreciation, plus an artistic talent that can be exploited, especially through such areas as music, art, writing, dance and drama. As you are responsive to the more subtle dimensions of life, and prefer more elevated ideals, your artistic creations are likely to reflect such perception and sensitivity and involve a high level of purified emotion and intellectual content. This quality of idealism and romance that can pervade your creations can be at odds with the real world, perhaps even a denial of those harsher experiences, yet if successfully expressed can indicate a future direction for people to aspire towards: a vision of beauty and harmony. You believe that much of value in life is found within a sensitive and sophisticated awareness, and that such cultural development deepens that sense of meaning and purpose for the individual.

You enjoy the company of others, and are usually an enjoyable companion, although due to your soothing and positive presence, you may find yourself placed in positions of having to support friends who are passing through times of crisis. You listen well, and can offer valid advice; friends feel that you do not condemn them for any failings and that spirit of acceptance of human nature is a healing power in itself. You express emotional empathy and understanding, and others feel safe and secure in your company, often confiding troubles and confidential problems to you. If anything, your permissive attitudes offered to others can be misused as an excuse to continue the path that they are taking; acknowledging human failings is compassionate and realistic, but helping others to become free from problems may often require advice that is more direct and confrontational in essence, mirroring back the answer that personally they may not want to hear, yet which is the real answer to their problem. True compassion is not soft; sometimes the solution involves taking a hard position.

The type of social company that you prefer to be associated with is that of similarly artistic and sophisticated individuals, those who are involved with personal development and expression and who express a dissatisfaction with much of contemporary society. There can be a preference for discussing the resolution of social issues, yet a lack of direct involvement in transforming them. Finding more appropriate channels to turn your responses into constructive means may be more satisfying. Sometimes complacency may rule, especially if your own lifestyle is basically fulfilling and immune from being touched by the more negative consequences of social decline and decay.

Becoming more practical is an ongoing challenge, and you need to link your inspired creativity towards that, otherwise your imagination may be wasted and rarely anchored in objective form. Your romantic life may be unusual at times, often with a feeling of 'inevitability' about partners and lovers.

VENUS–NEPTUNE SQUARE

With the square, there can be difficulties with the inhibition of emotions, creativity and relationships with others. Part of this difficulty arises from an extreme sensitivity of feelings which have never been properly integrated. The other main source is that of an unrealistic imagination which has a tendency to create escapist private realities, where you can avoid facing those aspects of life that you dislike or which are too painful.

The square is one of the Neptune aspects that stimulates those emotional-level fogs and mists, creating a consequence of being unable to see clearly, of being liable to make misjudgements, and which fuel tendencies of self-deception and mental distortion. Sometimes you even 'rely' on these inner fogs to prevent you from seeing the real and true situations regarding yourself and your relationships. Often these emotionally rooted problems are associated with impulses from the unconscious mind, and there can be a pattern of guilt, self-sacrifice and martyrdom operating within you at a deep unconscious level.

These factors tend to make you vulnerable to deception, prone to suffer from your own reality projections and filters, and from the choices and actions of others who may be similarly psychologically influenced. Due to this unease within your emotions, you can be almost belligerently defensive at times when you believe that others are opposing you; relationship or employment disputations are probable. There can be inner reactions against too much social or work company, often caused by that passive and unconscious empathy which can intensify the level of stress and tension in you. Such psychic currents seep into your 'aura' and mind at an unconscious level, and these will influence your state of well-being unless you recognise what may be occurring and then take action to release these intrusive energies from your body–emotions–mind system.

Intimate relationships can be a source of challenges, especially when you have made some form of emotional commitment, as often your choice of lover or partner results from misjudgement. Unless you have psychologically cleansed your distorting emotional level, you may discover that marriage may reveal a lack of honesty and direct relationship, and the impulse of attraction was founded solely on transient passions, illusions and the personal need to rely on another. It can be that a preoccupation with those inner emotional flows makes you less adept at dealing with the material world, and this can translate into unwise financial and business decisions, which can then have a negative impact on the economic foundations of a family and marriage.

Often there is a need to rely on others, or on an ideology or religion. You are basically idealistic, yet this is likely to attract you towards involvement with minority cults or foreign religions because of their glamours and strange fascinations. These can be a seed bed for additional confusions and distortions if not carefully approached, and you may discover that you have been too indiscriminate in your choices. In several ways these are symptomatic of an inner need of transformation, of the need to redeem negative patterns dominating your life. Sexuality as a powerful aspect of the impulse for relationships can be a prime area in which such dilemmas can be expressed. This can be revealed through needs for multiple partners, searching for a perfect though unattainable lover, yet being unprepared and unwilling to actually commit yourself to a real flesh-and-blood person. It may emerge through excessive sexual imagination, where unfulfilled sexual imagery and desires may be intertwined with underlying and repressed emotionally based complexes, or are practised secretly and conspire to build an area of denial in your life.

Changes are probably needed in order to integrate the Neptune energy into your life, so that it ceases to display its more negative face of unresolution. Your attitudes to others through relationships need to be redefined, so that any paranoia is dropped, as well as any tendencies towards exploitation by yourself or against yourself. Standing free and independent is preferable, at least as an initial cleansing process. Facing reality and turning experience into wisdom and insight is an essential step to move towards, so that your basic perception of your own nature and of others is reconstructed. Turning within through meditation or forms of self-therapy is an ideal path to take, so that you begin to release the old patterns, discover a new centre by cleaning out old illusions and see through new eyes. Meditation is a deconditioning technique, sequentially liberating through practice, and redirecting the energy flow of the mind inwards instead of outwards, where the energy acts as a penetrating disperser of restrictive psychological patterns. This will strengthen self-discipline, which, as energy is released through the resolution of inner conflicts and frictions, can free those channels of blocked creativity, and so enable you to take control and direction of your life back into your own hands. Accepting personal responsibility for your choices, decisions and actions will create a firm foundation to deal with the more complex sphere of the emotional sensitivities which, whilst it may take time and effort to clarify, is the point of resolution for the majority of conflicts in your life, and so is the key to a meaningful and satisfying future experience.

VENUS–NEPTUNE OPPOSITION

Whilst the square is associated with inner changes being stimulated by the pain of inner tension and frustration, the focus of the opposition is usually projected externally on to people and the world, from which it is often reflected back again as a source of conflict. How this tends to manifest itself in your life is likely to be through an underlying suspicion and distrust of others, perhaps based on actual experiences where you have been a victim of deception and deceit, or where you feel that others have badly let you down and reneged on actual or implicit promises. As 'Energy follows Thought', because you are projecting a pattern of suspicion and lack of trust into the world, it is likely that you are receiving back the consequences of your own inner pattern.

This is often formed by unresolved, unintegrated and unconscious factors associated with the influence of Neptune operating through a heightened emotional sensitivity and vulnerability. As the strength of imagination in you is potentially very potent, if it is misused or unrecognised, unconscious inner needs and desires create compulsive motivations formed around private fantasies and perceptual distortions of reality. These inner pressures affect the stability and content of your emotional level, so that one result can be moods and uncertainty regarding the consistency of your feelings. Obviously this will affect your intimate relationships, and can demonstrate its presence in a variety of forms of deception, within yourself and within the love affair. The 'enemy' that you often project 'out there' is hidden within yourself. Those Neptunian patterns of victim, sacrifice and martyr may emerge, either as experienced by you, or as expressed through you on to others, where you exploit any powers of sexual seduction that you possess for self-gratification. Sensual preoccupation may appeal to you, yet this could hold the seeds of your own destruction within it, as there is likely to be an addictive tendency operating which is associated with alcohol, drugs and sex. Surrendering to this pattern would be most unwise, and a reflection of an unintegrated Neptune.

Greater clarity and honesty in relationships is probably needed; or the consequences of this will emerge through deceit, by your own secret love affairs or by those of a partner. Certainly trust will be a casualty, and if not perceived correctly will only serve to add more fuel to the fires of your own suspicious outer projections. Marriage may become an uneasy battleground and a focus for inner pressures and stress. This is sometimes felt by others as an 'antagonistic vibration' which it is unpleasant to remain in close contact with for prolonged periods.

Learning how to recognise these projections is an essential first step: you realise how you are creating your own experiences, and how unconscious inner influences and motivational patterns are reflected back at you through external experiences. Reabsorbing these and accepting responsibility for them is step two. If this can be achieved to some degree, then energy will be liberated to enable you to access the positive nature of Neptune. You already have a form of idealism, yet this has been badly battered and damaged by the experiences of projections returned to you, so this needs to be restimulated and integrated, based on a new self-perspective. The fogs distorting that idealism need to be dispersed, and old unrealistic dreams need to be dropped. A creative potential also lies within you, relatively undisturbed and unexploited, and this too could be successfully awakened into action and expressed in your own unique manner. There is no reason why you cannot take effective action to transform aspects of your life, unless it is through willed inertia and apathy, or because you fail to see that taking control of your own life is your responsibility. When real transformation commences – even though it may be hard to generate the initial momentum – then minor or even major miracles occur in the inner life to add their support to the personal efforts being made to change. Life becomes supportive to the degree that it is appreciated and enriched by your personal contribution; what you receive is what you give out into the world. It's a simple message, but one which is often a key to resolving conflicts.

MARS–NEPTUNE CONJUNCTION

This conjunction can pose several difficulties: in choice of actions, where you may struggle to establish what your real aims are, in making that final decision to attempt to achieve them, and in ensuring that sufficient and persistent effort is then made to guarantee success. An unintegrated Neptune can dissolve that focused will, making decisive clarity difficult to maintain. Additionally, you tend to avoid accepting the consequences of your choices, and there can be a refusal to acknowledge responsibility when such actions lead to failure or negative results.

Part of this derives from lack of prior consideration and a willingness to sometimes jump into action on impulse alone; yet this is often used as a spur to be decisive. 'I didn't know it would turn out like that . . .' is used as a defensive excuse, and is probably true because possible repercussions were not evaluated. Yet continuing with such an approach is essentially avoiding personal responsibility. You may realise eventually that most actions you take on impulse go awry in some respect, rarely fulfilling your initial intention.

This issue related to choice and action is one which needs clarification and resolving. You may find it beneficial to pause before acting on impulse, sensible to slow down and take time to consider the likely results of your decision. This may then show you alternative routes to take, or may even dissuade you from taking action at all. As Mars will influence you to be more dynamically assertive, you need to take into account your effects on other people too, especially any family and those closest to you. This may then modify your more self-centred tendencies and ensure that through insensitivity you do not then create unnecessary pain for anyone.

You can be quite attractive to others, as the Mars–Neptune energies combine to create a potentially dynamic glamour, yet this apparent combination of action and sensitivity can often be superficial when the Mars characteristics are dominating the more subtle Neptune ones, which is more often the situation. Neptunian qualities come through disguised as a flexibility of personality, a set of masks and images that you almost automatically assume in your relations with people and in social or work environments. You recognise that these lead to some inner confusion, especially in respect of decision making, but they are also usable for self-projection. You quite enjoy playing with these masks and feeling that your real intentions are hidden within a secret persona; you do not really like others to know you too well.

This leads to the attraction of acting behind images, and there is often a dramatic side to your nature, perhaps through some creative expression or even theatre work, where imagination can flourish in an evocative situation and you can be hidden behind the mask, performing a role. Certainly you will develop a favourite image of yourself which is projected out for others to see you through. Some have affinities with medicine and healing abilities; even here you may hide behind the image of nurse, doctor, consultant or psychic healer. Alternatively, your dreams and desires about yourself could be unrealistic, and whilst you aspire to great status and achievement, your lack of will or application and your impracticality defeat you. Ultimately, your image of self-elevation may only exist within your imagination.

Steps can be taken to improve matters though. Feeling able to release your blocked imagination into daily life is important, because whilst initially such a move may be glamorous and ineffective, you can learn to direct it towards deliberate intentions, and so use it as a powerful energy to achieve your aims. Techniques of creative visualisation are recommended to take advantage of this process of mental imagination, and can help to re-create your life. Future planning can help you to gain greater control too, so that there is less opportunity for something unconsidered to destroy your intention. And working hard to actually achieve viable skills is another way of helping yourself; if you do not do this that unintegrated Neptune will serve only to dissolve those dreams instead of helping to fulfil them.

In intimate relationships, more awareness will probably be needed. A combination of impulsive Mars and the self-deluding tendency of Neptune may conspire to show you the pain of disappointing illusions in love. Mars can encourage you into sudden passionate affairs, caught within the glamours of a new lover, but when you are directed by purely unconscious motivations, the likelihood is that suffering will result, as a prompt to make you more aware the next time! Be wary of any personal tendencies towards self-deception and deceiving others or being deceived; these may be likely, and can be associated with the sphere of the conjunction's natal house. Try to remain honest and frank, as communication is vital in relationships, because you have a tendency to be both emotionally vulnerable and to have unusual emotional needs, so the quality of your intimate relationships should ideally be high.

MARS–NEPTUNE SEXTILE

The sextile offers a better balance between the characteristics of these two planets, so that the more positive qualities can shine through easily. That energy blockage which can cause problems in action and decision making in the conjunction is released and tends to flow into spheres of creativity and service to others.

The Martian tendency of impulsive passion is transformed into a basically generous and compassionate spirit, where you are aware and sensitive to the needs of others who are less fortunate than yourself. There is an effective balance of individuality in you that is poised between being excessively self-assertive or excessively passive; you are neither an exploiter or a victim.

Generally your energy level is high and vital, and this can find channels of expression through various routes. Healing is attractive, for you use that personal magnetic vitality to support a healing process, and others can feel convinced that you have their well-being at heart. There may be subtle abilities associated with psychic sensitivity that are present, or could be developed. As you have a sense of social responsibility, you can feel fulfilled by work which is in that sphere of life, where you are helping to meet social needs and improve the lot of people; certainly you will feel the attraction towards such involvement in some way. The commitment and inspiration that you offer can be uplifting to many co-workers and recipients of your contributions.

More individually creative channels may appeal, such as drama, dance and visual skills like photography and film. Physical culture is likely to be important, especially in your young adult life, and you can gain great enjoyment from expressing yourself through physical movement and dance, where fluency and grace may be present. In later years, this can become an interest in the body work of hatha yoga, maintaining a suppleness of body as well as improving body health. These types of preferred creativity tend to focus on either a developed use of the body or of the physical senses, rather than a more intellectualised form of creative expression.

Potentially, your relationships can be successful and fulfilling, and you will expend considerable effort to ensure that they remain so for yourself and for your partner. Your optimistic outlook helps you to perceive the highest qualities in a lover, whilst not denying the fact that people are human and prone to express much lower tendencies than an ideal. Tolerance and understanding of human weakness and tensions will be present, and your trust will be reciprocated. Much will depend on your choice of partner, and partly this will depend on a realistic appraisal of your own needs, especially those powerful physical and emotional ones, and on what is required of a suitable mate. Basically though, you have a 'give and take' attitude, and are reasonably relaxed and realistic about the pressures of living together in marriage. The quality of mutual communication is essential, and you highly value a direct and honest approach, which is always beneficial because at least each knows the nature of the current situation.

MARS–NEPTUNE TRINE

The energies of the trine should enable you to become a practical idealist, where the spheres of personal relationships and social obligations are highlighted in your experience. Mars will provide you with a powerhouse of energy to use, and Neptune will indicate suitable directions for expression.

This will be through a heart sensitivity to the problems of others, either individually or on a more impersonal, collective scale, and you will feel motivated to share in aspects of social responsibility. Fortunately, most of your personal aims can be achieved within such a framework, and so you may be attracted towards socially orientated work, especially in the fields of welfare, medicine, community aid and physical therapy. In such ways, you feel able to share your energy by supporting others who may be struggling in life, perhaps through ill health, disadvantaged social conditions, or family problems. There is a natural sympathy, and your compassionate approach will often lead to many sharing their problems with you. It may be that at times you will need to cleanse yourself of 'accumulated suffering' absorbed from such work, and forms of negativity-releasing meditations or psychic protection are advised; otherwise, you may experience your level of vitality dropping under the burdens that you choose to take.

Even if you do not adopt the Neptunian way as a profession, your closer social friends will recognise this quality of support within you, and will often turn to you for a helping hand and a listening heart, coming away feeling less burdened, more inspired and sharing in your confident energy that all will be right (or that they can at least cope successfully). This is an aspect of a healing energy that you can transmit, and which is often connected to an acute inner sensitivity to the environment and people's emotions. This empathy is a key to your potential effectiveness in relationships, an intuitive knowing of how to respond and what type of support can be offered. Some may consciously gravitate towards areas of spiritual/occult healing techniques, and this could be an effective channel to explore.

Your intimate love life should be reasonably satisfying, often with a strong emphasis on physical and heart energies, possibly with some intense and passionate romances. Once you settle with a stable partner, you will appreciate those deep emotional bonds, those subtle empathies and feelings of real relationship that can be established through mutual love. Generally, your partnerships are honest and direct: friendship and goodwill for each other are strong, and genuine feelings for people with whom you have shared intimacies can still persist even after a relationship has ceased. Some relationships end in perpetual bitterness and mutual conflict; but whilst recognising that love can fade, you prefer to separate on good terms. People can benefit through contact with you, and finding a suitable partner can offer you an opportunity for considerable mutual inner growth and enjoyment.

There can be an attraction towards more dramatic expressions of the energies of these two planets, perhaps one where flamboyance is possible, such as the theatre, acting, dance or where physical culture is emphasised. In some, the Martian energy to act is focused through spheres of Neptunian creativity, design, art, literature, film, photography. The trine often appears in charts of creative people, as the energy helps the process of anchoring the idea, vision or intention. You should find that you can achieve your goals, making the most out of the potential and opportunities that are presented to you; allowing scope to your imagination and then acting on it is the key to success.

MARS–NEPTUNE SQUARE

The square aspect can pose a variety of inner tensions and compulsions that are difficult to acknowledge and integrate properly. It is indicative of the inner conflict and stress which often affects the nature of your relationships, especially emotionally and sexually.

Most of your impulses arise from the unconscious mind, and so it can be difficult to perceive them correctly or to understand their nature. Squares involve frustration, and here both the energies of Mars and Neptune are mutually inhibiting, creating distortions in both their favoured ways of expression. Even the inner energy flow is distorted, with the Martian energy taking on an intermittent current, ranging from an obsessive urge for action (or release) to almost disappearing at times, leaving you with a minimum of motivation and vitality. Often the Neptune energy emerges in its distorted nature, in that there can be disconcerting emotional impulses, strange imaginations and obsessions, or negative types of habit-patterned behaviour, which can be essentially self-destructive through a vulnerability to the Neptunian addictions of drugs, alcohol and compulsive sexual obsessions.

As there can be an inhibition in consistently and effectively expressing your self and your aims, this eventually creates a build-up of frustration, leading to internal pressures and stresses. This can form personality splits, where more negative aspects of the unintegrated unconscious mind erupt into the conscious personality and begin to dominate, almost as forms of possession. You can feel impelled to act in certain ways, and whilst you feel in a state of confusion, those hidden powerful motivations are directing your choices.

There tends to be a 'vicious circle' in action, often due to that belligerent and aggressive way in which you can attempt to be self-assertive. Because of those unresolved inner conflicts, your style of emotional expression and your relationship with others is often tainted by vibrations of aggression which are registered and usually rejected by others. The result can be a rejection of your outstretched hand and of your aims. Yet as this becomes a repetitive pattern, your inner conflicts become more intensified and part of your energy field which is sensed by perceptive people. Alienation can occur.

Because of inner blindness, you can fail to understand what is occurring and thus enforce a developing pattern akin to paranoia, where you begin to imagine additional rejections by others, become extremely touchy regarding all social contacts and imagined slights, and then become defensively belligerent too as a form of protection. There is considerable self-deception happening, in that you fail to see the process within you. Through looking outwards, you fail to see the source of your difficulties.

Sexual relationships can be a major battleground, and a central point for many of these tensions. The nature of your sex life and sexual desires is likely to be distorted to some degree. Sex and emotions are closely tied together, and it may be essential to achieve a redefinition through understanding. This may become the core of your obsessions and compulsive behaviour, stimulated by a highly active imagination. There is unease, anxiety and confusion related to your sexual impulse. This can arise from a lack of intimate opportunities, leaving the frustrated energy little option but to circle around within you, activating a variety of stresses and splits that ideally should be healed rather than widened. It could be that your imagination becomes over-active, creating unfulfilled sexual imagery and desires. Or it may be aspects of your natural expressions of sexuality that you are refusing to acknowledge, and so repressing. It is certainly an area of inner contention.

This often leads to an overshadowing guilt pattern developing, where you are attracted towards illicit affairs, or sexual activity which you believe is morally wrong. Resorting to unsatisfying sexual expression may be attempted, such as the purely physical release of the energy and pressures, as with prostitutes for example. This need for sexual release is a crucial one for you to come to terms with; it is essential to discover an approach which is fulfilling and which does not re-emphasise your inner conflicts.

Relationship failures may be common until you begin a reorientation, a re-channelling of your energies into more suitable directions. You may find that your experience of the stresses inherent in this aspect is one of degree only, but much depends on the rest of the chart, and even then some degree of modification will still be required, especially if other aspects are challenging to Mars and Neptune.

What is necessary is a confrontation with reality, where you assume self-responsibility for your situation and inner life. This is an acknowledgement of inner conflicts without feelings of guilt, denial or personal condemnation. Acceptance is the first step; this may be quite difficult to achieve, yet it is the first step towards a resolution of the problems and to allowing inner healing to occur. Stop mentally pointing at others and projecting any blame for your failures on to them; yet conversely, do not blame yourself either, just resolve to change things for the better in the future. Because experiences have led to the creation of repetitive patterns frustrating you, it does not mean that this situation has to persist. The potential is there for you to change it. Study the techniques of creative visualisation, take control over the areas in your life that you want to change or resolve. Begin to look for ways in which the energies of Mars and Neptune can be integrated together, where using your imagination creates bridges instead of more uncrossable abysses of neuroses, paranoias, illusions and obsessive sexual desires. Change your attitude to people, be willing to take a risk in re-creating your life. Instead of looking to take, look for where you can give, as this will redirect that Neptune energy into constructive channels, withdrawing it from the distortions of Martian energy and from overstimulating sexual desires. It is a sacrifice of an attitude that is necessary, and it is one that poses problems for you; in releasing it there lies the opportunity for a rebirth to occur.

One key lies in the correct use of emotional and sexual energy, discovering a direction that can soak up its excessiveness and negativity, transforming it into a positive asset rather than a guilt-ridden obsession. Discover creative channels to pour it into, express it through the physicality of dance, through art, literature, music, drama. Even if the original creations are not beautiful or harmonious, be assured that over time their quality will change as your inner healing proceeds through the release of those frustrating poisons. Instead of being controlled by the energy, take control of it, plan and direct your life so that it moves in your chosen way. Eventually, with persistence, the pieces of the new jigsaw will fall into place and you will emerge into an experience of life that satisfies you. Fight those inner battles and those conflicts can dissipate.

MARS–NEPTUNE OPPOSITION

The opposition is focused more on your outer relationships with people, although inner projections are often the key to their problematic nature. As with the square aspect, there is the presence of the unconscious mind being activated by a frustrated Neptune, which leads to distortions in action and expression. Inner motivation is often unclear in respect of its true nature, and often compulsive desires are hidden behind a facade so effectively that even you are often essentially unconscious of why you act in certain ways and what is actually making those decisive choices for you. Self-clarity can be difficult to achieve, especially in the areas of emotional and sexual desire, which can have a compulsive quality to them, and which can dominate your options. These areas may become highly emphasised in your life, excessively so and out of a healthy proportion and perspective.

You probably lack trust and faith in life. Suspicion is a constant companion, and you see others through such a filter, yet this is often mainly composed of your own nature projected out like a shadow over the world. How can you trust yourself when you do not fully comprehend you own motivations and desires for actions? Yet you often mean well, but are let down by your own tendencies of secrecy and manipulation. Your own attitudes are reflected back at you, so that mutual suspicion is often created, and you lose even more trust in people. Sometimes you tend to withdraw from social activity due to this. A refinement in how you choose to assert yourself may be necessary, as well as a withdrawal of these conditioning negative characteristics.

Confronting reality is essential, so that by acceptance a more realistic balance in relationships can emerge, one where your desires are less dominant and threatening, and where the emotional dimension is more integrated and explored. This will help to modify and redirect the blocked Neptune energy so that relationships become deeper, more satisfying and a bridge to renew your experience of social relating. Evaluating your ambitions in life can be more productive once the projections are being withdrawn, and using intellect and common sense can be more effective in realising them than following a path of glamour and compulsive desires which, whilst perhaps more temporarily exciting, leads to a dissipation of your self and your objectives. Avoidance of unnecessary stimulants is also wise, as these will not help, and a more perceptive insight into the nature of glamour and illusion will also be highly beneficial. This is especially so if you have become involved in the occult or spiritual realms of life, where there are always many candidates to take advantage of those who are more gullible and susceptible to the power of 'secret knowledge'. Those who have the desire to be 'special' are often abused physically, emotionally, mentally and spiritually.

The nature and quality of your relationships can be transformed, provided that you deal with those problematic areas of your inner nature, trust, emotions, sexuality and illusions. Perceiving how you can negatively condition your experience is the key to realising how you can positively transform it too.

JUPITER–NEPTUNE CONJUNCTION

This conjunction occurs approximately every thirteen years, and tends to create characteristics that are often similar to the Pisces temperament, where both the positive and negative qualities of both planets are present and highly active.

Tendencies towards excess, idealism, creativity and naivety will be evident. The Jupiter impulse of expansion may encourage you to reach beyond your actual capabilities. Whilst this can aid in stretching you – and in some cases you will succeed to a greater degree – the likelihood is that when it is combined with a Neptunian distorted perception of your abilities you will fail more regularly than triumph. Over time this can become a repetitive and inhibitory pattern which lowers your self-confidence.

The sphere of relationships is likely to be a source of many lessons for you, and to reflect back several of your own tendencies towards those less realistic qualities of Jupiter and Neptune that are present in an unintegrated personality. Whilst faith and trust are potentially positive qualities to possess, life experience often demonstrates that placing our confidence in everyone will unfortunately and inevitably lead to disillusionment. In the ideal world this would be possible, but in our current reality there are many who will self-centredly take advantage of others' naivety and innocence (and ignorance too!). A more realistic appraisal of the motivations and nature of others is necessary; an unconscious automatic offering of your trust and faith in the goodwill and fine nature of others will lead to your abuse. Discrimination is always required, so that you can recognise those in whom such fragile qualities will be rightly respected. Blind faith is an innocence waiting to be ruined; and many will be queuing up to take their pickings.

Yet this ideal of relationships will still persist, often despite many disappointing experiences over the years. It is probably wiser to be more careful in your more personal and intimate relationships, because unless you are aware of what is occurring, your love life could be painful. As you have a natural impulse to care and serve others, you could be exploited by less scrupulous individuals, taking advantage of those tendencies of sacrifice and martyrdom that hide within the Neptune influence. This also leads you towards illusions related to the feelings of others for you, where you convince yourself that they are a strong and true love, and then allow yourself to become deeply committed to the relationship; you may be correct in your assessment, but it is an area in which you are very vulnerable to self-deception, and perhaps more caution and less haste should be advised. Time taken in establishing others' motivations and deeper nature is often time well spent; resorting back to a blind faith, trust and assumptions founded on satisfying your own needs can be a recipe for future problems. A careful evaluation of the other is necessary, otherwise under the pressure of actual marriage or living together other aspects of the other's nature will emerge which may not suit you (or vice versa). Many relationships flounder today due to mutual self-ignorance, where inner projections of illusions and the *anima–animus* patterns overlay the real nature of the participants, until time dissolves them and each partner wakes up to realise that they are living with a stranger.

It is not suggested that you become overly sceptical or cynical, but that a deeper and discriminatory look is made, both into your own nature and that of any proposed partner. It may be that those tendencies of faith and trust should be applied in a more impersonal sphere, where instead of having to believe in individuals (who are always capable of letting you down) it becomes more abstracted into a belief in the essential goodness of humanity that is slowly evolving and being anchored in the world. Certainly your experience of relationships will be a testing ground, and one where many lessons can be realised and hopefully where your evaluations will become more acute and realistic.

When disappointments strike you, there is a tendency to retreat into a private fantasy world. This can be positively used as a self-healing technique, but you must avoid any temptation to use this purely as an escape, for if you do so you risk losing contact with reality. A place to consider the implicit lessons and meanings for you, yes, but not one where you elevate withdrawal as a means to remain ignorant and persist in any illusions.

You may have desires to experience 'sublime feelings and emotions', an intensity that is not commonly found in everyday life, and an expansion beyond your normal boundaries of existence. This can be a latent mystical proclivity, which you search for in love affairs. You may be similarly attracted towards involvement with drugs, alcohol or spiritual cults. Certainly the addictive attractions should be avoided, and if you do look towards the spiritual scene, be careful of illusions related to gurus, cults and the like. Discrimination is vitally necessary in these realms too.

Throughout your life, there should be a fertile imagination at work, which may find means of expression in art, music, literature or by an absorption in religion and philosophy. Suitable channels for this imagination need to be established, or else it will just amplify your inner dreams and distorting illusions.

Idealism will remain strong, although there can be a lack of real practicality and common sense, where through a lack of persistent self-discipline you often fail to deliver what you are capable of doing. As a result of your high emotional sensitivity, you may be attracted towards work related to a feeling of social obligation, where social welfare and aid for others becomes dominant. Such spheres as medicine, nursing, mental health, teaching, community welfare or voluntary service could satisfy this need. You may have to guard against becoming too personally involved when you offer sympathy and support, or else your own ability to serve will be weighed down by the weight of the world on your shoulders. That type of martyrdom which turns you into a victim is often an unnecessary sacrifice, and can be avoided by a different inner perspective.

JUPITER–NEPTUNE SEXTILE

The sextile includes several of the themes of the conjunction, but often develops and defines them more clearly within the individual, and so they are probably more easy to deal with and apply in daily life.

In personal relationships, that tendency towards gullibility is still present, aided and abetted by powerful sensitive feelings and emotions that encourage you to believe in the commitment of your partner who satisfies your needs and desires. Your evaluation of the status of your intimate relationships may be unrealistic, and there are bound to be times when your belief in the aptness of your choices is later seen to be merely self-deception; wherever your emotions are involved, they are the source for many illusions and much vulnerability. Standing beside you in the shadows of love is always the prospect of disillusionment. Take more time to know someone, be more cautious and check with them how they feel about the relationships too; do not just assume that because you feel in love and happy they feel the same. They may . . . but the rising divorce rate seems to indicate that the reverse is, regrettably, often the real situation.

The theme that is more defined in the sextile is that of optimism, imagination and idealism. The likelihood is that this will be more focused within your mind, and that your lifestyle will reflect this more clearly. In you, faith and trust becomes a more optimistic spirit looking towards future prospects and opportunities. The sphere of expansion is in that direction, and much attention is likely to be paid to contemporary social problems.

This vision is probably radical in nature, and often veering to the 'New Age' perspective. You are alert and aware enough of social conditions, desires and needs, yet you also add a broader perspective to what is currently occurring and what needs to occur in order to build a brighter future. You are capable of an analysis of modern social problems, seeing intrinsic dangers there, and can be articulate in raising these issues. You may become involved in groups that are public voices for such concerns, those minority pressure groups that perform such an essential public service in the Western world. The failings of established political, religious and social power blocs should be recognised, although you may choose to work within them as an influence for inner change.

You value individualism highly, and see how others can be unconsciously swept along by powerful ideologies and socially acceptable ways of behaving. This can encourage you to make your own stand against any negative social ideologies that are currently powerful, even those emanating from governments and the churches. You may become a publicist for your ideas and those of affinity groups in an attempt to alert public attention to what is occurring. Idealism will be vitally important to you, and you will feel quite passionate about those ideals.

Yet what can let you down is the fact that you are essentially a theorist, in that activity is via a mental perspective, and the ability to ground your vision is often lacking in basic common sense and practicality. At worst, you may recognise social problems, acknowledge that you do have a social responsibility and then fail to take any action about it. Your innate altruistic and humanitarian nature can remain inhibited.

If this is happening, and it is partly a symptom of an unintegrated Neptune which dissolves the will to act, then you may need to give yourself a shake. Certainly social change does need visions and mental theories, but ultimately these have to be anchored on this level, and that inevitably involves a transformation of their nature, often compromising the initial pristine vision. They never come through pure! And they often come through channels and areas of life that are surprising and unexpected. There are 'thinkers and doers' and ideally the two need to work together; but even the thinkers can become more practical, even if thinking is their real task and not just an excuse for doing nothing. One simple step is to transfer money towards those who are 'doing' and support them in that way. Or you can evaluate your skills and resources; you should have an articulate imagination, which could be positively applied in the publicising of vital issues, be inspirational, or express positive social ideals. These are possible channels for you to work along which will be beneficial to yourself and others and will avoid any tendency to retreat into isolated reactive theories, a private monastery of the mind. We can all complain about aspects of life; but the issue is, what are we doing about them? We can all do something, and even if our contribution is apparently small and insignificant, collectively we can make a difference.

JUPITER–NEPTUNE TRINE

The trine aspect between these two planets offers the most fluent and the easiest ways of expressing that inner potential, and has several similarities with the characteristics of the sextile.

There is likely to be a natural religious and spiritual affinity, whether orthodox or unorthodox, and possibly pursued through a more mystical orientation, an interest in occultism, or by your own heightened psychic sensitivity. You tend to recognise that spiritual insight and attitudes can help to infuse supportive foundations in the lives of those who are responsive, and can enhance meaning, purpose and life direction. These need not be traditional religious philosophies or theology, but are a personal path which unfolds from your own insights and values, emerging from that ability to understand life and people that seems to be a part of you.

This approach is less intellectually biased than with the sextile aspect, focusing more on feeling, emotion and intuition, and so the path of the mystic and of contemplative meditation may feel more natural to you. Exalted emotional experiences are of an intensity that you welcome; and it is the evocation of such sensations that can draw you towards communal and religious activities that enhance ceremony, atmosphere, communion and a touch of dramatic mystery. It could be the appeal of the High Church that you find attractive. It is the love and relationship aspect of the spiritual life that motivates you, rather than the knowledge or wisdom dimension, and indeed you may lack discrimination to some degree. Even so, you do succeed in successfully integrating your inspired knowledge so that it is absorbed within your optimistic outlook on life and serves to add richness and variety.

There is likely to be a deep sensitivity to your local and world environment, and a strong sense of community spirit. Your basic attitudes are positive and progressive, in that you see the light imprisoned even within the deepest darkness, and have faith that it can be released into constructive activity. It is this essential trust in life and people that can give you strength, both in your own path through life and in supporting others when times are hard and challenging. Your generosity of spirit is one which can be relied upon when friends and family are in need. In several ways, you will both grow and feel fulfilled if you are engaged in service to others, when something real, constructive and positive can emerge from your efforts, and this can lead you into the medical and nursing professions, community welfare and forms of teaching or into developing beneficial social programmes which increase the opportunities for others to release their potential or enjoy life more. Attempts to refine and improve society are likely to be your most effective channels to work through, although you may also do this through creative means too, such as art, music and literature, where your expansive imagination can find ways to be anchored in objective forms. You recognise that there are always causes which can benefit from your support and energy, such as international aid organisations.

In intimate relationships, ideally you require someone who is essentially compatible with your outlook and attitudes, someone who can understand and respect your sensitivity and refinement, and who acknowledges, values and supports these qualities. Because you have much to offer, there may be occasional inner clashes between a few self-centred demands and needs and your higher ideals; following the path indicated by your ideals will prove the most apt way, and ensure that the positive tendencies of these planets shine through.

In a few, the spiritual and mystical worlds may be extremely attractive, so much so that the ties of mainstream society fail to bind them into a traditional lifestyle. In such cases, a withdrawal into the world of contemplation may occur; a monastic life or one of non-materialism may greatly appeal. Some prefer to remain free and wander without too many ties or possessions, and adopt a travelling Bohemian lifestyle like the 'New Age travellers' scattered across the world, free to listen to their own inner inclinations and to experience the boundless nature of planet Earth by exploring alternative cultures.

JUPITER–NEPTUNE SQUARE

The square aspect tends to indicate great promise which is usually frustrated by the more negative qualities of these two planets. It is the potent dream world that you create which is both the source of your creative potential and the cause of your challenges in actual achievement. The problem is that often your dreams remain just dreams, an inner world into which you retreat, a world that you invest much energy in maintaining. Dreaming becomes too addictive for you, and your life becomes just an unrealised dream.

This frustration is often caused by a lack of self-discipline and too much self-indulgence and time wasting. Concentration is poor, and discrimination in decision making can be virtually non-existent at times, as well as being hampered by an unconscious attraction towards flawed ideas and projects. The influences of others are powerful, and you are often pulled from side to side as alluring ideas take control of your dreams. Confronting reality and accepting responsibility is not your favourite activity as you prefer to be absorbed within your current 'castle in the sky', which feels emotionally satisfying. You may be capable of spinning great yarns about what you are going to do, but time reveals that usually you are incapable of actually doing anything, except to dream.

Even when you begin to anchor an idea or intention, what occurs is that it is soon revealed to have flaws, in that faulty logic and reasoning have already eroded firm foundations, and it is seen that those ideas lack real substance and an ability to deliver. Financial awareness is another area where you are rarely at your best, due to the distortions stimulated by Neptune and the expansive over-reaching of Jupiter. By unwise actions and lack of preparation you can create financial problems for yourself quite easily. Your nature is a little other-worldly, running away from the realities of the physical-plane life, and you may have an ongoing struggle to shore up a collapsing ordinary life when your attention has been elsewhere for too long. You tend to become lost in cloudy visions, unable to see clearly through those mists and inner fogs. The real world can feel oppressive and too restricting, and you want to shake it away, yet really you need to properly face it or you will receive many more rude awakenings from those inner dreams.

Yet you are often generous and sympathetic with others, having a good heart which is also liable to be abused and taken advantage of by less understanding people. You can lack discrimination towards those in whom you place your faith and trust. That tendency to be gullible and naive will be present, and you may find that others use you as an excuse for their own failings, placing any blame on your shoulders. There can be the 'victim syndrome' operating through your unintegrated Neptune. Because both of these planets have similar characteristics, it is likely that you will express both of their more negative dimensions. This can cause a blockage in action, a hesitancy over decision making. You can become like a seeker of a dream, frustrated by always looking and never finding. Eventually you may even become apathetic at the failure of your attempts and surrender hopes of ever achieving success.

Relationships can pose problems; distortions and misunder-standings may be common, your consistency questioned, or a liability to be emotionally abused is likely. Offering your heart to unsuitable lovers is probably inevitable at some point. What keeps you going? Dreams . . . you dream of exotic adventures, exotic lands, exotic mysteries. You find it very difficult to settle in this world. A tendency of restless wanderlust is common, on physical, emotional and mental levels. Contentment is rarely found. Yet it need not be like this, as many of these frustrations are of your own making, and certainly the potential is there waiting to find channels of expression through a disciplined control being applied. It may be difficult, but facing reality, conforming to its restrictive limitations and learning how to be more practical could be the key to success. Some of those private dreams could become real if you became more concentrated and dedicated to achieving one at a time, instead of withdrawing when the going gets tough. The first step is to become aware of your receptive patterns, to see how they operate, see what consequences occur, see the point where things fall apart. Then, resolve to change that pattern, put more thought into building the dream, more realistic self-evaluation, more discipline and effort placed into making that intention successful. By slowing the process down, and by applying yourself more consciously to what you are doing, you may be able to transform this pattern of frustration into one of future success – it would be well worth the effort!

JUPITER–NEPTUNE OPPOSITION

The opposition has several similarities to the square, but here the source of 'contention' is projected externally on to the outer world and people. There is the difficulty of 'follow through', where intentions and plans are often thwarted by an inability to actually realise them, despite your original aims; things are started but never completed in any satisfying way. You tend to resent and resist any external pressure that can be placed on you by others' expectations of your performance and abilities.

Conflicts often arise in interpersonal relationships, especially with other work colleagues, who may attempt to take advantage of your skills or persuade you to take on responsibilities which may be thankless tasks, or in which for reasons of their own advantage they expect you to fail. There is often a lot of manipulative activity in work places, and you can become a victim of this if you are not aware of the hidden motivations of others. You can become paranoid and suspicious of people, perhaps as a result of previous experience, and there is often a kernel of truth and validity there; yet equally, part of this is a projection emanating from you based on the tensions inherent within this opposition. You tend to either oppose or antagonise others, sometimes by being too direct in your comments and attitudes; there is little social diplomacy in your style of expression, and sometimes you can be very tactless and too adversarial.

There can be a blind spot in your character that is often unrecognised, and is related to the sign and house positions of Jupiter and Neptune. Whilst you may fail to fully comprehend your own nature and what you 'should be doing', you still express yourself forcefully and with a tendency to be authoritarian. Yet you also often challenge the dictates of those in positions of authority, questioning their perceptions and rights to wield power. There is less of a social awareness and conscience here with this aspect, as most of the energy is tied up in an external uneasiness; you do not have any great trust in the good nature of others, which, whilst possibly more realistic, is also symptomatic of your own inner fragmentation and stress – you cannot relax and trust yourself either. You need to learn how to accept others as well as accepting yourself; the two are intertwined, and if you can manage this then stress will be diminished and all your relationships will improve as you correspondingly feel more at ease in your own nature.

Intimate relationships can pose difficulties until the step of personal integration and resolution is taken. Your choices of partners may be unwise, especially where those *anima–animus* projections are superimposed on the partner, apparently turning them into the ideal lover who possesses everything that you believe you desire and need. When these projections collapse, you are liable to be emotionally distraught and see that person as another one who has deceived you; in fact, it may have been your own illusions that have been self-deceptive, and so the consequences of a hurt heart should not be taken out on your partner in any emotional or physical aggression. Resorting to the Neptunian addictions of drugs or alcohol must be avoided at such traumatic times.

Some form of religious or spiritual life and aspiration is likely, yet this too can suffer from some distortion and invalid projections. Your spiritual attitudes may lack a practical dimension, or even be seriously applied by yourself in everyday life. There can be a greater attraction towards the glamours of more exotic religions, which offer a colourful fascination and mystery that appeals. Cultism and an idealised surrender to gurus can be a temptation, despite your resistance to forms of authority, and can seem to offer a way out from the disappointments and stresses of your life. Alternatively, you may dream of foreign travel or pilgrimages across the world as an antidote to the lifestyle you feel trapped within.

Realising that much of what dissatisfies you in the world is a reflection of an inner lack of integration would be a major step forward. Reabsorbing those powerful projections, allowing yourself to re-own them can only strengthen you and give you back the ability to redirect your life in ways that you want it to move in. Taking such control and self-responsibility is crucial, unless you want to persist in the likelihood of unsatisfactory relationships with others, where your need for development and expansion is perpetually thwarted by 'external resistance'.

SATURN–NEPTUNE CONJUNCTION

This aspect only occurs approximately once every thirty-six years, during this century in 1917, 1952 and 1989.

The effects of Saturn have a beneficial influence on the tendencies of Neptune, helping definition, stability and ease of expression; the potential is for practical idealism and an ability for positive application of the ideas and imagination emanating from

Neptune. This is useful for creativity, as the inspiration of Neptune can be given adequate form and manifestation by the concrete tendencies of Saturn, and so the imagination is not left swirling in an inner world of dreams and fancies but is released on to the physical plane to be shared with others.

There is less of the delusive nature of Neptune present with this aspect, and there should be a greater perceptive clarity than usual, one that is especially sensitive to issues of deceit and glamour. You are less prone to make mistakes through such reflective blindness, and tend to be self-protective mainly by a careful and wary distancing that you maintain with strangers or new acquaintances. This is part of the Saturn contribution of caution and unease with anything that is unknown. Trust needs to be progressively developed in you, whether in people, circumstances or situations, and you are usually reticent in making any firm commitments until you have thoroughly evaluated any set of choices. You tend to rely on a faith in facts, an impersonal judging of what seems to be the wisest choice to make; this can be beneficial in your life, privately and in a career.

It is probable that the Saturn energy will be the dominant one, with the Neptune energy occasionally repressed for practical reasons. If you allow Saturn to be too emphasised, then opportunities may be lost through excessive evaluation and lack of decisiveness; that fear of the unknown will also act as a restrictive and inhibiting factor. You are likely to erect a well-defined lifestyle and personality structure which allows relatively little space for the Neptunian influence to be expressed, as it is more anarchic and expansionary. What can occur is a sense of confusion regarding your own personal limitations, where they begin to feel imprisoning and Neptune agitates to dissolve those barriers and to experience those repressed dreams that you are attempting to ignore. A careful balancing of both these planetary energies is essential, both for inner harmony and for external success. Otherwise degrees of distortion and lack of perspective will increase, as the Neptune influence demonstrates its repressed presence through more negative characteristics.

For those exploring the spiritual dimension of life, this aspect offers several valuable assets, in that there is a questioning of dogma and assumptions, a tendency to deglamorise through a more earthy perspective, and a developing ability to rely on the inner guidance of intuition rather than on external 'authority sources'. This stage may have been reached as lessons learnt through earlier phases of gullibility and submission to teachers, possibly through religious or parental conditioning which you begin to cast away as inimical to your own development. Discrimination is important in life, and especially so when contacting occult teachings, where the likelihood is that through a lack of real personal experience only genuine ignorance exists, and the tendency of most is to fill that void by passively accepting whatever teaching is making an impact on them.

As you continue to develop, especially through standing alone and living through your own light, a greater maturity and perception will unfold. Insight and compassion founded on living experience will be gained, and if you practise meditational techniques, then your own power and light is likely to shine brighter as your inner clarity emerges. Effective concentration and meditation should be possible, and some signs of psychic abilities may also emerge from the Neptune energy being released. You may become a channel for the transpersonal energies to enter these levels, and there will be a sense of social responsibility and of the context through which they can operate.

Your intimate relationships are likely to be deep and enriching, partly as a result of your careful evaluation of suitable partners, and in those relationships where your heart becomes involved you will tend to be cautious before opening to a full commitment. Relationships are important to you, and you place great emphasis on continually working at them to ensure that they are mutually beneficial and a source of evolutionary growth. You believe that 'right choice leads to right action', and this is a key to your success and to your procedure of careful evaluation of options and decisions.

SATURN–NEPTUNE SEXTILE

Working successfully with the sextile aspect often involves action related to that strong sense of social responsibility and duties that you recognise. This sensitivity to a social role that requires performance is a major component of your motivation, and one that should not really be denied. There can be a tendency to acknowledge its presence and then fail to actually do anything about it, but ideally this should be overcome by more deliberate action. At least you can always help by funding those socially active groups whose ideals you can support. This characteristic is a combination of Saturn duty and the Neptunian social collective ideal.

The element of careful discursive planning should be evident where the right foundations for future action are established, and efficient organisation is seen as necessary for a successful conclusion. There are likely to be strategic skills which can be exploited in order to achieve those intentions, whether purely personal or socially orientated. Consistency and determination are usually well applied, and your schemes are characterised by their realism and achievability; Neptunian over-expansiveness is tempered by Saturnian caution and a sense of stability and limitation.

What can inspire many of your efforts is a reaction against social injustice and foolishness. Fairness is one attitude that you support, and opposing social aspects where unfairness and injustice is being expressed can almost become a personal crusade. Social discrimination and taking social advantage of those unable to resist can cause your passions to rise, leading to social activism designed to resist such encroachments on individual rights and liberties. You dislike seeing the waste of resources, social and material ones as well as the waste of human potential. This can lead to supporting human-potential-raising groups, or ecological activists calling for new atttitudes towards the excessive negative exploitation of nature's reserves. You tend to have a social vision of harmony, where equity is achieved and social respect for all is found, rather than any unbalanced divisive situation of haves and have-nots. Concepts of the values of community or global thinking will be preferred, and you like to believe that what you are attempting is beneficial to others.

If you become active in such ways at an early age – perhaps through a career choice – then you may find that it absorbs most of your energy; it is a never-ending task! This may affect your intimate relationships, especially when a partner needs to hold similar viewpoints to your own. Ideals are important to you, and you try to live in a way that maintains rather than opposes or compromises them. Your passions are firmly fixed on issues of social concern, and even within personal love relationships your energy is too diffuse to focus just on one partner; it flows out as a feeling of social relationship too, and you often fail to understand why society is as it is, and why people are so passive in allowing negativity and indifference to flourish, even in those in high and powerful social positions of influence.

Concentration and visualisation abilities should be present, and can be applied through contemplation of issues or meditation. You may become effective if working in occult or socially active affinity groups committed to generating beneficial change. There is little ego gratification in such work for you, and you tend to expect a high degree of probity and idealism from others engaged in similar self-chosen roles.

SATURN–NEPTUNE TRINE

The high idealism of Neptune and the awareness of social responsibility of Saturn will be prominent, and will stimulate an inner motivation intent on sharing in the ongoing work of social improvement. You should have a natural insight into social issues, and this coupled with a keen perception can help you to indicate those core problems that require resolution; in addition, you are able to offer constructive solutions to such problem areas, and are able to work with or within existing social organisations or governmental bodies to influence suitable changes to be made. In particular, you enjoy restoring 'order from chaos' and making use of forgotten and ignored resources.

There can be a tendency to sit back and observe social decline and contentious issues without choosing to become more actively involved, but this would be a waste of your own talents and a denial of that sense of social obligation. Your idealism has strong moral and ethical roots, and you could feel uncomfortable if you ignored those inner promptings. Direct activism may not be your preferred mode of involvement, but you may find your role perhaps through communicating to others the facts about certain problematic social issues, especially through the medium of writing and analysis.

You tend to have an absorbent intelligence, which accumulates considerable information and knowledge easily, and which is a resource that you should be able to utilise. The level of imagination is high and active, and this too can be personally used in a variety of ways, giving a spark of life to the ideas that you have for personal and social development. You may have difficulty in deciding exactly how to use your own resources, and the ideal may be to become involved in work which has a definite social dimension. Such work can include community welfare, law, social services, environmental concerns, finance, management, media, film, photography.

Friends find that you are a reliable support in times of crisis, and you are equally willing to lend a helping hand when necessary. Neptune inspires you towards compassionate feelings, both for people you know and strangers.

If the spiritual quality of Neptune is active (and not so overshadowed by a dominating Saturn), then you are likely to be attracted towards spiritual or occult groups, where your talents can find ways of expression. Meditation and visualisation work should be enhanced by Neptune, and anchoring the energies in suitable forms should be enhanced by Saturn. Learning to trust your intuition will lead you to rely on it even more over time, and this could be a vital step forward in your own development.

SATURN–NEPTUNE SQUARE

The square indicates inner tensions and frustrations, and it is likely that Neptune will be inhibited from true realisation and will be bound within the unconscious mind by the barrier-forming restrictions of Saturn. This will cause Neptune to be agitatory, stimulating unconscious fears, anxieties, phobias, morbidity and guilt feelings arising from an overactive imagination which lacks suitable channels for a more healthy release.

The consequences of this inner pressure and disquiet tend to create feelings of inadequacy, incompetence and inferiority. These may be quite illusory and unrealistic, yet they have a powerful influence on your actions and choices. As time passes and you perpetuate these tendencies, you continue to create negative results, which convinces you that such inferiority beliefs are actually true. You become a self-defeatist, and lack confidence in your own abilities. This negativity can spread until you begin to run away from accepting responsibility or challenges; you can become afraid to even try. Obviously this begins to severely inhibit your life experiences, as you are increasingly trapped within the parameters of your own inner phobias and lack of self-love and self-confidence. If this is allowed to persist, then this form of imprisonment will only intensify as you cut yourself off from the richness of life, and forms of depression can occur.

Such a situation can be allowed to happen where inner blockages of energy generate stresses of compulsive behaviour which are internally felt as real yet are the symptoms of denying aspects of self (as symbolised by the planets which are inhibited); with this square the probability is that Saturn's activity will become distorted too, over-emphasised by the erection of excessive boundaries and limitations. Tendencies of anxiety and guilt are also self-perpetuating and these expand to form a web of energy which absorbs the individual's freedom of choice, and creates circular loop patterns of repetitive thought processes. There is emotional agitation, overly stimulated by inherent negative attitudes, yet there is no apparent ability to deal with them. Dissatisfaction and confusion is to be expected, yet any impulse to change the situation can also be inhibited.

The degree to which this inner psychological environment develops will be dependent on the rest of the chart; there may be mitigating factors which diminish its potential severity. Yet certain issues will be present in those who have this aspect, and several corrective and releasing acts can still be valuably taken to prohibit any likelihood of such tendencies developing.

Accepting your own nature is vital. Denial of any aspect leads to its suppression into the unconscious mind, where it is likely to fester, slowly releasing poisons into the personality within the appropriate level of natural affinity, distorting body, emotions or mind. Such a forced cutting away of part of your nature is never wise, and is as foolish as cutting away an arm because there may be an unsightly mole on it! Often these tendencies to 'cut away' are indicated by square aspects, and symbolise probable inner tensions and blockages of energy which need release; yet in doing so, they can often become 'great friends', giving energy and power to enable you to achieve your aims. They are keys to real personal development, spurs to stimulate necessary integration.

In accepting your own nature, self-forgiveness is required, and a refusal to compare yourself to any illusory ideal of perfection. Why feel guilty because you are not like an ideal? You never can be, and your real task is just to become yourself, warts and all, and coming to terms with that is a great freedom and liberation in itself. Face those fears of failure; everyone fails in some way, why should you be any exception? But some fail (repeatedly) and yet still carry on, gathering more successes as time passes and achieving their ambitions. There is success waiting for you, just shake yourself down and carry on, and when you arrive, it will taste very sweet, and you'll know a valuable secret! Talents are there within you, they are just hiding out of sight; find that pot of gold around the corner, and perhaps with a bit of support from others, you'll learn how to really use it. All of those inner illusions, guilt trips, inferiority complexes and phobias can dissipate like chimeras in the sky. The self-imposed barriers of Saturn will collapse, and Neptune will flow through, healing you and inspiring you to find a new way. Why stay in a self-created prison when there is no locked door? Stop being self-indulgent. Walk through and emerge in a new world. And isn't that worth struggling for? Remember, your life is basically what you make it. Don't throw it away, enjoy it!

SATURN–NEPTUNE OPPOSITION

What occurs with the opposition is the projection outwards of inner attitudes, so that life reflects that inner state back to you. Usually this includes elements of distortion, which with Saturn and Neptune tends to involve fears of failure, suspicions of motives, cloudy judgements, deceit, caution and wariness. These are the more negative qualities of blocked planetary energies, and yet you often fail to realise that the world you are perceiving is a mirror image of your own attitudes. Take another look. Do the world and people reflect your own views? Are they pessimistic and perhaps threatening or frightening? Do you feel that you have to be extremely self-protective? These may, of course, be genuine fears, and can depend on the environment in which you live, but equally they may be illusionary and self-created.

This fear of failure is inhibitory to some degree, and it is likely that you will withdraw from situations of competition, retreating into feelings of inadequacy, imagining various types of conspiracy being hatched against you in secret. You don't really trust people, and that attitude is communicated intangibly to others, so that a vicious circle is perpetuated. Your relationships can lack depth, human warmth and real contact, often staying unsatisfyingly superficial, in that you are afraid that others may take advantage of you. The problem is that this may well happen (or has in the past), and since then you have been too wary and too aware of your vulnerability to risk deeper relationships. Certainly you are vulnerable emotionally and financially to people, and one lesson that may need learning is that you should look closely at the nature of others before you become committed in any way.

Saturn's barriers are firmly established for self-protection, yet they also block many valid experiences and opportunities for self-development. Neptune remains partially released, but liable to display its presence through experiences of persecution and martyr/victim complexes in your life. The results can be that you isolate yourself, become a solitary loner, immune in your imprisoning cocoon of self-protection, perhaps feeling the repercussions of your choice through depressive emotions or psychosomatic illnesses.

You can look out on to the world and secretly want status and involvement, yet be self-restrictive in actually attempting to achieve those ambitions. Or you may perhaps resort to cunning, subterfuge and devious behaviour, believing that is the way everyone else achieves their desires.

The fact that your world analysis may be incorrect could hold a solution to your frustrated energies. The world holds all shades of behaviour and attitude, and whilst there are many who accurately embody reasons for your cautious perspective, there are others who are not like that at all. You need to find a bridge to contact those people of goodwill, and then you may realise that your interpretation of the world is only partially accurate; the others hold a key to your transformation. If you can find an intimate partner who does not let you down and is supportive, then that frustrated ideal may be reborn, and in accepting another as they are, you discover that this is the way for healing and mutual love to occur. The nature of relationship in your life can be renewed and reperceived through more optimistic eyes; Neptune has replaced the barriers of Saturn.

Sometimes Neptune plays a stronger role than Saturn, and if this is the case, then the relationship inhibitions and distortions may be less evident. The focus will be transferred towards that of social duty and obligation, where the lesson deals with responsibility. You may experience a feeling of 'social guilt', a personal responsibility to put right social evils, a personal crusade which you need to follow in order to absolve yourself from this inner feeling of guilt that haunts you. For some reason, you know that this is your duty, and that some form of social service needs to be done in response to an inner compulsion. Some may consider this to be 'a rectification of Karma', but whatever, it can be an inner pressure and related to the Neptunian tendency of sacrifice in the social sphere of Saturn. The battleground is seen to be the world, but the source of the battle is within your own nature. Check this out thoroughly before you go tilting against any windmills; try to isolate those conditioning projections and discover what you may be really fighting against. It could be your own unintegrated aspects, Neptunian ideals versus Saturnian realities, and the middle path of wise balance may be the most suitable way to follow.

URANUS–NEPTUNE CONJUNCTION

This conjunction aspect occurs quite rarely; the last was around 1821–3, and the next will be in 1992–4, allowing a two-degree orb. Aspects involving the transpersonal planets focus more on the generational and social dimensions of life, where the attitudes and experiences of the individual are intimately linked with social changes.

Nobody currently alive has this aspect, but a new generation who will be born in the early nineties will demonstrate these characteristics as they mature. There will be a strong degree of identification with the collective mind and group consciousness, which in some cases could revert back to fervent nationalist affinities in countries that have a powerful controlling religious, racial, political and social structure. Yet in most cases, it is unlikely that this will result in the emergence of charismatic demagogues as in recent examples of the manipulation of the masses.

There will be a directing sense of social responsibility, and an awareness of participating in a social community, which will be expressed in positive ways for the betterment of all. The merged energies of this conjunction will inspire concepts of brotherhood, which will reflect the ideals of Uranus and Neptune, as a form of revolutionary mysticism emerging from an acute mental and emotional sensitivity connected to an intuitive imaginative faculty.

Personal freedoms and rights will have a high priority, and there will be a new perception of 'leadership' being formed, which can dissolve those old patterns of a powerful leader and hundreds of following 'sheep'. There is a distrust of leaders, based on an intuitive perception of their real motivations and characteristics, which will also develop into a new understanding of authority and power in society. Those born under this aspect will be willing to 'fight' for the maintenance of personal freedoms and rights if they are under threat by the decisions of social leaders. A new balance of power between the people and the state will begin to form, and a new politics should rise into view that reflects this increase in individual rights and power. Generally, this should be a period of spiritual and scientific development, where break-throughs occur in the exploration of nature and mind.

As these planets conjunct in 1992–4, at a time which will see the birth of the generation that will become socially influential during the period when Pluto is in Aquarius and Pisces at the end of that transit cycle, it is expected that signs will emerge then that point to the new world which this new generation will inherit. Changes that will become inevitable by 1994 will have to be more fully achieved and realised by that future generation, imbued with a more conscious spirit of human unity and solidarity.

URANUS–NEPTUNE SEXTILE

Most of the characteristics of Uranus–Neptune aspects involve the element of distrust for leaders, organisations and power elites. Those born with the sextile aspect tend to object to establishment secrecy and the withholding of information from their people or their electorate. They consider this manipulation of information to be a deliberate and iniquitous distortion of the truth which should not be allowed by their leaders. Often such people would support a 'freedom of information' cause, believing that the state should be the servant of the people, and not the other way round.

There is an anti-establishment attitude, together with an objec-tion to state autonomy in which the person is steam rollered by the weight of state bureaucracy. There is a need to reassert indi-vidual power and freedom from state interference, and such at-titudes will often oppose authoritarian dictates. An attraction to-wards social revolution and changing the nature of state control can develop a revolutionary and evolutionary philosophy which champions the people's right to power within their own society.

An optimistic belief in people and their potential will dominate, which some may consider to be too naive and idealistic, but it is founded on the right to be able to choose for oneself, and to deter-mine the sort of personal lifestyle to live without being inhibited by social repressions (provided that it does not harm others). It conceives of a society aimed towards personal development and fulfilment, through individual creativity and uniqueness, in contradistinction to one which conditions people to unquestioning fulfilment of economic roles and adherence to social convention.

Essentially, it asserts the right to be self-determining, rather than meekly and blindly following the guidance of leaders who often gain such positions through money or heritage alone. An active involvement in social decision making will attract, especially in ways designed to make some progress towards those brotherhood ideals which so appeal to the mind and emotional levels of those with this aspect.

URANUS–NEPTUNE TRINE

The trine aspect was made roughly during the period 1941–6, and features in the birth-charts of a generation born during war time. This tends to condition their perception of life and people, which in effect can sometimes veer towards pessimism and cynicism, especially if they were born in the early years of the trine when the world war was at its height and the result still hung in the balance.

Underlying this is still the idealism of these planets, but with possibly insufficient personal faith in their actual manifestation, together with an ambiguity about their own personal role and responsibility in society. There can be a tendency to follow personal goals irrespective of social needs and obligations, and a preference for personal gain and ambitions. Yet this too can be a source of personal development, and it is still perhaps too early yet to be sure how such individuals will use any social power and influence that they may have acquired.

As the trine is a reconciling factor, this generation could be seen as a 'bridging group' where both the past and future tendencies co-exist, probably uncomfortably at times. They have grown up in a rapidly changing world, though childhood conditioning would still reflect pre-war attitudes; they are thus able to serve as mediators in society, knowing the older world and yet attuned enough to the dawning of the new world.

There should be sufficient intellectual capacity for them to evaluate the implications of ideological belief structures for themselves

selves, without the imposition of authority; this should result in the development of genuinely held personal views irrespective of their nature and content. If they don't feel convinced, after careful consideration of the validity of an idea or belief, they will usually be unable to give whole-hearted support for it – unless they compromise themselves for personal gain.

They are aware of the dangers of gullibility and of a lack of public discrimination regarding leaders – as the German people in World War II demonstrated – yet are not fully convinced by the intent of any leaders who use truth as an expedient to be employed only when it suits them. In many ways, this generation is faced with a need to resolve certain inner conflicts and opposite world views, almost as a 'trial run' for the way in which society can achieve this on a larger scale. There are paradoxes on both mental and emotional levels that should be resolved and integrated, because too often such people are caught in the cleft stick of their own indecision and confusion over which 'face' to present – the face of the older ways, or the face reflecting the emerging changes in the world.

URANUS–NEPTUNE OPPOSITION

Like the conjunction aspect, the opposition is made approximately every 171 years. The last one was during the period 1906-10.

What seems to occur with this aspect is a domination of the conscious mind by a social-conditioning programme, which makes the individual and the collective less aware of what is actually happening in the collective mind. The transpersonal planets stimulate an agitation in the unconscious, so that areas requiring release and resolution are brought out into the open through encountering crisis.

It is a phase when the conscious mind is absorbed within the status quo, firmly fixed in its world views, ideologies, religious beliefs and social lifestyles. Basically, life is running along clearly defined 'tracks', with relatively little questioning or dissidence; yet under the superficial calm, there is brewing a maelstrom of repression and restricted energy searching for release and expression. In many ways, the individual is too identified with collective groups, and is losing the ability of self-determination and freedom of choice. This involves a relinquishing of personal responsibility,

and transfers collective power into the hands of those who volun-
teer (for various reasons) to be social leaders.

There is likely to be a misplaced optimism and illusions concerning the well-being of society, because the dynamic of change and
the struggle to achieve a high ideal is being denied full expression.
Inwardly, both within the individual and the collective, there is
a conflict between the emotional and mental levels, where there
is no real meshing under the directing influence of a focused will.
It is as though a comfortable pattern has been established, which
is conformed to with little discriminatory awareness. There is
mental tranquillity, but this somehow denies a satisfying emotional dimension, which causes that energy within to fester. Eventually it will re-emerge as motivation, creating mind desires which
will generally embody a separatist attitude. This was seen in the
nationalist and economic greed that emerged prior to World War
I, and was repeated in the later war of 1939–45.

This can be a confusing phase, in which the real activity is
stirring underneath the surface, ready to erupt. The individual
becomes swept along by major social changes, where real choices
eventually have to be made as a consequence of confronting the
results that emerge from the inner tensions. Sides have to be
taken, and instead of apathy, a real struggle can ensue in the
attempt to secure the preservation of the essentials of the state
lifestyle against potential aggressors, who could be either internal
or external. Yet change cannot be ignored, and a revolution of
some kind will happen. Three examples of this are the Russian
Revolution and the world wars, all of which led to permanent
international change.

URANUS–NEPTUNE SQUARE

The last square aspect happened during the period 1952–6, and
influenced the people born during that phase. This was the second
phase of post-war children, born into a time of relative stability
and reconstruction, when the memories of the war were ebbing
away into past history, even though the Korean War was rekindling some of them.

This group received a psychic impression from the collective,
which embodied a form of social confusion then prevalent which
was reflective of the collective mind. Social direction was the
issue. The defeat of Churchill's government after the ending of

the war, a government which seemed to represent the past, and the introduction of the post-war Labour reformist policies such as the Welfare State seemed to herald a new vision and direction. But the collective was torn between dreams and fears of a new world, and a rejection of painful recent memories of man's inhumanity; a clash between the future and the past, the unknown and the known.

Reflecting this collective conflict, the individuals born at this time received a pattern of rebellion (Uranus) which was mixed with confusion (Neptune) over what to do, which direction to travel in, how to achieve objectives, even what these objectives actually were. The only model that could be absorbed was that of their parents and peers, which offered conflicting and confusing social messages.

The problem in later life would become ambivalence; they would be torn between a need to revolt against authority and the establishment, and a need to feel socially secure. Purity of ideals would become a challenge, especially when confronted with the pragmatic demands of economic and family life.

With this aspect there is an aversion to leaders, who, it is felt, lead people into blind obedience and conformity, which to the Uranian spirit is anathema and opposed to the Uranian principle of freedom. Personal freedoms are paramount, and their repression may lead to a struggle to assert them. Yet this group eventually fragmented into various types. Some were reluctant revolutionaries, eventually being reabsorbed into the social mainstream; some were 'rebels without a cause', social misfits with no direction except that of aggressive reaction. Members of this aspect group were attracted to the existing hippie and drug counter-culture, in the later phase after 1968; others became early leaders of the mid seventies punk movement, an anarchic reactionary youth revolt again conformity; and perhaps most significant of all became part of the spreading of the New Age movement which incorporates the ecological Green political groups.

In fact, many of those who were early adherents of the hippie ideals have become part of the New Age culture, which is expanding throughout society through alternative health therapies, mind training, healthy foods, and an ideology of individual and collective wholeness. It is in this way that the core group of those born during the period 1952–6 are active in taking control of their own lives and influencing society.

PLUTO–NEPTUNE SEXTILE

During this century, there is only one aspect made between Neptune and Pluto, and it is interesting to note that the sextile commenced in the midst of World War II during 1942. The influence of this relationship would be expected to have global and generational effects, and like all of the transpersonal planetary energies, would be a directive force stimulating the development of the evolutionary process within time and space.

Neptune will attract an almost mystical exploratory search from those responsive to it, and since the sextile commenced science has reacted in two distinct and complementary directions: effort has been poured into developing space travel and satellite technology, exploring the vast outer universe through radio-telescopes, for example; while the complementary exploration of inner space – investigating and probing the building blocks of matter – and quantum physics has emerged at the forefront of scientific enquiry.

The attempts to understand the nature of the universe, its composition and size, the possible creation of the universe and the 'big bang theory' reflect the traditional Western way of looking externally. What has paralleled this tendency has been the birth of an opposite movement amongst people, that of self-exploration, the inner mystical way. This has been through the New Age movement, humanistic/Jungian psychology, occult techniques and rebirth of magical attitudes towards life. It has also involved the grafting on to the Western tree of many of the attitudes and knowledge of Eastern philosophies and religions, a merging of the two hemispheres, a potential unification of belief structures reflecting the scientific movement towards a more mystically orientated quantum physics.

As the outer universe becomes vaster, and the inner universe becomes a mysterious vastness of space, the only point in which the outer and the inner can become reconciled is in the human being. At a time when the immense destructive power of splitting the atom can be used to commit racial suicide or genocide, the old Mystery School injunction of the ancients is the key to the future: 'Man, know thyself.'

The generations born after this aspect commenced, or those especially receptive to its influence, are aware of the basic tendencies emanating from it. They are life-enhancing: the need to protect the world's environment from senseless devastation, the need to extend individual rights and freedoms, to unfold international co-operation and to move beyond an embracing consumer materialist dominance in the West. The recognition that potentially a higher quality of life can be had in the world for the majority of people through a redirection of resources (if the will is there) can lead to radical change.

The energies of transformation are present, and much depends upon our use of them, individually and collectively, for negative or positive results. The challenge of 'free will' is the nature of choice and decision which determine, in the present, the nature of the future.

NEPTUNE EXALTED IN CANCER

There are several signs and planets connected within this exaltation: Neptune, Jupiter, Venus, the Moon, Pisces and Cancer, all of which emphasise aspects of love, the heart, collective consciousness, the group humanity, emotions, the Mother and the astral plane of desires, images and imagination.

In esoteric teachings, Cancer is the gateway through which mass incarnation is to take place, and it is interesting to note that Neptune is the planet most closely aligned to political and spiritual philosophies of group unity. This grouping of zodiacal influences coalesces around the element of Water, where Neptune is the God of the Oceans, ruler of Pisces and at ease within the watery sign of Cancer. The old co-ruler of Pisces is Jupiter, which is also exalted in the sign of Cancer, and Neptune is now considered to represent a higher harmonic vibration of the Jupiterian expansionary tendency. These exhibit characteristics of social expansion and religious or mystical interests, and are the bonding energies of social cohesiveness, with Jupiter especially strong in the areas of family, society and religious or ethical affairs.

Cancer is associated with deep sensitivity and feelings, often psychic in nature and attuned to unconscious tides which influence an often moody human temperament. The exaltation of Neptune in this sign intensifies the emotions, heightening them to empathic peaks which can be difficult to contain for some people, and the attraction towards a mystical reclusiveness or otherworldly lifestyle may predominate. Such an emotionally rooted attunement can create a sensitivity to world suffering, registering everything that impinges on that sensitive awareness, perhaps being easily influenced by others or by inner, unconscious motivations, or even attempting to walk the path of the World Saviours and acting as a channel for redemptive energies.

It is through Pisces that Venus is exalted, and these four planets (including Jupiter, Neptune and the Moon) have affinities to vibrations of the energies of love in the universe. Jupiter is the social and communal bond; Venus relates to personal, separative love and the polarity of sexual duality; the Moon (ruler of Cancer) relates to our early experience of love and bonding to the Mother, forming emotional patterns, habits, needs, expectations and disillusionments; and Neptune in its higher guise reflects the non-separative love for all, a transcendental union with divinity and the expression of universal love. Through each of these connected channels comes the Neptunian influence, especially the subtle and illusory qualities which are often more apparent than the higher vibrational qualities. Despite the liking for habit and repetitive pattern-making of Cancer and the Moon as building security and stability, Neptune will constantly dissolve all inhibiting structures and so liberate the imprisoned life and allow vitality to be renewed in new forms.

Neptune as Significator of Practical Director

The Significator of the Practical Director of a natal chart is determined by noting the planet that immediately precedes the natal position of the Sun. This has also been termed the planet of oriental appearance. For instance, in a chart where the Sun is placed at seventeen degrees Scorpio and has Neptune at twelve degrees Scorpio as the nearest preceding planet, thus Neptune is the Practical Director.

When Neptune is in this position, it tends to heighten the role of that planet in the personality, and it is often the case that the Director is a highly influential planet through aspects, rulerships and the like. The qualities and talents associated with Neptune can be especially directed through the natal house position, and will take on an even greater importance and need for expression when Neptune is the chart Director.

For the individual who has Neptune performing this role in

their chart, this indicates a particular talent for a natural spiritual affinity and inner contacts. Intuitive feelings are usually powerful, potentially serving as a means of ongoing life direction and guidance, especially at those times where crisis points are reached; a strong impression of the right way to travel is usually registered. Personal energies can be easily focused towards ambitions related to spiritual evolution, insight and realisation, and the likelihood is that to some degree the individual will be expected to serve as a transpersonal channel.

Interests will probably veer towards creativity and mysticism, although as is often the case with Neptune, there may be some difficulty in integrating Neptunian perceptions into daily life and ensuring that any evaluation is cleansed of distorting glamours and illusions first. The problem of diffuseness may occur, and learning how to focus that will be required in order to achieve a full expression of those Neptunian talents. As Neptune tends to draw people away from conventional realities, there can be an ongoing struggle to find a satisfying type of employment, and the clash between Neptune's dreams and any current reality can often be painful and frustrating. Many who respond deeply to this planetary influence often gravitate towards more creative and artistic lives, or towards the emerging lifestyles offered by the expanding New Age movement and the market place, where they can live more in harmony with their inner needs and spirit.

RETROGRADE NEPTUNE

The retrograde position of natal Neptune implies that the individual will be extremely sensitive to the inner life and to messages from his unconscious mind and higher self. Intuitional empathy is probable, and this can bring its own difficulties as well as blessings. There can be tendencies towards types of prophetic insight, sensing future events before they occur.

There will be an other-worldly tone to the personality, which adds another dimension of complexity, and which will prove puzzling to others' perceptions. Individually, there may be a problem establishing a distinct life direction due to the fact that the Neptunian imagination is a constant source of dreams and fancies, and being able to choose any one dream to pursue can prove almost impossible. A clearer evaluation of realistic possibilities is essential in order to make progress.

There is a dilemma relating to inner needs and the demands of the outer world, in that the natural tendency is to look for meaning and purpose in all endeavours and daily life, and yet the outer world can prove strangely resistant and inhibiting to that personal need, especially by weighing the individual down by the obligations of social life and economic restrictions. This creates friction and internal tension, and a careful balance needs to be established to satisfy both inner and outer demands. Greater adaptation to daily life and the physical plane may be required, and there is a constant temptation to want to run away from life demands towards those attractive lands of inner dreams and fantasies.

Much depends on the level of development and integration of the individual as to how Neptune is dealt with and received. With those who are more consciously sensitive to this higher vibration, there will be a great stimulation of the spiritual impulse towards unity with the self, and to express a life which is in the world but not of the world. For such individuals, perceptions are received from intangible sources too, with psychic intuitions and impression-conveying states of empathy with others becoming common; sensitivity becomes highly refined as does the feeling response to life.

Following the Neptunian call, the individual may break free of conventional living and orthodox behaviour, treating his life as an 'artistic creation', renewing and re-creating himself. Ideals are likely to provide a guiding light, but these can also prove to be illusory; great care needs to be taken to distinguish between reality and illusion, as Neptune stands on that razor edge, simultaneously looking both ways. Being true to the self becomes a necessary path to take, but finding balance and integration on the road to the vision of Neptune can be extremely difficult, almost like trying to walk on water. Yet, for everyone, there is eventually no other choice available.

CHART EXAMPLES

Marilyn Monroe

The chart of Marilyn Monroe is an interesting one to consider from the perspective of a powerful Neptune influence, as her life tends to embody several of the major associative themes of that planet. The relevant astrological Neptune aspects are oppositions to the Moon and Jupiter, square to Saturn, and trine to Venus, with Neptune placed in Leo in the 1st house.

Monroe is still one of the immortal Hollywood 'stars' of the film world, and is a symbol of the glamours represented by that type of mass adulation often bestowed on charismatic actors and actresses of the screen. Monroe has been identified as almost an archetypal sex symbol, providing an image of desire for men, and a role model or figure of envy for many women. Impressions from her films conveyed the message that she was just a 'dumb blonde' starring in several light-entertainment and comedy roles.

Her death reflected a Neptunian pattern. In August 1962, she died of an overdose of barbiturates, and the nature of that death has since been surrounded by a variety of mysteries and speculations, especially in connection with the American President John F. Kennedy and his brother Robert Kennedy. Here we see the perpetually fascinating glamours related to film stars and powerful political characters, and Monroe has been identified since as fulfilling the roles of victim, martyr and sacrifice, depending on the individual point of analysis.

She succeeded in making use of her Neptunian talents of drama and personal expression, rising to become a worldwide star and media personality, yet the cost to her was enormous as she became an increasingly discontented and tormented soul – even at the zenith of her public fame – and in her private love life she was to become regularly embroiled in painful and failed relationships with a variety of lovers. Psychologically and emotionally she grew more distraught and fragmented, suffering from the strains of insomnia as her inner life began to collapse under the pressures and tensions of her high public profile. Severe depressions were quite common, allied with a reputed suicidal tendency over many years. In fact, her unprofessionalism, regular lateness and erratic dramatic performances eventually culminated just prior to her death in her being fired from the film *Something's Got to Give*. Her star burned brightly, immortalised on celluloid for future generations, and then was suddenly extinguished, like the posthumous sympathetic eulogy expressed in Elton John's 'Candle in the Wind'.

Astrologically, she had a Gemini Sun which can often indicate

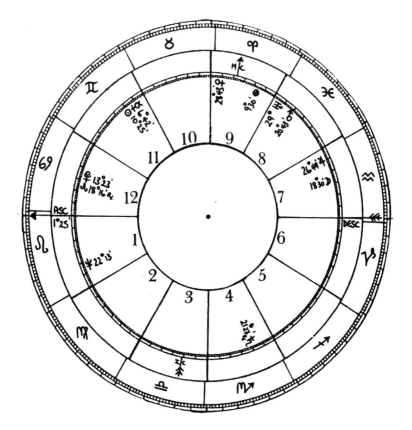

MARILYN MONROE
Born 1.6.1926 Los Angeles 9.30 am P.S.T.

the existence of two distinct personae within the individual (as
reflected by the image of the Twins) and which reoccurred in her
conflicting private and public realities. Publicly, she was a woman
to be admired, a world-famous film star, successful and receiving
the projections of public adoration; privately, like any woman
struggling to deal with battered emotions after a series of failed
love affairs and marriages, she was strangely isolated from everyday realities and just wanted to be loved and to love someone
with whom she could relax and settle down – she needed stability
and security. She lacked the element of Earth in her chart, and
this did not help her need to be materially and psychologically
anchored in life.

The opposition aspects to the Moon and Jupiter and the square to Saturn indicate inner stresses and tensions, where projections are made on to the external world and reflected back by other people. As the Neptune–Moon opposition suggests, she essentially lost her own individual centre through displacement into an image of herself as film star, losing that distinction between reality and illusion, of truth and fiction, and these conflicts took their toll in her private love life. Escape was looked for in the loss of self through sex, drugs and alcohol abuse. As the Jupiter–Neptune opposition suggests, the choice of partners may be unwise, with in Monroe's case *animus* projections being made on to unsuitable men whom she hoped could provide her with a type of solid father figure and protector. The Saturn–Neptune square requires degrees of self-acceptance essential in resolving that inner denial and blockage of free-flowing energies; the result of continually reinforcing negative inner tendencies can be to diminish self-confidence and this can lead to a sense of being trapped within personal neuroses and the lack of self-love and self-acceptance.

The trine of Neptune and Venus indicates those artistic and dramatic qualities, in her case the image of a seductive and sexually vibrant symbol of ideal femininity, an impression of sensuality and allure that the screen enhanced instead of reducing. The 1st house position of Neptune reveals that life-long problem with defining her own identity, a challenge that was never resolved and ended in tragic circumstances.

In several ways, her function in life was to serve as a Neptunian sacrifice, by reflecting the common needs, attitudes and perceptions of the ideal epitome of a film star. By dying whilst still young and beautiful, and before the tarnish became too obvious on the gold as older age ravaged her beauty, Monroe became an artistic film medium, a public open channel serving as an image for the people, because much of the sacrifice asked of her by Neptune was to universalise her identity by relinquishing her own distinct and separate personality, even at the cost of her own life.

To gain a deeper sense of the Neptunian influence on Monroe's inner psyche, please refer to the appropriate sections of aspects and houses.

Sigmund Freud

Sigmund Freud was one of the pioneers of the psychoanalytic

movement, and his theories are still the foundation of the Freudian school of psychology. These have been extremely influential during this century.

From a contemporary perspective, Freud's psychological doctrines are often viewed as providing a partial analysis of the complex totality of the human psyche, but during his own life he believed that he had discovered the path to resolving the mysteries of the psyche. Indeed, he made an important early step and opened the way, but he was dismayed when several of his most important 'disciples' left to lead breakaway analytical movements based on their own theories and doctrines. These included Adler, Jung and Assagioli. Both Jung and Assagioli are now well known in the astrological and humanistic fields, as interfaces between their work and self-development techniques are now firmly based. Assagioli became the founder of *psychosynthesis*, a psychological approach founded on the reality of an inner self and a spiritual dimension.

Freud helped to introduce those familiar methods of free association of ideas using the on the analytical couch and he developed a doctrine which asserted that the sexual impulse is the key to understanding human motivations and reactions. For him, the determining factors in the unfolding of the personality were instincts, sex and past events, especially childhood experiences and relationships with parents. He used the term 'id' to describe the primitive, impersonal and wholly unconscious part of the mind which also embodied the inherited instinctive impulses of the individual, and was especially associated with memories and fantasies evolved during the experiences of infancy. Freud tended to replace the image of God by these deep-rooted components of the psyche, and from his Jewish ancestry almost substituted his concept of the id for the Hebrew Yahweh as a tribal god. He also adopted the use of the term ego as signifying the part of the mind that is the conscious thinker, where organisation arises, and which creates a sense of a distinct separate identity. The ideas of the Oedipal complex also came from this school of thought, which manifested itself as infantile sexuality related to parents, based on an attraction towards a parent of the opposite sex, and a rejection or jealousy of the other parent.

In the context of society at the time when Freud's ideas became public, these psychological analyses were considered quite shocking, and Freud needed all his spirit of tenacious endurance and

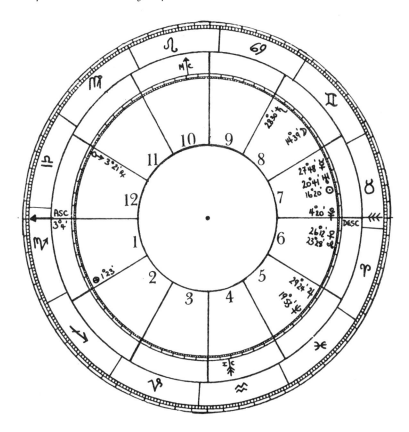

SIGMUND FREUD
Born 6.5.1856 Freiburg Moravia 6.30 pm L.T.

an uncompromising stance in order to resist the harsh criticism
aimed at him. It must be remembered that these ideas came out
of a society conditioned by Victorian attitudes, during the early
phases of the Edwardian era in European culture, and to suggest
that active sex was an essential and important part of the normal
human life and that any repression of those energies was
psychologically dangerous caused many a raised eyebrow and
look of distaste. It was not considered socially polite to discuss
sex in public.

Yet Freud's insights and persistence eventually broke down the
socially erected barriers of thought related to human sexuality.
His argument that beneath the civilised veneer of European culture and sophistication was a subconscious level of psyche which

was primal, instinctual and a fount of chaotic compulsions, obsessions, hidden motivations, sexual drives and repressed energies became known as the unconscious mind, a sphere that Jung was to explore from a different perspective by revealing that hidden archetypal structure. Freud openly stated that there were negative personal implications to be drawn from the deliberate repression and frustration of the energy of the libido. These medical attitudes of liberation were quickly seized on by the artistic community as justification for the performance of their own natural tendencies, and would emerge during the twenties as a liberated set of social attitudes where sexuality became a little more respectable (although writers like D. H. Lawrence still found considerable resistance to several of their literary themes). Sex is still a contentious issue today.

It is as if Freud had a mission from Neptune to release such doctrines, because the depths of the unconscious are realms in which Neptune rules and is active, linking them to the mythical Neptune's proclivity for rampant sexual activity, and also to glamours and illusions. His Neptune is placed in Pisces, a doorway to the unconscious mind, and Freud acted as an opener of that door, releasing the floodgates of a collective repression of sexual energies. The natal position is in the 5th house, emphasising creativity and sexual love, and Freud certainly developed these themes as well as over-exaggerating them due to the associative glamours attached to them. As the analysis of the 5th house Neptune suggests, Freud created a new understanding and redefinition of roots, foundations and family through his psychological doctrines, and almost turned upside down the nature of parent–child relationships by looking at the hidden sexual dimension. He transformed his own heritage of social attitudes, values and beliefs, and chose to follow his own lighted path through life, which in itself was no small achievement. He explored the mysteries of life, and moved deeper into investigating his own inner depths, sharing his results as a common collective experience to illuminate the psyches of everyone. The sextile of Neptune and Sun indicates this desire to be creative and to act positively in the world, so that a beneficial contribution is made in service to all.

His impulse to be anti-authoritarian is indicated by the Neptune–Uranus sextile where through his doctrines he opposed the weight of social attitude and belief, and where he was attracted towards making his presence felt in 'social revolution', through developing his own revolutionary and evolutionary philosophy which was eventually to develop into a great social influence. The Neptune–Moon square may indicate areas in which the childhood experiences of Freud served as a basis for his later theories, in that there are indications of some type of emotional conflict, discontent and dissatisfaction with his parental relationships, especially to his mother, and perhaps indicating an Oedipal situation. The existence of inner pressures and stresses are also indicated here in this square, eventually emerging as a creative response and emphasising Neptune–Pisces and the 5th house interests.

As 'father of the psychoanalytical movement', Freud's influence has been great, laying a foundation for many later developments and derivatives of the human potential movement, as well as influencing a school of art – the Surrealist movement obsessed with dream life and releasing the contents of the unconscious mind into view. Freud's life ended in 1939 just as one eruption of the repressed collective unconscious nearly shattered the world through the focal point of another Austrian, Adolf Hitler.

Alice A. Bailey

Whilst not having such a high personality profile as several other occult teachers, the influence of Alice Bailey has been extremely powerful in the realm of esoteric teachings, through her functioning as the scribe for the Tibetan, one of the Trans-Himalayan occult brotherhood. In several ways, she was the focus for the continuation of the teaching that emanated from Madame Blavatsky, and was a precursor of the modern fashion for 'channelling' spiritual teachings. In her case, however, the claim was that the Tibetan was physically alive and serving as an abbot in a lamasery in Tibet prior to the Chinese invasion, rather than as a disembodied inner-plane communicator. Her channelling was more of a high order of telepathic rapport, and her life was devoted to esoteric service and the anchoring of visionary and transformative teachings.

In Bailey's chart, the sextile of Neptune–Mercury suggests her suitability for a role as amanuensis. In the analysis of the planetary aspect, there is the statement that this sextile helps to build a close connective channel between the conscious and unconscious minds, where information can be transmitted between them to the rational mind, with experiences of telepathic communication possible. In her lifetime, she spent thirty years dedicated to discipleship service in such a communication with the Tibetan.

The square of Mars–Neptune and its more negative lower expressions appear to have been transcended by her spiritual path, although in her earlier life and first marriage several of these areas of emotional and sexual contention were present and active. According to her *Unfinished Autobiography*, this was an especially testing time for herself and her young family, and she needed to directly confront many of her intrinsic tendencies in often embarrassing situations. This time of her life required much stripping away of the inessentials of her childhood upbringing, which was reflective of upper-class Victorian society, and was necessary in order to prepare her for later tasks.

It is likely that private issues of sexuality and emotions may have plagued her at times, and that these stresses were later better integrated, especially when all of her time and energy was absorbed by her esoteric mission. Yet there is a story regarding her second husband, Foster Bailey, who when he suggested that they should get married, received the response that if the horse over there nodded then she supposed they should — which it duly did – and they did marry. By then, however, she was committed to her tasks as the rebirth that Mars and Neptune indicate had been achieved; she had successfully fought her inner battles and those conflicts had dissipated. The implication here is that it was a marriage for the *Great Work* rather than for personal needs and desires.

Her Neptune–Uranus trine occurred during an earlier period than mentioned in the aspect analysis, yet the themes of acting as a bridging agent between the old world and the incoming new one are pertinent, as is the service of mediators in society. The development of a personal intellectual vision and viewpoint is highlighted, as is the need to stand free in her own light and understanding in distinction to a mental acquiescence and gullibility regarding those who elevate themselves to be public leaders. A spirit of individual enquiry is essential, especially with discrimination when linked to the spiritual path, and passively accepting such teachings as gospel is rarely the way to discover the truth for yourself – all you receive is a reflected light which may, or may not, be true for you. As the Tibetan commented 'A Master is a rare efflorescence of a generation of enquirers'. The key is

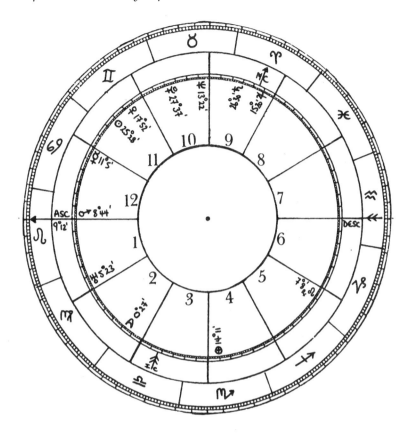

ALICE A. BAILEY
Born 16.6.1880 Manchester, England 7.32 am

that of questioning all assumptions and teachings, and not to assume that because Christ or Buddha are reputed to say something it is true. Always find out for yourself; although that is by far the hardest path to take!

Bailey's natal Neptune in the 10th house displays that she succeeded in achieving a career of community service, aiming to manifest that Neptunian idealistic utopian vision of the New Age, where she became devoted to the cause of the Masters, and offered her life as a sacrifice to their inspiration. She became a channel for that something greater which lies beyond the parameters of the separate self, and became a spokesperson for her visionary perception. Bailey managed to give birth to her new self (the spiritual twice-born) and this was 'a self which is intimately connected with the well being of a wider society and one which is connected to the impulse of the emerging Aquarian Age'. Of interest is the fact that each of her transpersonal planets of Uranus, Neptune and Pluto are all placed in Earth houses, almost as if insisting on an anchoring of the transpersonal vision on the material plane.

The Bailey/Tibetan vision is one which underlies much of the current New Age consciousness, and as one of the great occult pioneers her work has proven invaluable to many following enquirers, and is an often unrecognised seminal influence in modern esoteric and psychological teachings, as for instance in the formation of psychosynthesis.

Dion Fortune

Another famous charismatic occultist of this century was Dion Fortune, the pen name of Violet Mary Firth, which derived from her family motto of *Deo, non fortuna*, and was adopted at her initiation into the infamous Hermetic Order of the Golden Dawn.

Fortune stands firmly in the line of modern women occultists who appear to form an initiatory group for the magical Aquarian current, although her own interests would begin to move towards the Western Mystery Tradition and especially the role of High Priestess and the Divine Feminine aspects. She was highly psychic, mediumistic and another early channel for inner-guide communications, such as *The Cosmic Doctrine*. Her life became devoted to the pursuit of magic, and increasingly took on otherworldly aspects and personae, as if by her rising on the planes she returned with characteristics of her assumed god-forms and archetypes. In her own words, she said: 'I had my dream of moon magic and sea palaces, and day by day I lived more in another dimension where I had that which I knew I should never have on earth, and I was very happy' (*Priestess*, Alan Richardson, Aquarian Press).

Fortune developed several of the strands of Golden Dawn teachings into an attempt at restoring the fading Western Mystery Tradition, and much of this activity was focused on the group which she later formed as an independent entity, the Fraternity of Inner Light, which had its roots in a community house in London

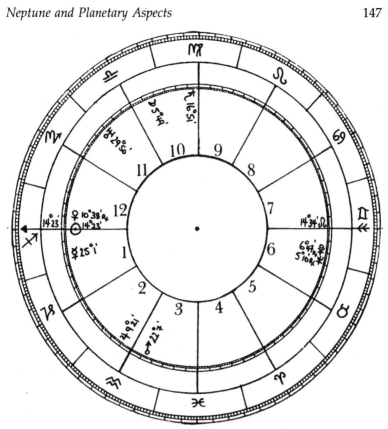

DION FORTUNE
Solar Noon Chart born 6.12.1890 Llandudno, Wales

and on the slope of Glastonbury Tor in Chalice Orchard. Fortune acted as the heart and guiding light of this group, and increasingly evoked additional power through regular ritual and pathwork-ings, performing her chosen role as mediatrix and priestess. In several ways, she came to embody characteristics of her favourite goddess figures, one of which was the Egyptian Isis, and another Morgan le Fey of the Arthurian legends. It is arguable whether she became too personally identified with such archetypal per-sonae, and evidence suggests that the female lead character of her two most famous novels *Moon Magic* and *Sea Priestess* were slightly idealised versions of how she perceived herself. Past lives and the role of Atlantis were other preoccupying themes, both of which indicate a Neptunian influence in her psyche, as do her dramatic ritual robes and performances and her larger-than-life personality. Like Aleister Crowley, she lived as a spirit of high magic, publicly and theatrically.

Magically, she saw part of her mission to reinvoke the power of the Great Goddess and to reinvigorate the sleeping spiritual power of sacred Avalon. Certainly her work and influence lives on, and has been highly influential for those who follow associated traditional paths. Rumour has it that even after her death, she continued to guide the development of her esoteric group for several years until her presence came to inhibit further changes, and so she was encouraged to let go of the controlling strings. Like many other occultists, she claimed to be inspired by inner-plane communicators, and informed opinion has it that her own inner guides are still contactable today.

Astrologically, we lack any time of birth, so a solar chart has been raised. The Neptune–Moon trine indicates her natural creativity potentials, and her psychic and prophetic tendencies. Her creativity was expressed in her occult writings and novels, and the two previously mentioned are well worth reading as they offer several keys to the nature of her self-images and personal compulsions applied in a context of magical ritual work. The opposition between Neptune and Venus emphasises that emotional imaginative personality, and also reveals inner stresses related to her personal relationships and marriage to Thomas Penry Evans ('Merlin'), which whilst successful as a magical partnership in the early days, was to prove a source of pain and suffering later.

Fortune had difficulties integrating her emotional and sexual natures properly, and as a result of drawing through her inner *animus* into her psyche often came across to people as surprisingly masculine for a woman. Assuming goddess forms in ritual failed to make her especially feminine, and Fortune seems to have been asked to sacrifice a satisfying human relationship in exchange for the powerful magical one. In this she is not alone amongst famous women occultists, as Blavatsky, Besant and Bailey all made similar sacrifices; partly this may be due to the fact that they became such powerful and assertive women with a mission that any personal needs were transcended in favour of spiritual service.

The trine of Jupiter and Neptune is revealing too in her appeal to the occult path and the values of spirituality in life, where heightened emotional exaltation leads to experiences of unparalleled intensity, especially through ceremony and touches of dramatic mystery. The use of a lift in one of the London houses into the ritual room was tempting to her, as it enabled her to rise up as Isis before her priest's vision and so make a dramatic entrance. Sometimes occultists can become impersonal, but it is those human and eccentric touches that make them so fascinating and appealing!

Irrespective of her capes and her liking for dramatic colourful robes and broad-brimmed hats – and why not indeed? – Dion Fortune was a powerful magician and worthy of a place in the occult pantheon of heroes and heroines.

The planetary aspect of the conjunction between Neptune and Pluto played a role in her life, and summed up her magical function. This is a rare conjunction, the last occurring around 1888–90, and it is one of the highest of all planetary vibrations, which if integrated can offer a high sense of spiritual understanding of the nature and psychic foundations of the human psyche. It is very subtle but extremely powerful, dissolving old entrenched and outlived social attitudes and belief systems, replacing them with new and more suitable visions for the next steps, and often indicates a turning point in the rise and fall of national states. Often the religious status quo is challenged by new approaches to the religious impulse, and there can be the death of old concepts; a process which is embodied in the work of certain individuals who have 'a high spiritual mission'. Dion Fortune was one of these, and her pioneering work in restoring both the Western and Women's Mysteries has proven to be inspirational to many.

Israel

The national chart that is worth considering from a Neptunian perspective is that of the state of Israel, which was founded in 1948 as part of the reconstitution of national boundaries in the aftermath of World War II, and was created out of land previously known as Palestine.

Throughout many centuries, the response to the Hebrew and Jewish people has been oppressive, ranging from Egyptian and Roman domination to persecution and civil pogroms (organised massacres) across Europe in varying states and at varying times. The Jewish people have almost traditionally been a victimised race, often accused of social crimes and dissension whenever a social scapegoat was required, and the punishment meted out to them has been severe and brutal. They have been a wandering people even from the biblical times of Moses, who led them across the wilderness in search of the Promised Land; being the Chosen People of God has never proven to be an easy cross to bear.

The modern state of Israel was the culmination of years of international political effort made by the Zionist movement since 1897, and was the successful result of the great visionary dream of the Zionists who conceived of a permanent home on ancient land, where Jews could return again to the Promised Land and finally settle. After the horrific attempt at genocide by the Nazi regime, many Jews decided to return to the new state of Israel to aid in the building of their new society in 1948.

Israel is still a land of tension and conflicts, with contemporary friction and belligerence towards Palestinians and surrounding Arabic nations such as Jordan, Syria and the Lebanon. The dove of peace has still not descended on the land, and the Israelis live with the mentality of a persecuted people under threat; defending their interests and homeland is a major preoccupation, and their conception of state interests tends to spread across the world, with several examples of interference in foreign lands.

Astrologically, we can note those Neptunian tendencies of victim, martyr and sacrifice being firmly fixed in the historical traditions of the Jewish race and within the collective consciousness of the people. It is interesting to observe that the national natal chart of the modern state of Israel has a noticeable emphasis on Neptune aspects, as if this is a continuance of a previous pattern. Neptune trines Mercury, sextiles Saturn and Pluto, squares Venus and MidHeaven, and conjuncts the Ascendant, and is placed in Libra in the 1st house.

The 1st house position indicates some conflict and confusion within the national identity, where the real nature and definition of the national self requires clarifying. This is partly due to several disparate national views concerning the most apt way to proceed in establishing the state of Israel on firm foundations, and in their relationship with the rest of the world, especially with surrounding states. In addition, there is internal confusion regarding their religious heritage, with groups representing the old Hebraic traditions and attitudes which are opposed to the more contemporary secular attitudes of many modern internationally sophisticated Jews. The fact of being Jewish evokes a variety of conflicting reactions even within Jews, and there is often an uneasiness

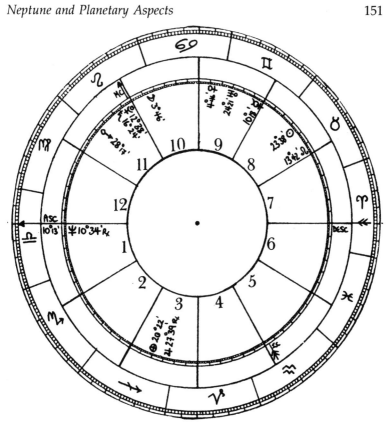

ISRAEL
14.5.1948 Tel Aviv 16.30 L.T.

related to that racial identity. When an inner insecurity persists, there are often exaggerated external reactions to the hint of a threat, and Israel is extremely touchy and aggressive towards any encroachment into its territory.

The Neptune–Mercury trine expresses itself through Israel's powerful advocacy of its national position and interests throughout the world media communication channels. Israel currently has a very forceful and direct style of political assertion, stating a clear position and holding its ground against much vacillation or international pressure. In foreign nations, there are influential groups of Jews which act as pressure groups on foreign governmental opinion, and so ensure that the Israeli position is understood.

The Neptune–Saturn sextile evokes that powerful sense of social responsibility and national identity, where the building of the state (and its protection) are considered to have top priority. Saturn desires fixed and firm boundaries to work within, and so the issue of territory will remain important, although the tendency of Neptune to break free of boundaries does and will prove problematic in that volatile area. Israel's strategic skills and manipulative organisation are indicated, as are wilful consistency and determination in achieving their aims. At present, one of the main obstacles to peace in Israel lies in an excessively self-centred perception; this may be quite understandable in the light of recent and past history, but this still works against satisfactory relations with neighbouring states.

This tendency re-occurs in the Neptune–Venus square, and in the conjunction to the Ascendant and natal position in Libra. The square indicates problems in relationships and the creation of illusions, glamours and self-deception where unconscious motivating factors can be projected out on to the external world until the state sees only its own negative reflection returned as threats to security. That aspect of belligerent defensiveness is highlighted, and the real need is to eventually resolve those negative inner patterns so that clarity and harmony can be restored, and freedom made from those patterns of guilt and victimisation that are prevalent in the Jewish psyche. The conjunction to the Libra Ascendant and Neptune's position in Libra is one key, where the need is to establish correct relationships with others, not just for their own self-protection and peace, but also on behalf of the international balance of power and world tensions, especially as conflicting states have opposing supporters in the USA and the USSR.

Establishing a balanced viewpoint seems difficult for Israel at present; it is still a young state, and tends to move towards extremist positions due to its own fears and insecurities. It is a melting pot for world religious, racial and political tensions and conflicts, a crucial area in the pivotal balance of the Middle East. What is needed is a lowering of the barriers of the national personality so that real contact can be established with neighbouring states. Remaining locked within the parameters of its own often distorted perceptions of a separatist vision will continue to create additional difficulties, but feeling strong enough to offer a hand of friendship across territorial divides may be the way forward to the next stage of the Promised Land.

If this does not happen, Israel may fall deeper into the trap of acting like its own previous persecutors by instituting racial, religious and territorial oppression of a homeless minority such as the Palestinians. The liberating shock to the national Israeli personality may come as they increasingly see reflected back at them – from international opinion – the fact that they are starting to imitate those who victimised them. This can then stimulate the process of deeper self-enquiry that Neptune offers from its 1st house position, an enquiry that, if successful, will also transform their international relationships and their persona as perceived by other states.

CHAPTER 5

Neptune in the Natal Houses

THE NATAL HOUSE POSITION of Neptune often indicates one of the main areas for the individual experience of the Saturn–Neptune polarity, and is a point where those transpersonal energies of dissolution can touch the Saturn structures of the egoic personality. The house position directs attention to those types of life experiences that can lead to a transformation of the personality boundaries, and which can usher in mystical and transcendent insights. Periodically emitted through the natal house channel – as Neptune aspects and transit movements are activated – come those whispers from the beyond that so tantalise and evoke deep yearnings within the hidden spiritual self, and which bring radical changes and confrontations to the individual.

It is through the natal house position that the individual unconscious mind (as reflected through the function of Neptune) is slowly revealed, as by dreams, creative inspiration, aspiration and the more negative characteristics of glamour and illusion. The house displays the route that Neptune will take in entering our conscious lives, those areas that will attract and those in which the seeds of our own transformative undoing are to be found.

The Neptune house is considered to be the individual Achilles' heel, a point of vulnerability in our egoic shell, where the separate identity can be connected to the universality of life, and Neptune is the planet dedicated to the loss or transcendence of the lesser identity by merging with the greater whole through dissolving boundaries into formless unity. Grasping hold of Neptune is impossible, and it is in the house position that the ego is liable to disintegrate, enabling a rebirth to emerge through being opened up to broader vistas of life.

Because of the depths or heights to which Neptune can take the individual, personal reaction to its presence varies and often polarises strongly. Some prefer to re-evoke the protective barriers of Saturn against the Neptunian erosion, whilst others seem willing to follow the Neptune sea breezes wherever they may go. There is a need to be adequately grounded before consciously opening the psyche to the Neptune vibration, because its effects may be extremely potent, although this may not be immediately obvious when one is initially experiencing its seductive fascinations. Any form of personality and psyche dissolution can be difficult to endure, and many collapse into a chaotic panic as the experience intensifies in an inexorable way; this leads to Neptunian associations with mental and emotional breakdowns under the inner stresses.

Neptune creates an unfocusing in areas of the psyche which are represented by planets and signs, and touched by Neptune activity through aspect and transit movements. This is its function, and whatever Neptune contacts begins slowly to change, losing previous solidity, and egoic security and stability are diminished as past patterns lose cohesiveness and reliability. Through inner 'gaps' created by this process, the unconscious mind – individual or collective – begins to extrude into the conscious mind, and there is a tendency to attempt to repress this invasion, stimulating additional pressures rather than making an effort to integrate this into the widened personality structures. An unknown world opens up, feelings intensify and the world takes on a more mysterious glow. Some react against this, feeling terrified, and others welcome and surrender, becoming more humanitarian and universalised in attitude and perspective. Receiving the descent of grace can sometimes be a traumatic experience; rarely are individuals ready, yet it is through this natal house position that Neptune attunes us to that potential for transcendence, and where life can be felt most directly and exquisitely intense to a degree never previously conceived.

For those inclined towards the transpersonal path, the house position implies ways in which the individual may be expected to serve higher spiritual interests, as forms of personal creative expression or transformation. The requirement is that of a selfless impersonal service to the whole. Through this house, we may receive messages related to our purpose and direction in life; by dreams, intuition or inner visions. The Neptunian urge to expand may be given safe expression through meditation, visualisation, prayer, creativity and service to others.

Often those themes of victim, martyr, sacrifice associated with Neptune are especially activated through the house position, and many individuals unconsciously perform them through the appropriate house characteristics. It is here that we unconsciously create those life situations in which we are forced to adopt a wider perspective, perhaps through circumstances which necessitate a more sacrificial attitude to others or a situation that is beyond our control. We can learn to live easily without our personal needs and desires being paramount in determining our choices; in effect, we live for the benefit of the whole.

The Neptune house is often where we build our imaginary utopia, where we look for paradise on Earth, the source of a purifying redemption. The need for a personal saviour can be found here, and a search for a Zeus–Jupiter type of rescuer can emerge. This often happens as a consequence of repeated disillusionments and disappointments in life, failed ambitions or relationships which can stimulate that inward turning of attention and direction. In some cases, the absorption and performance of the Neptune energy transforms the lives of individuals into a group demonstration of an embodied ideal, image or collective wish fulfilment, as in examples of 'superstardom', social scapegoats, archetypal representations and film star myths of 'gods and goddesses'.

For many, Neptune acts in a purely unconscious manner. The natal house acts as a sphere of confusion, deep unease, and often veils an intrinsic problem area in that individual psyche which requires resolution. Reactions against Neptune are common, and escapes are often attempted to evade its presence and to deny any confrontation with that inner presence. Deep inner fears are likely, and are tied up with unrealistic attitudes, dreams and self-projections, where private fantasies are preferred to the stark reality of things. Evasion leads to those attractions towards drugs, alcohol and sexual activity, which appear to promise the illusion of a satisfactory life or to appease boredom. Personal responsibility is often rejected, and sometimes the preference is for the collective mind to take the strain of individual thinking – by absorbing pre-formed social attitudes and values – or by a passive surrendering to political and religious belief structures. Often the root of a personal crisis or problem is indicated by the underlying meaning of the natal sign of Neptune, and the quadrant of the house wheel reveals the general type of growth that the collective requires from that individual; his basic direction in life.

NATAL NEPTUNE IN THE 1ST HOUSE

With Neptune in this position, there can be a challenge related to the nature and definition of your own identity. The difficulties of this lie in the dissolving quality of Neptune which will affect any sense of a unique and separate identity, and so make it hard to establish any kind of fixed and firm centre within the personality structure. The need for this can manifest itself in search for self, and may eventually lead you towards a religious or spiritual quest which you hope will satisfy your dilemma and sense of inner unease.

You will often find it difficult to perceive your own nature, as every time you try to probe inwards, it seems as if a new inner landscape appears, reflecting a new combination of inner selves back at you. Your attitudes, beliefs, values and emotions can regularly change – as if on shifting sands – and so you find it perplexing to evaluate your own uniqueness, let alone attempt to understand that changing complexity. What you may begin to realise is that these inner shifts are partly stimulated by external influences, as you can be highly impressionable to the personal expressions of others, and it is often their attitudes, beliefs and opinions that are absorbed and reflected out by you as if they were your own.

There is a powerful reflective quality to your personality, almost like a reflection created by still waters, which can emerge as an unconscious mimicking of others as you take on their characteristics. Your persona (or social mask) is often shaped by your current influences and associations, and to others you may appear in the guise of a changeling or chameleon-type personality, hard to fathom and lacking in consistency. You can try to be all things to all men, where your identity forms itself around others' needs and wants, and perpetually moves its ground of being. There is a tendency to move beyond boundaries, in that your private sense of a separate identity becomes extremely diffused and begins to adopt a more inclusive perception, although in distinction from the mystical position; your expression of this could be in becoming dependent and relying on others. Sometimes in being so sensitive to the needs of others, you can become sacrificial in attempting to satisfy them, and in so doing lose your own purpose and direction through a misplacement of your identity.

You often respond to more subtle and psychic influences, and can be strongly affected by the quality and tone of your environment and the company you keep, at home, at work or socially. Registering hidden, inner realities and motivations is quite common for you, and this can create some confusion, especially if you are receiving conflicting messages from an inner perception of a person as distinct from their social expression. You learn to trust the 'vibes' and have faith in that. Because of this heightened sensitivity, you may be able to act as a channel for spiritual or healing energies and an empathic understanding helps to create a connectedness with others so that healing can be transmitted.

There can be artistic abilities and a need to be creative, both as a form of self-anchoring and as a way to express and release all the impressions that move through you. This could be as a reflector of collective needs, visions, attitudes and perceptions, where any creation 'speaks to many' as a common experience; many musicians can tap into this area of universal human experience, and lyrically reflect emotions and feelings that are extremely resonant. You could become an artistic medium – like an open channel – serving as a voice for the people, because much of the sacrifice that may be asked by Neptune is that you should universalise your identity, and this is why it can be so difficult to maintain an independently unique and separate personality.

One challenge that may be hard to overcome is that of commitment and persistence, in that you have problems in establishing a chosen direction and focusing your energies on following it until success is achieved. As there is self-confusion often allied to insecurity and inner deceptions, your objectives are elusive and prone to regular fluctuation. You may need to struggle to build a satisfactory degree of singlemindness in your endeavours, but this will partly be formed through a more defined and grounded identity. Yet the way to achieve this is not through merely reflecting whatever is around you, but by opening more fully to become a channel for some higher impulse to work through you, so that the visionary nature can shine and be inspirational.

Use of drugs or alcohol is probably best avoided, especially with those tendencies of excess, as these will just serve to fragment an already fragile identity and stimulate the negative face of Neptune into action. There can be a strong charisma around you, an enigmatic and mysterious persona (because of its apparent depth and reflective nature) which can intrigue many who desire to investigate your secrets. This can lead to unusual relationships, which can be very influential – positively or negatively – and you may be wiser to exercise some discrimination in this sphere, especially as your judgement may not always be too accurate. Some could take advantage of your mutability; for instance, by seeking to mould you into their own preferred shape. If this is allowed, then you could experience the Neptunian tendencies towards victim and martyr. The real way forward is to move towards the whole, and not become lost by reflecting just the parts of life.

NATAL NEPTUNE IN THE 2ND HOUSE

The issues with this Neptune position revolve around the themes of money, resources and possessions, topics that are central to modern Western capitalist and consumer thinking.

Money is often the main symbol for success in the world, and most of man's activities are designed to generate this commodity, both for essential survival needs such as food and homes, and for the satisfaction of additional desires such as luxurious and extravagant living, enhanced security and the accumulation of possessions which enrich life.

Neptune may stimulate several contradictory attitudes towards money and resources, but one common thread underlying them is the need to develop a new understanding of their relevance in your life, a deeper perception of their significance and meaning.

There may in some be a preoccupation with money, resources and possessions, where money is elevated to a position of supreme importance and where all ambition is consumed with the desire for more. Here the tendency is to excessive consumption, extravagance, the need to feel secure by being surrounded by the material forms of purchases, and external displays of having money. There is a continual dissatisfaction which always demands further satiation through buying and acquiring more; more cars, TVs, bigger houses, holiday homes etc., and there is a resulting lack of appreciation and value. Some may have that 'financial knack' where, like Midas, everything that is touched turns to gold and money accumulates with little effort or through wise business acumen.

Another tendency can be a lack of financial sense; one wastes money through careless impractical schemes and foolish dreams, or by failing to generate sufficient self-application to ensure that a potentially viable business project eventually succeeds. Speculations can be wrongly made, money lost through depending on others, either fraudulently or through an unrealistic trust.

Some may believe that life should fulfil their every need without their having to do anything in return, becoming social parasites and dependent on state generosity without due reason apart from laziness.

Others may imbue the issue of resources with an idealistic vision, whereby excess money and possessions can be shared within a social context, perhaps through donations to favourite causes and charities, or where unwanted possessions are freely given to those in need in the world, thus creating a freer flow of the energy contained in money. This can sometimes emerge as a feeling of 'guilt in the mind of the successful liberal', but is a prompt towards social responsibility.

Neptune asks you to reconsider your attitudes towards money. Does it condition your life so that everything else is secondary? Do you really appreciate and value what you have now? Could some possessions or money be released to help others in greater need than yourself? Are you irresponsible with money and do you waste it? Do you derive a sense of self-worth, value and identity from your accumulated possessions, and do they act as a status signifier for you? What is really important to you, and is a search for more money merely a substitute for something else that is lacking?

Neptune may strip away all forms of externally based security if that is the lesson required. What is necessary is an inner re-evaluation, where value is placed on less material substitutes and possessions, where actual use of personal qualities and those inner resources such as gifts and talents is made, so enriching the life in that creative way. Many personal attitudes and beliefs are reflected by our money attitudes, and in changing either the other can be transformed, such as where inner insecurity relies on external possessions for strength, or where stability in life is looked for in bricks and mortar. Much of the personal identity is tied up in status-ridden employment for many, as is witnessed in the attitudes of personal superiority that many managers possess whereas, in truth, often those lowest in the hierarchy are much finer people and less obsessive and unbalanced!

The power of money is considerable, and its influence on contemporary choices is profound. Social transformation is similarly linked to changes in our personal and collective attitudes towards money and resources, and in this lies one of the fundamental keys to the future well-being of the planet. The visionary dreaming of Neptune can help us choose our attitudes wisely, with balance and discrimination, and with awareness of global repercussions. It is a re-evaluation that all concerned with the New Age ideal need to make.

NATAL NEPTUNE IN THE 3RD HOUSE

The issues associated with the 3rd house involve those of the mind and communication, and can manifest themselves in a variety of ways.

Neptune may have the effect of interfering with the mental faculty, especially affecting concentration, focusing and rationality. This creates the dreaming mind, absorbed within imaginative fantasies, inwardly turned and preoccupied, where the mind lacks a consistent cohesive centre, becoming vague and impractical. A certain degree of distance from the everyday world is observed as the inner dreams are much more attractive and absorbing, so that attempts at study and learning are often disrupted by the inability to concentrate.

There can be difficulties in finding suitable forms of personal expression, where traditional verbal and literary means are felt to be inadequate, perhaps too gross to reveal subtle nuances that are perceived to be equally important. This can lead to problems of connectedness, where that psychic attunement of the Neptune vibration can clash with the physical-level challenge of perceiving the part within the whole, or by reverting to the 3rd house tendency to analyse and separate. Another approach to this is to discover other more suitable ways of communication, perhaps through Neptunian artistic channels: film, photography, drama, art, dance.

You may find that Neptune works as a highly receptive quality in your mind, where it becomes extremely absorbent to all influences, so that the reflected nature is paramount, and you easily mirror back all dominating impressions made on you. At worst, this could mean that you have no thoughts of your own, only those of friends, or collective attitudes and beliefs. The undercurrents of life will be registered, although how you respond to these and in which way they are interpreted cannot be easily defined.

Making decisions may be hard at times, as you can see so many options and angles on your possible choices that judgement becomes difficult. Always be wary of possible Neptune distortion, because there is a preference to see only the beautiful, and such conditioning mental selection can inhibit a more realistic analysis. There can be a great attraction towards study and knowledge, based on the hope that by acquiring more information you will understand the world more effectively, as well as yourself. This may help, but true perception and insight do not rely on knowledge at all, and in fact a mind full of such information may block true understanding. Amongst those on spiritual searches, many fail to experience a genuine spiritual transformation because they believe that they already know 'the answers' which are invariably second-hand and book absorbed.

The ideal that Neptune may be trying to lead you towards is a re-evaluation of your mind, so that you could become a channel for collective inspiration to flow through. Knowledge can be communicated to others, and there may be a connection to forms of mass media as the means of sharing. The focus of this will be related to connecting the parts to the whole, establishing some type of unifying context within mental perception where hidden meanings and patterns to life are illuminated. You are likely to have a good image-making mental faculty, and telepathic or empathic receptivity, which could pose a few problems of integration and understanding of what it is that you are receiving. Exploring such dimensions of existence will lead you towards occultism and the spiritual life, even if initially it is from an intellectual or scientific perspective. Such positive uses of this Neptunian energy can be particularly beneficial for artists, writers, film makers and creative or mystical people.

NATAL NEPTUNE IN THE 4TH HOUSE

This position of Neptune gives an emphasis to personal roots and foundations in life, and can often indicate deep unconscious ties to family, parents and social traditions, and a need for security and stability which is opposed by the Neptunian tendency of dissolution and expansion.

Motivations, attitudes, beliefs, value structures and personal identity will tend to have foundations in your earlier life. The influence of parents upon you will be considerable, and many of the conditioning emotional associations will be closely intertwined with that parental relationship and your childhood. Some degree of idealism or distortion is likely in your memories and family connections, and it is possible that you have a desire to return into a golden age where the womb-like embrace of the family offered security and protection.

It may be, however, that your early life experience was unsatisfactory and unfulfilling, where expectations were disappointed and the home life was more unsettling and unstable, and that this pattern has been carried over into your adult life. The father is associated with the 4th house, and part of this insecurity could be connected with his role in your life. Child idealistic projections on to him could have been later disillusioned, or he may have seemed distant from you, offering little emotional comfort or relationship, or he could have left or been rarely at home when you needed him there. Some type of unbalanced relationship is indicated by this placing of Neptune, and in many instances this implies a divided marriage situation or a broken home.

Neptune offers great emotional sensitivity, and you are likely to have absorbed into your unconscious mind most of the underlying psychic currents present in your family home. These can be parental frustrations with an unhappy marriage, the denial of ambitions or dreams for successful futures for their children; whatever they were they have made an impact on you as you received that 'atmosphere' into your unfolding nature. A parent may have been very dominant, so much so that their way of perceiving life has never left you, and you have difficulty in breaking free of the parental embrace and umbilical cord, so that you can stand free as an individual in your own right. Or you may have received 'family traits', delusions and challenges passed down through genetic lineage, repetitive family patterns of behaviour and attitude, like a family adherence to religious conditioning or political beliefs.

Many of the themes that will be highlighted in your adult life will have their roots in your childhood. It is quite likely that in some way you will tend to repeat similar paths and patterns which were present in your parents' lives. The challenge is to transform them, so breaking unconscious repetition and avoiding becoming a victim to such tendencies. Your adult marriage and family life could be the sphere of this repetition. Where Neptune is involved, the need for sacrifice in some way is often found, as are the themes of victim and martyr. You may need to consider whether you are unconsciously duplicating the tendencies and failings of your father or mother, because they were your early role models of behaviour. You may be required to be self-sacrificial in your domestic relationship, perhaps through the illness of a child or partner, or as a result of a partner's need to pursue his or her ambitions, and you are usually willing to become a protective and embracing parent figure, even to a partner.

A new understanding and redefinition of family, roots and foundations in life is required. Neptune may ask that you surrender your family, perhaps through the dissolution of a marriage, or just through a transformation in your heritage of attitudes, beliefs and values as you learn how to stand free in your own light and follow your own path through life. The need for stability, security and roots needs to be expanded, so that reliance on a limited conception is transcended, and Neptune opens out into a wider space for exploration. For those attracted towards the spiritual dimension and the search for universal and eternal roots, the challenge may lie in trusting the goodwill of the universe, having faith in its guidance and moving beyond any dependence on rational thinking and protection of the limited self. This can develop into a determined exploration of the mysteries of life and yourself, moving ever deeper into the inner depths. Failure to accept this challenge of re-evaluation and transformation can create psychosomatic symptoms of ill health in later years, and static regressive repetition of received patterns from childhood. There can also be a withdrawal from social activity and a preference for isolated privacy, especially if the home life fails to fulfil, and you attempt to retreat into an inner idealistic dream world where life should be as you prefer to imagine it to be.

NATAL NEPTUNE IN THE 5TH HOUSE

This position of Neptune is closely concerned with personal creativity, romance, life enjoyment and children.

Romance and love affairs are likely to be very influential in your life, and you may need to be careful in respect of the glamorous and illusory facade that Neptune can cast over others and upon your own perceptive clarity. This facade shimmers and sheens, but all may not be as it appears; where Neptune is concerned, always keep a wary eye open for images of deception. Romance will be coloured by idealism and that search for perfection which evokes the presence of *anima* and *animus* projections from the unconscious mind, overlaying the actual reality of any partner.

You are probably attracted to people who have an aura of mystery, intrigue and fascination surrounding them; this may be real but equally they could just seem that way to you if your inner projections have been activated. The allure of illicit and secret relationships is strong, as are any which promise glamour in some way, perhaps through association with status-rich people, or a more stylish and fashionable lifestyle. You enjoy situations that include a chance to be in the dramatic spotlight, and can sometimes resort to playing too many games to be fully trusted. Yet beneath that dramatic flair is someone who really wants to be loved and appreciated, although you may often act in ways that prevent this from happening successfully. Much will depend on the nature of aspects made to the natal Neptune.

Romances may not progress smoothly, and it is possible that a succession of failed love affairs can generate additional problems in your life, perhaps through children or unresolved emotional ties. Children could be a weak spot, and Neptune may demand a sacrifice from you in this area, prior to changes occurring in your life. More clarity is needed in this sphere of life, where in order to achieve your real desires of partnership you need to resist the lures of more glamorous tunes played by siren-like lovers. Try not to place lovers on unrealistic pedestals, or chase those who are not available; these can be just futile endeavours, dramatic perhaps, but strangely unsatisfying, unless you want to become the emotionally tortured *artiste*!

As with romance, your creativity may also be blocked from fulfilment. Neptune will give you a fertile imagination which can be used in very creative ways, but a way to release this may need to be found before the floodgates open. There may be natural talents in music, drama and art which have an inspirational source from the muses, and you will certainly feel more fulfilled when you are being creative and self-expressive, releasing emotional and imaginative energies into the world. This could be a key to transcending any blockage. Neptune may want you to move to a higher vantage place, so that there is less emphasis on purely personal creativity for more selfish aims and where the new perception is one of service to the greater community. Until you move in that direction, your aims may be frustrated. In offering something of value to others, you may be simultaneously offering a sacrifice to the inner gods, which will be rewarded in their own way – through your transformation and rebirth into a 'walker between worlds'.

Natal Neptune in the 6th House

The influence of Neptune in this natal house is concerned with the themes of work, service and health, and there are several personal adjustments that are likely to be required before you are able to experience the positive dimension of Neptune.

The nature of any aspects made to natal Neptune will be important indicators of how your Neptune will feel in this position because this is the point of detriment and so can be uncomfortable and struggling to express the planetary nature through you.

Work will be a challenging sphere, and it is probably essential for you to try and discover a satisfying type of employment; otherwise, it can prove to be an area of inner conflict, especially if the aspects are squares and oppositions. You may find that you do not enjoy your work, that its repetitive nature irritates and bores you, that your potential is not released but only constantly repressed, and that it is only continued because there seem to be few other options to take. Neptune will intensify your natural sensitivity, and you will find that you are attuned to the atmosphere of fellow-workers and the work environment, which may not enable you to enjoy work any better because invariably in most employments people would prefer to be elsewhere and there is a constant current of underlying tensions and pressures in the air.

It may be that you fail to reap the rewards at work that you believe are due to you, and because you have invested so much time and effort feel almost betrayed when promotion is offered to 'young high flyers', leaving you feeling disgruntled and wondering if it was all worth it. You may be vulnerable to being the 'fall guy' when things go wrong at work, others blaming you for their inefficiency – the victim aspect of Neptune. You may be made redundant, and struggle through a period of unemployment with the stresses that it brings to finances and domestic life. Certainly the sphere of work will be a key one in your experience, personally important to your development and one which is liable to have periodic disruptions caused by a blocked Neptune.

If Neptune has favourable aspects, then you are more likely to find suitable employment, which offers reasonably interesting work and decent relationships with co-workers. The types of work that can appeal and would fulfil this Neptune energy include creative ones, and work which involves service and aid to others.

If your experience of work is unsatisfying, then Neptune will be confronting you with the issue of change. How can you become free of an imprisoning situation? What type of work do you really want to do? Are you capable of doing it? Do you need extra study and qualifications? What are your essential family obligations? Can you take steps to reach your dreams? What resources do you have that can be used? What personal talents can be exploited? How can you earn a living in a more fulfilling way that is beneficial to others too? You may need to consider such questions prior to making changes in your life; there are always alternatives; yet we are often conditioned to believe that there are none, and so persist in imprisoning ourselves unnecessarily.

There is a more humanitarian, altruistic and service-orientated side to the Neptunian work ethic of this house, and in several ways it helps to express that energy more fully. This involves a devotion to community development, the healing of the individual and society, and will appeal more to those touched by the New Age vision. This can include a more *karma yoga* attitude, where the spiritual life is fully integrated into the everyday world and all life experience is perceived as an ongoing 'Mystery School', all work is seen as an offering to the Divine and part of the anchoring of the biblical Kingdom of God. Communities such as Findhorn embody such an attitude.

The power of a spiritual vision on Earth is indicated in Gandhi's expression of *Satyagraha*, his philosophy of non-violence, the application of the power and force of Truth, and the social changes that this can stimulate. Acting from a spiritual perspective, work becomes transformed, and so possesses a deeper meaning and importance to the individual.

It is possible that if you succeed in releasing the Neptune energy you may discover a natural healing ability which can be offered as a means of service and livelihood. Alternative therapies may fascinate, and the philosophy of the body as a living temple of God will open up a new dimension of life for you to explore. You will become aware of the influence of inner states on the health of the body, and will investigate the psychosomatic effects of separatists and unintegrated attitudes, beliefs and emotions, and attempt to develop a working concept of the whole-man therapy.

You could approach alternative health concepts through personal illness, where they offer a more satisfactory way to self-healing, and Neptune may take this route to lead you towards a personal transformation. You may realise that suppressed emotions are causing corresponding physical ailments, and that inner work can be therapeutic in allowing a cathartic release to happen, so liberating blocked energies.

It is a delicate balance that needs to be established to gain the best out of Neptune in the 6th house, because there are innate conflicting tendencies operating. Neptune prefers to expand and move beyond barriers, and the Virgoan 6th house prefers to define, impose boundaries and order. Connecting to a spiritual attitude and transforming your own life and work in the context of social change could be the ideal answer to aim towards.

NATAL NEPTUNE IN THE 7TH HOUSE

Neptune in this position indicates that the issues of relationships and partnerships will play an important role in your life. In addition, it also implies that there are likely to be a variety of inner projections and glamours surrounding these themes.

You will probably have an idealised perception of love, where any partner is seen through rose-coloured spectacles, placed on a romantic pedestal and is believed to be everything you have ever dreamed about – the perfect partner. This may be, but the odds are probably against this being a true perception; your clarity is dimmed by those active inner dreams and illusions, as you see your dream figure rather than the more imperfect real human being before you. These are the *anima–animus* projections from the unconscious mind, and can affect your perception and relationship with a partner in a variety of ways.

If Neptune has challenging aspects with other planets, then this sphere of relationships can pose personal difficulties through unsuitable liaisons, marriage partners, deception, emotional trauma and uncertainty, where the overshadowing glamours ensnare until reality intrudes and shatters any illusions, leaving an unsatisfactory relationship in their wake. Personal insecurity can create a partnership of dependency, where through emotional confusion you may prefer to rely on the presence and strengths of your lover; the danger may lie in any possible unreliability of a partner, who may act as a foil for the Neptunian pattern of deceit to be reflected back at you, designed to encourage you to become more self-reliant. Searching for needed qualities through attachment to another person is not the right way to proceed with such a task; they need to be evoked from within your own nature.

Those Neptunian tendencies towards sacrifice and towards being a victim and martyr, will probably be more active with challenging aspects, as you may be expected to sacrifice something to your partner.This can be a situation that is easily abused, and life is full of many examples of passive sacrifice to an unappreciative and unresponsive partner. It is that impulse to be absorbed in something greater than the limited self which is activated, that urge to surrender in order to be transformed. Often the partner is elevated to an almost 'divine position', where they are perceived in the guise of god or goddess, and through the spell cast by the inner projections they are highly idealised and worshipped in a strange manner as intermediaries to that 'something greater' which is so evocative of the Neptune patterns.

There can be a conditioning ideal of selfless love operating which, apart from the giving aspect, can often move towards the pursuit of the unreachable and unattainable dream partners, where love is never fulfilled and worship is made from a distance; the obsessional devotion towards media stars is such a symptom, although such private fascinations can equally be projected on to work colleagues or friends. Neptune has a peculiar attraction towards pain and pleasure in love, with intensity of feeling being the main desire that is sought. That martyr aspect can enjoy the exquisite emotions of tortured love, seeing it as a path towards redemption and healing through suffering. Pleasure can be elevated into mystical raptures, universal beauty and goodness, a glimpse of that which lies beyond. Some may prefer the saviour trip and be attracted to people with problems, believing that through their support and help salvation can be achieved for the other. Such a path does provide meaning, purpose and direction, and can indeed be extremely helpful in improving the lot of others; yet equally it can be strewn with many delusions, and it can be a razor edge to remain balanced upon.

With the more harmonious aspects to natal Neptune there is a greater likelihood that a satisfactory relationship can be made, although those Neptunian patterns will still be active. It is probable that partnerships will include a carefully defined spiritual and creative dimension, where the higher values of mutual relationship will be applied as effectively as possible, turning it into an environment of growth and spiritual development. The partnership may have complex elements at play with it, and phases of ongoing transformation will characterise its nature for all participants. Continuance of the intimate relationship will depend on the mutual stripping away of illusions and glamours, and an appreciation of the reality of each other as well as equality between the partners.

As Neptune is in your 7th house, it will be important to reach a realistic understanding of your relationships if they are to be satisfying, and also to see what your innate tendencies are attracted towards – sacrifice, or being a martyr, a victim, or a saviour – and to those inner fantasies and glamours. You may find it difficult to limit your affections to just one partner, and this can create some problems as those projections will inevitably be made to someone who expresses a mystery to you, rather than on a partner of several years' experience. Balance in the relationship may need to be made to avoid you either needing to possess a partner or to be possessed by one; neither situation is ultimately harmonious, and steps may need to be taken to create a form of relationship that is beneficial to both of you. This can include the integration of new ideals of relationship that are present in the New Age vision. Service to the greater community can help to channel some of the positive energies of the partnership, and satisfy your altruistic spirit as well as expanding the influence and parameters of a successful relationship.

Natal Neptune in the 8th House

The issue of sexual identity and activity is one which Neptune will confront you with in this position, and this is probably related to that impulse to transcend separatist boundaries of self and body that connects to the realm of the mystic and occultist which is also highlighted here.

If Neptune has challenging planetary aspects, squares or oppositions, and perhaps the conjunction to some degree, then there may be a fear of losing control in sexual intimacy, a blockage prohibiting any abandonment of self to passion and physical sexual activity. Because of an inner inhibition, there can be disappointments in this form of adult sexual behaviour, where the social fascination and emphasis on sex creates an expectation that is rarely fulfilled. Or there may be some confusion related to your own sexual nature, a lack of confidence or experience, a lack of knowing and understanding your own sexual preferences and choices, or of integrating that powerful aspect of your nature into your self-image.

Many inwardly keep their sexuality at arm's length, only allowing it to be present in restrictedly allowable circumstances, and not openly acknowledging that dimension of their being; this often occurs when heavy psychological conditioning has influenced their earlier development, such as religious or moral teachings, or feelings that 'sex is dirty and animal-like'. Neptune certainly does not make a definition of sexual feelings and attractions easy to make; it is too fluid and changeable, capable of a variety of different expressions and adaptations, and how one is with one partner can be entirely different with another. Intimacy touches in different 'inner spots', evoking quite varied reactions, often to the surprise of the participants. Part of the challenge facing anyone with this position is to begin to understand what it is they really want from sexual relationships.

This can be further complicated by the activation of Neptunian imagination in themes of sexuality, death, occult mysteries or mystic devotions that can add deep undercurrents to sexual intimacy. A search for peak experiences and total intensity (if they are allowed) can lead to a lack of contentment, as you believe that there are always greater experiences waiting if only the right partner could be found. This can create sexual promiscuity or the impulse to be sexually sacrificial and giving in an unrestrained manner, which can also merge with the need to lose the self in an ecstatic moment, and in so doing to forget the mundane limitations of everyday life.

Human sexuality is a complex theme reflecting a variety of possible psychological patterns; where Neptune is involved, it is virtually impossible to accurately predict the particular way in which it will manifest itself; also patterns can be transformed over time, shifting from one being dominant to another being so, depending on what is evoked by any sexual partner. Desires of being possessed and absorbed in self-abandonment may persist or the desire to possess and control another may be dominant. That overshadowing by a 'greater force' and overlaying of a mystical dimension may be the operative fascination, where sex is perceived in terms of a mystical quest for union, as in the Tantric traditions, or in aspects of the Western Grail and Arthurian Mysteries. Another extreme could be the conscious renunciation of sexual activity, as in celibacy or monastic attitudes, where personal sexual intimacy is offered as a sacrifice to an ideal, given for the reward of purification and redemption to be received as a transformation. Certainly a degree of understanding and integration of Neptune in this house is essential for personal well-being and psychological health.

Occult interests are likely to be attractive to you, there is probably a powerful psychic nature that you can access and you may receive information from inner guidance. You may be very psychically open, and this can cause certain problems of absorption of energies and impressions from your environment, but these can be filtered out by means of psychic protective actions. Loss of separative boundaries may occur as the individual consciousness merges with the universal one, especially if you are following a path of conscious development through meditation and occult experimentation. At least, glimpses of something other than and beyond the material world will become common, although you may have to be wary of occult glamours and illusions leading you into a fool's paradise and inflated sense of ego. Discrimination is vital in such inner enquiry, as is a sense of humour which is deflating and a lack of pomposity and tendencies towards self-aggrandisement!

Death may exert a peculiar fascination, as can the more taboo areas of life, and there can be self-destructive tendencies too, although these are often common in the strange inner worlds of mystics and occultists as part of the impulse to transcend and live intensely through the rush to experience 'as many lifetimes worth of experience into one life as possible'. The taboo attraction can be summed up as 'if anyone tells me not to look at something, then I'll be first in the queue, and will not leave until I have satiated my thirst for the forbidden'.

Money and legacies may also be reflected by this position of natal Neptune, and there may be distortions, contentious issues, deceptions associated with this, or simply an inability to become clear as to your own personal values regarding money and the material level of existence. Greater clarity may be required, and care must be taken to maintain good family relationships if inheritances become a disputed issue.

NATAL NEPTUNE IN THE 9TH HOUSE

In this position, Neptune is active on the level of mind, especially in the realms of philosophy, religion, morals, ethics and spiritual teachings. Belief systems are important to you, and you need to feel secure in the one that you have adopted as a guideline in life; or alternatively, you are searching for one that you can believe holds satisfying answers to those burning inner questions.

It is likely that you will feel a need to rely on some form of external teaching, and this can draw you towards involvement with specific religious groups, or mystical cults and guru-figures. As your mind is quite open and impressionable, and influenced by the Neptunian imagination, your clarity regarding such groups may be distorted by a desire to achieve redemptive salvation through association with a belief structure that promises universal answers.

This can result in a negative form of surrender, where your fantasies, clouded judgements and desires encourage you to submit to an external authority or acquiesce in an imposed belief system, creating a situation where you feel absolved of any need to think for yourself, as all the answers have been given to you. This is an abrogation of real responsibility, and no genuine teacher should demand absolute adherence to their teaching, or inveigh against any who disagree or choose to leave the self-selected elite. The type of dangers involved in such a course include spiritual inflation and self-delusions, guru imitation, and obsessive beliefs in being 'right' in your opinions and world view.

Neptune can lead you into such a philosophical minefield as a consequence of your own confusion and lack of direction, and by the need for some type of spiritual search for a higher unifying knowledge. The underlying intent may be to confront you with a collapse into disillusionment with that external search for answers, forcing you to turn within and to discover that what you are really looking for is hidden within your own nature.

The types of philosophy, religion or belief structure that will appeal most to you will often include themes of sacrifice, redemption, purification, martyrdom and self-transcendence: the themes of Neptune. You will need to express incisive discrimination in walking this path, as you are liable to reflect these Neptunian patterns quite unconsciously in your choices. Distinguishing the real from the false can be extremely difficult, and unintegrated natural tendencies will attract you towards the mysterious and glamorous, but as you should recognise, all that glitters is not the alchemist's gold.

Spiritual aspiration will be powerful, and you are likely to possess refined, mystically orientated emotions aching to achieve a transcendent and embracing unitive state of existence. Psychedelic drugs may appeal for similar reasons, as a means of opening doors to alternative realities, but great care needs to be taken where Neptune is involved, and mixing these with spiritual development techniques is unwise. Meditation, contemplation, yoga and psychic unfoldment are likely routes which will interest you, or those more intellectual occult systems like the Qabalah and the Seven Rays, which offer considerable scope for mental fascination. Whilst you have a tendency towards daydreaming and fantasies, such an inward turning can make you more receptive to inner guidance and intuition, and in some instances this can develop into you serving as a channel for inspirational teachings to be transmitted into the world. Today, there are many of these, and a broad mixture of quality too, reflecting the mediumistic and mediatorship nature of Neptune, with both high and spiritual visions and lower astral and illusory ones being presented to an avid public.

Part of your own challenge will lie in unfolding your own path, relying on your own insight and understanding to light the way, and in being able to clarify your own direction and exploit that latent mind potential. Creativity through artistic expression could be useful, especially the sort which attempts to reflect spiritual values and vision into everyday life. The real spiritual path is never one of escapism from life, even though you may feel tempted to do that through travel, pilgrimages and by surrendering to a higher temporal authority as a guru figure. Neptune in this house can lead you towards the highest flights of consciousness, or restrict you within self-chosen realms of delusion; it can be a narrow line separating the two, but ensuring that your feet are firmly fixed on the ground is an important aim to maintain.

NATAL NEPTUNE IN THE 10TH HOUSE

The themes which are indicated by this position include social status and influence, careers and leadership. How Neptune will operate through you in terms of your public or community life can vary, and may be reflected by the nature of planetary aspects made to natal Neptune.

The more negative aspects include a lack of achievement, acknowledgement and status. This can be due to an inability to clarify the direction that you should travel, Neptunian confusion and indecisiveness, and the work environment failing to satisfy for some reason. Perhaps through a lack of defined ambition or persistence in achieving aims, a lack of expressed talent or interest, your career life may be frustrated. You may lack practicality or just be erratic and unreliable in application, shifting with those fluctuating inner tides of Neptune and failing to be consistent at work or even in your relationships with professional colleagues. Attempts at manipulation or deceit may work against you, a transparent self-centredness may restrict opportunities coming to you, or scandals and whiffs of impropriety may circulate, tainting you by association or involvement.

Positive aspects can include a career of community service, where you become respected and appreciated for your efforts and social contribution, and this is an expression of a Neptunian social conscience seeking for that ideal utopian vision. You may become devoted to a cause, some type of idealistic social movement, and dedicate your time to its development. This can serve as a sacrifice to an inspiring ideal, where you offer yourself to be a channel for that 'something greater' which lies beyond the separate self. In this way, you may become a spokesperson for a visionary perception; spiritual, ecological, humanistic and altruistic in content. For some this occurs through embodying such concerns within artistic creations, artistic, musical, or literary, and so communicating them to others as an inspirational channel. The struggle may lie in finding the appropriate form which fits the message and the need for right livelihood, and discovering this can involve you in a transformatory path of its own.

Having social power and influence can be a challenging role to perform, and you may need to understand the dynamics of such a position and the concepts of personal empowerment to ensure that you do not abuse any influence that you may achieve. Remember that Neptune's influence can lead to distorted perceptions, and always keep that sword of discrimination ready to use.

This position can also indicate an inner resonance with the Mother figure, your own or as an archetypal image. Associated with this are the typical Neptune themes of sacrifice, victim and martyr, and it is possible that your mother had to relinquish many of her own personal desires in order to raise her family. Many adults are unconscious of the sacrifices and demands of parenthood until they become parents themselves, then the realisations begin to dawn, and a greater understanding and appreciation of their own parents is born. Some adjustment of this mother image and ideal is probably needed, especially in order to realise your own nurturing and protective instincts, and to harmonise your emotions more effectively. It can reflect a need to give birth (mother) to a new self that can emerge from within you, a self that is intimately connected with the well-being of a wider society and one which is connected to the impulse of the Aquarian Age which is now emerging.

NATAL NEPTUNE IN THE 11TH HOUSE

This indicates an emphasis on the sphere of friendships, group association and idealistic social ambitions, and it is likely that the compassionate humanitarian spirit of Neptune will be highly influential in forming your eventual social activity.

Neptune will encourage you to build high social ideals which are utopian in essence, and where your dreams involve only the beautiful, the good and the true. You probably feel an empathy with life on Earth, and are concerned with its well-being and continuance; this can lead you into joining groups which are also concerned with promoting similar idealistic visions.

It is important to you to feel involved in such social endeavour, and is an expression of that sense of relationship to your fellow-men and the other kingdoms of nature. From this altruistic heart projection you attempt to develop the concepts of group brotherhood, which are so prevalent in this house and connected to the emerging Aquarian impulse, although you may disguise your compassion by concealing it within an intellectual or abstracted type of expression; even so, your moral outrage at man's foolishness and separatist thinking will still shine through. This indicates a receptivity to the inner spiritual nature, and if this becomes more powerful within you, will guide you towards a lifestyle which is designed to be socially influential, serving as a transmitter of spiritual values and vision. This sensitivity to planetary needs will also attract a corresponding type of friend to you, based on an affinity with an idealistic world view. Some may become involved with mystical or occult groups, especially for additional training in specific transformative techniques.

If Neptune is more artistically expressive, then you may choose to work along this line, using art, music and literature to serve as a means of communication to display your social concerns. The theme of healing may become prominent, perhaps through a study of whole being healing techniques as is currently pioneered through alternative and complementary health therapies, or as a unifying concept to synthesise your social activity: the healing of self and society.

If the planetary aspects with Neptune are more challenging, then whilst these themes will be present, there are likely to be several distortions occurring. Ideals may be impractical or too utopian to stand any chance of being manifested at present. Ideals act as an evolutionary spur for mankind, and are often imposed or overshadow the collective mind, serving to inspire humanity to progress in certain directions. Unfortunately the obstacle to their achievement is mankind, who either refuses to change or only does so in a slow laborious fashion as a result of consequences of prior avoidance. You may need to struggle with the issue of fine intentions and failure to actualise those golden romantic dreams. More clarity and effort will be required to actually achieve anything, or else those impossible dreams will just disintegrate as chimeras in the air, totally insubstantial.

Establishing your chosen direction could prove equally problematic, as you may find it difficult to clarify the direction you wish to travel, and whilst you may have a fine visionary perspective, you may need someone more earthy and pragmatic to hold you down from those flights of fancy, to guide you step by step into making those dreams real.

Groups may attract you solely for inner reasons of sacrifice and escape where those Neptunian inner patterns are searching for some way to be released, and where you believe that through such association you can either lose yourself or find meaning and purpose in life. It may be best to be wary of looking for a group which promises you salvation and redemption, because if you do have a real need for that, then you can be vulnerable to the psychological influence of such a group. The power of world religions rests on this human need, although for the 'exchange of redemptive salvation' there is a price to be paid, and that usually involves undercurrents of guilt and a diminution of free thinking. It is an understandable need to have answers to the questions of life, but just to fill an aching void with a group belief structure may placate and act as a panacea, yet rarely transforms the individual to discover his own light. Many New Age groups still perpetuate ancient patterns of human need for answers, persuading people to enter psychological dependency and to absorb without question a variety of 'spiritual teachings'. Flexibility of world view is usually healthier, and liberates the open enquiring mind.

Apart from involvement with such groups, friendships can also be distorted if Neptune has challenging aspects. Discrimination is always required, as you are very susceptible to powerful influences, and choosing unsuitable friends may lead you into wrong directions or cul-de-sacs. Be wary of possible deceptions, and avoid any attractions towards types of addictive behaviour.

NATAL NEPTUNE IN THE 12TH HOUSE

The 12th house is considered to be Neptune's own house, and so both the positive and negative qualities are found in this natal position. The influence of the unconscious mind is especially strong, and the effects of this may be dependent on the rest of the chart and the type of aspects made to Neptune.

For those who are relatively unintegrated individuals, or who lack an effective self-development or spiritual path, Neptune can stimulate considerable unease from this sphere. There are disquieting undercurrents, irrational fears, phobias, compulsions, and obsessions which can arise. Imagination is extremely active, and the feeling-emotional nature is highly stimulated and prone to impressionable influences and changes of moods. Memories of the past can still carry blocked energies or contain 'unfinished business' that affects the present; a generally negative, insecure and unstable outlook on life and self may dominate. Confusion and vagueness may afflict decision making, and passivity and feelings of lack of control restrict any full experience of life.

The sense of personal identity feels eroded and dissolved from within, and there is no firm inner centre to rely on; this diminishes the ability to consistently apply the will to achieve any aims. There can be an avoidance of responsibility, a tendency to withdraw from life, and a strange juxtaposition of the external reality and intrusions from the inner unconscious mind may develop. This can create confusion regarding interpretation of reality, as the reception of 'messages' conflicts; this is heightened by the psychic sensitivity activated by Neptune, where intangible sensations are also registered as co-existing within human reality.

Whilst you can be extremely sensitive to the impact of the environment and people, and prefer to live within a beautiful and harmonious lifestyle, you still desire to escape and retreat into those private inner worlds which you attempt to fill with images of security, stability and protection. You recognise that – for you – the world will never fulfil, and certainly will always fail to match your utopian vision, thus withdrawing into daydreams and fantasies is a way of recompense. You may indulge in impressions of previous lives, especially if you are familiar with the theories of reincarnation, and can become intrigued and fascinated by pondering the workings of karma, attempting to discover what has led you to this point, and being careful not to generate more negative karma through unwise actions. This can be another way in which you inhibit your experience of life.

More positive integration of Neptune into the psyche, which is aided by favourable aspects, displays the positive dimension of this sphere, where forms of channelling of hidden wisdom and insight may be achieved. Psychic sensitivity can destroy a life just as it can enrich it; much depends on the individual reaction to its influence, and the degree to which balance and integration can be made. Intuitive accessing of inner stores of knowledge is becoming more popular again, and can often be highly inspirational, although great care must be made in opening inner channels because the energy and experiences that can be unleashed are extremely powerful and transformative, and many become victims of their own repressed unconscious mind which, like a dam bursting, floods the separate personality, dissolving protective barriers.

There are likely to be distinct mystical and religious attractions through this position of Neptune, possibly a monastic type of impulse, where the idea of retreat from the world or relative seclusion is most appealing. Periodic withdrawal can be beneficial, especially when it is done as a form of inner cleansing and designed to re-empower the self. Compassion will be a motivating tendency, and some with this position become dedicated to a life of service and care for those who are disadvantaged in life, those who are ill or are social rejects. Some type of service to the world is probably the most effective way to release this energy and cleanse any unconscious patterns which otherwise may affect the conscious life; selfless service can be highly purifying, offering meaning and purpose in life, and for someone with this natal position of Neptune it may prove to be the best direction. Certainly learning to accept life with its good and bad, its light and darkness, and coming to terms with inner conflicts and disillusionment in the world are crucial steps to take because these help to restore balance and clearer perception. Remaining in anguish because the world fails to match your expectations is a waste of time and energy, and is a futile task. Discovering how to use your gifts to help the world to move towards your vision could be your most worthwhile contribution.

CHAPTER 6

Neptune Transits through Houses and Signs

THE TIME PERIOD that Neptune takes to pass through a full transit of the signs and houses lasts for 167 years and 5½ months, and is the second longest of the planetary transit cycles, after that of Pluto. Neptune takes almost fourteen years to transit each sign, and so the sign distinctions are more relevant and identifiable when one is considering the influence of Neptune on society and generations rather than on the individual. During each year, Neptune has a seven-month direct movement followed by a five-month retrograde.

The majority of people only experience at most half of the full Neptune cycle, which even then takes eighty-four years to complete, and will cover the transiting effect of Neptune only within a range of six houses from the natal position.

Much depends on this natal Neptune position in relation to the other planets in the chart as to future transiting aspects that are made. Conjunctions are likely to be made once to each planet over a time period where planets are placed in that six-house range, and similarly oppositions will be made once to planets placed in the other six houses. Squares, trines and sextiles are likely to be made to each planet either once or twice and this depends on that natal position of Neptune relative to planets in that six-house range.

Any planetary aspects that are made adjacent to the change of station are usually repeated either three or five times over a period of time as the transit movement changes from direct to retrograde motion. Over this change-of-station period, Neptune can aspect a planet three times over one year, or five times in a two-year period. Such aspects have an influence that is effective from the time of the initial contact to the end of the last repeated aspect, and so should be carefully considered with regard to their likely impacts on the individual. When Neptune is transiting at its maximum speed of movement, there is a two-month period of influence of a planetary aspect, where there is a one-degree applying and a one-degree separating to partile. During the change of station, there is a slowing of movement, and the aspectual orb time lengthens to approximately four months. When making aspects to any planet, it is often the case that when transiting Neptune is moving direct, it has most influence on a natally direct planet, and that a retrograde natal planet is most influenced by a retrograde transiting Neptune.

Important phases of the individual life cycle related to the transiting Neptune are: age 28, transiting Neptune sextiles natal Neptune; age 44, transiting Neptune squares natal Neptune; age 56, transiting Neptune trines natal Neptune; and age 84, transiting Neptune opposes natal Neptune. At 14, an age associated with puberty and the onset of adolescence, a semi-sextile is made.

The impact of transiting Neptune on an individual through the houses or by the forming of planetary aspects can be quite variable, and often depends on the individual attunement to the more subtle dimensions of life and on the rigidity of their personality structure. Even personal responses to transit aspects and their registration within consciousness varies considerably. Some who are highly attuned to the currents of their inner life can register a slowly forming aspect whilst it is several degrees away from becoming exact, perhaps up to a year away in time; others, whose preoccupations are more materialistically absorbed, may only begin to register a creeping disquiet within one or two degrees from an exact aspect, perhaps within a two-month period. Such sensitivity – or lack of it – can often rely on individual affinities with specific planets too, those which play a more important role in their natal chart and life. For those engaged in spiritual pursuits, any aspect made to one of the other transpersonal planets could prove important and powerful. Any planetary transit to natal Neptune is often important for those on spiritual quests, as Neptune can represent a state of passive quiescence which requires waking by another planetary stimulation.

There can be difficulties in attempts to accurately date Neptune's transiting influences. Obviously times and phases of planetary aspects can be defined, as can transits through the houses, and crossing the angles, but apart from indicating these and likely personality effects, most Neptunian influences are subtler, deeper and more encompassing than many recognise. Similar to Pluto, Neptune moves so slowly that defining a Neptunian effect can be problematic, as it is a period or phase of life that is affected as the transit moves through a quadrant or half of a chart.

What are the types of Neptune crises? And how are they likely to affect individuals?

Unlike the impact of Uranus, with its tendency to enter with a rush, often with surprising, traumatic and dramatic effect, turning the life upside down and leaving the shell-shocked individual spinning like a top trying to assimilate what has just hit him, Neptune enters with a more gentle disguise, slowly permeating the inner consciousness, its watery nature slowly seeping through fissure like cracks in the mind's surface. The changes that Neptune brings are slow and thorough, often associated with a sense that 'something is going on', a puzzlement and bewilderment, shadows in the mind that evade every attempt to grasp hold of them, wispy elusive mists that disappear as attention is turned towards them. Neptune prepares the person for a Plutonic rebirth, through a process of slowly dissolving the familiar patterns of personality and expression and initially replacing them with an unfamiliar scenario, both of personal feelings and relationships to people and any established life structure. It is disconcerting to feel that once solid ground of self and life dissolving from inside, especially as it may be impossible to discern exactly what has triggered off this process, and much of the life may superficially be the same as before. It can be like an inner collapse out of proportion to any external influences, and will invariably be connected to that level of emotions, feelings and values that are often personally used to define the boundaries of the separate identity.

What tends to change is the personal perception or relationship to an external situation or partner, and once the process commences, then there is little that can be done to withstand its inevitable effects. Some tend to project the cause of this crisis externally, seeing someone else as responsible for their own feelings; these are often individuals who have an outer focus, perhaps indicated by appropriate natal planetary aspects, houses, tendencies and the like. Some are more naturally introverted, locking these changes deeply within themselves, perhaps withdrawing more through personal uncertainty and vulnerability. Certainly whatever is touched by Neptune is vitalised, sensitised and opened up – planets or house transits; this is achieved through that universal solvent dissolving any fixed and inhibitory patterns of behaviour, thought, attitude and lifestyle. For those who are more attuned to the transpersonal spheres of life, the inner awareness of the intangible realms is emphasised; whilst this may be the goal of many who seek to discover the path of spirituality, it can equally be disconcerting to actually enter a phase of changed perceptivity rather than just imagining and dreaming about what it 'must be like'. Learning to function from a transformed consciousness can at an early stage be an extremely sensitive and vulnerable experience, until time and familiarity make their own adjustments.

It can be both exciting and frightening to have a sphere of life suddenly changing and opening up to receive a new impulse from the transiting Neptune. The area of life represented by each house is often a fairly established pattern by adulthood, so changes stimulated by Neptune in such an area are often as unwelcomed as accepted. Initially the need for change is indicated by feelings of discontent, confusion, uncertainty and desires for escape from whatever we feel is oppressing us or a source of pain in our lives. Clarity is often the first casualty of the Neptune influence, and irrationality is the mind's response to the conflicting and confusing signals it is receiving from agitated feelings and emotions. Some who have been repressive and tightly self-controlled can dissolve into psychological pieces as their imaginations and mind begin to whirl out of control and into new orbits, displaying a lack of awareness, attention and practical efficiency. These are often indications of transiting Neptune's aspects with natal Mercury, Mars and Saturn. With natal Mercury, the old patterns of the mind begin to break down, the mind is opened to new experiences and ways of perception or interpretation and reliance on the old foundations falls away. With a natal Venus, the transiting Neptune influence can be focused on the sphere of partnerships and love relationships, where existing illusions may dissolve, revealing the actual reality of a partner, or where there is the opportunity to unfold a deeper and more realistic perception of love. Aspects made to a natal Sun could be more powerful, especially in the sphere of personal identity, which could become extremely fragile in some, or be exalted in others, realistically or not. The nature of the planet to which Neptune makes a transiting aspect will evoke the appropriate tendencies, either purifying and refining them, so that greater sensitivity and appreciation can be enjoyed, or dissolving those old forms indicated by the nature of the planet that is being transited.

It is usually the conjunction, square and opposition aspects made by Neptune that are harder to deal with, or more powerful in their impacts, especially when they aspect any of the personal planets or the Ascendant in the majority of people. The strongest degree of impact and influence of an aspect occurs as the aspect is applying (moving closer to the point of an exact aspect), as the initial encounter with the new is faced; as the separating aspect (moving away from the exact aspect) proceeds, the act of assimilation is required.

Similar to the transits of the other two transpersonal planets, Uranus and Pluto, it is often the more challenging effects of Neptune that are experienced first by the majority of individuals. This is probably inevitable, and due to the fact that most establish a fairly rigid persona and fixed lifestyle built on attitudes, values, beliefs and personal desires. The pain and confusion that can result from those inner movements of Neptune are the symptoms of resistance to necessary changes and attempts to release outgrown patterns of behaviour. 'Spaced out' sensations are often common with the effects of an activated Neptune, a lack of focus and inner centre.

Some respond to the Neptunian influence by immersing themselves in 'dreams and fantasies'; phantasms of desire are created as substitutes for the frustrations of unrealised expectations in daily life, and they prefer to remain with such dreams rather than risk exposing themselves to actually experiencing them in life. In some cases this can be personally and socially beneficial, yet there is always the danger that such unfilfilled dreams can become obsessive on an individual and collective scale. There is a narrow dividing line between recognising that these are compensatory personal fantasies and failing to maintain a demarcation line so that the fantasies degenerate into restrictive glamours and illusions, self-deception, confusions and states of addiction due to the loss of discrimination and ability to truly confront the real reality. What tends to occur then are personality splits, where the aspects of life that are unacceptable are rejected and replaced by the overshadowing fantasies to such a degree that distortion is inevitable. These fantasies can become excessively dominant, slowly bringing about a degeneration of the personality as their motivation intensifies to actually experience them.

A negative reaction to Neptune always has the effect of exclusion, where some aspect of self or life is denied and rejected, and where a separate ego resists the prompting to live by those more universal and compassionate values that Neptune symbolises; a positive response to Neptune involves the tendency to be universally inclusive. In order for Neptune to be positive in the individual, there needs to be some conscious awareness of feeling part of a greater whole, so that the inclusive tendency leads towards an enhanced identification with life. Some expand their sense of compassion and identification with the unnecessary suffering of other people, both in their own country and internationally. As a progression in human evolution, this has been a most noticeable development since the discovery of Neptune in 1846. Based on this sense of inclusiveness, Neptune intensifies the need for forms of collective action and group awareness where the needs of the whole are paramount.

Neptune has been termed the 'planet of social obligation', and is a major indicator of how the individual experiences and responds to the social and collective group. Usually if Neptune is highlighted in a chart, then the personal life is often closely associated with the life of the collective, perhaps negatively as a victim, martyr or sacrifice or positively as an agent of Neptunian transformation, through expressing a more inclusive vision, artistically or spiritually. All of the transpersonal planets work together in an inner harmony, where the Uranian intellectual and intuitional vision of the greater life is complemented by Neptune's faith and feeling of connectedness and inter-relationships as preparatory steps to the total Plutonic transformatory rebirth.

The process which occurs is that Neptune is the main influence on the emotional and feeling nature. What the transit is liable to affect are feeling responses and motivating values, so that any restrictive old order is gradually dissolved in order for the next step to be taken (as is often indicated by a Uranian-type vision). Being aware of the next step also needs confidence and faith in actually taking it, which is the Neptunian contribution as it dissolves the Saturnian limitations in our personality. Through insecurity and fear, we often restrict ourselves from taking opportunities or gambles in order to achieve some long-cherished dream or desire. Uniting both Uranus and Neptune in harmony can give us the momentum for the transformation to be made. If that wilful act is not taken through dominating our personal insecurity fears, then the ability to function as an integrated individual is progressively diminished. This is one of the negative consequences of becoming too influenced by and reliant upon collective attitudes, beliefs and values, where essentially the person becomes a passive slave to a collective consciousness and unable to think and act for himself.

The positive dimension of Neptunian transits is the way that new opportunities are opened up, especially through the realisation that the intangible realms do exist and that existing attitudes and values can be successfully refined and attempts made at actualising ideals. Often experiences happen which encapsulate 'universal lessons', so that what is learnt, realised and understood can be applied across a broad spectrum of life, and so can come to have a profound influence on future life. For those who are mystically or artistically inclined, Neptune transits can be a source of inspiration and creativity, unlocking doors and revealing hidden treasures that can be positively used.

Common challenges which confront the individual from a transiting Neptune include the following:

1 Learning to accept the dissolution of outgrown feelings and emotions, perhaps the replacement of old values by new and more inclusive perceptions, the releasing of old atrophied relationships in order to create the space for new relationships.
2 Learning how to ride the tides of confusion, insecurity and 'spaced outness', being patient in waiting for the new to become more distinctly defined.
3 Learning how to access that innate creative potential, manifest it into some external form and allow imagination to permeate your life in every way. Our options are severely limited by the degree to which we can allow ourselves to imagine alternatives, and society does not emphasise or encourage such ongoing changes. Essentially, look for ways in which life can be more vital and enriched.
4 Learning to live from the perspective of the compassionate heart, that living sense of connectedness to people and the whole of life, moving towards a giving and service orientation, rather than a separatist 'taking' attitude.

5 Learning to use imagination positively and constructively to recreate your own personality and life in a pattern that is more harmonious and satisfying.
6 Learning to avoid misapplying imagination and wasting that energy in distorting fantasies and personal glamours, of becoming lost and content in a private dream world immune and impervious to the real world.
7 Learning how to trust that the light will dawn when it all seems to be collapsing around you, as illusions shatter and your values, ideals, and beliefs are seen to be unsuitable or too restrictive, and you do not know what to replace them with in that empty void.
8 Learning how to allow your feelings to flow without repression, whilst protecting yourself from the negativity of certain aspects of life and the vulnerability of oversensitivity.
9 Learning how to guide your life by the light of inclusive ideals and a global vision, and how to co-operate with the higher self.

These are all challenging lessons that Neptune may ask you to learn during its transit phases, and are the positive dimensions of the Neptunian vibration that you are expected to embody. Achieving these would transform your life.

NEPTUNE TRANSITING 1ST HOUSE

As transiting Neptune crosses the Ascendant, a new cycle commences in the influence of this planet on your life. It is likely to become an inwardly disturbing period, feelings of disquiet and anxiety will begin to emerge, even though you may find it difficult to define to yourself exactly what is causing these sensations of discomfort. As Neptune has crossed your Ascendant, activating your rising sign, and is now positioned in the house of your personal conscious identity, there is a corresponding agitation deep in the depths of your psyche. It is the changes in your psychological undercurrents – reminiscent of sea tides – that are stimulating this unease. Those personality foundations and fixed structures of thought patterns that are the essence of the separated self are slowly being dissolved. You may feel strangely threatened somehow, possibly projecting externally on to others these feelings, seeing them as the causes for your discomposure.

It may be difficult to correctly perceive yourself, your relationships and life with realistic clarity at this time, especially in the phase of dissolution prior to the next stage of re-integration. The influence of Neptune on the separate self is to stimulate tendencies to build up fantasies, to encourage you to become immersed in mind-dreams of an escapist or unrealistic nature. Whilst in the hands of a trained, psychologically adept person, Neptune can be used in extremely positive constructive ways, but for the majority of people its influence tends to appear negative. Changes that Neptune is attempting to promote are unrecognised and are resisted, which stimulates more agitation and disruption in the inner life, rather than being acknowledged and co-operated with as part of the ongoing cyclic process of the individual life.

What will emerge with greater clarity during the initial impacts of Neptune entering the 1st house is the recognition of an impulse slowly developing and forming that is asking you to discover a new way of living and experiencing your life. Psychologically, you will still be looking backwards through the established lens of existing personality and thought patterns. But now you have to re-orientate yourself towards this new cycle that has opened. Inner questions will arise concerning your own nature and personal identity, and it is likely that your sense of confidence in your ability to deal with life will seem to be dissipating. Life may suddenly begin to display dimensions and subtleties that you had never previously recognised as existing. Inner sense and sensitivities may open up, causing problems by tuning you into vibrational frequencies associated with psychic abilities. Your old familiar world of solidity and predictability may shimmer and fray at the edges as an unknown dimension peeks out at you and begins to interpenetrate your established reality.

So what is this 'new way of living' that seems to be the intention of this transit? The initial reaction to feelings of personal unease is likely to attract you towards something that appears to offer stabilisation. This could include relationships, especially in the context of dependency on another, but the main sphere that is highlighted is towards social groupings and group beliefs, attitudes and ways of thinking and living. Such social groupings offer – in their own particular ways – a sense of security and belonging, which are two very relevant needs in your present inner life. Being a part of some social tradition is often an easier way of creating an anchor in life, probably offering 'answers' that you absorb as true, saving the effort of searching for your own light, and by trusting in the attitude that suggests that if millions believe the same traditions or ways of social living it is also a guarantee that the tradition is right. This is the majority path.

As Neptune works through the channel of the collective mind, these initial impacts will influence you to look towards those collective social values, attitudes and beliefs which are prominent and which serve as guiding standards for a majority of people. These may not be exclusively related to your own national society, but can also relate to your possible involvement in any sub-group, such as political, racial or religious groupings. Basically your personal identity will tend to be receptive to those influences emerging from larger social groupings. The possibility is that you may need to guard yourself against either a misunderstanding of these powerful influences, or against absorbing them without any conscious evaluation and discrimination of their truth and relevance to your personal life in the overwhelming need to discover an anchor and safe harbour from the stormy inner seas.

Illusions concerning ideals, beliefs, attitudes, values and traditions are likely to occur through such misunderstanding and their intrinsic glamours; essentially, you will not want to see the real truth that may be hidden within them, or equally, you may not be able to see the truth. Even if you step out of more mainstream and socially acceptable traditions towards the New Age ones, there is the same problem. As many New Age spiritual approaches are so dogmatic in their presentations of 'spiritual truth', the glamours and illusions are still extremely present. Just absorbing New Age ideas does not transform an individual.

The inspiration of many beliefs is always more pure than their actual expression in life. As Neptune is an inspirational planet, you will be internally fired by its active presence. Being aflame with spiritual or ideological fervour does not, however, often lead to clarity of mind. You are likely to find it difficult to both perceive and evaluate your self-worth during this transit, and this can lead to either a complex of superiority emerging fuelled by discovering 'the way for everyone to follow', or by inferiority if you remain in a lost and confused state. The real truth is that you are neither superior or inferior, and that essentially you are still the same person passing through a changing time! You will experience an underlying discontent with yourself and the world, and will often be confused and uncertain as to what to do about these feelings. Usually you will display indecision and erratic commitments, unless your feelings of being at a loss are so great that in an effort to alleviate them, you throw yourself into some great cause in order to forget your own problems.

A phase where old structures are dissolved is never easy, and Neptune rarely casts a spell where crystal-clear clarity emerges. It is often hard to grasp what is occurring, and there is a lack of clear perception. The possibility is that through applying discrimination and self-awareness to the best of your ability, you could move through this phase gaining considerable personal insight into yourself and into the nature of society and its traditions. It could become a liberating period, one where you are able to take full advantage of those opportunities that will arise. What will attract is some form of social vision, humanitarian or mystical in nature, which will challenge you to truly look at yourself and others. Your idealistic tendencies will be stimulated, although you will need to temper these by retaining a practical approach to everything. If you can take the open-eyed positive approach through this transit, then you are less likely to be englamoured by any restrictive alternative structure of mental conditioning. Being aware of the ways to experience Neptune's sea mists can be a key to working positively and constructively with this energy.

NEPTUNE TRANSITING 2ND HOUSE

For those of us living in the captalist and materialistic Western societies, the main thrust of the social conditioning upon our lifestyles and life directions is towards possessions and exploiting resources, especially external resources. We are encouraged to be consumers, chasing after glamorous acquisitions and status symbols of success and achievement. The accumulation of wealth and high spending is proposed as a meaningful goal and purpose in life. Most people struggle on an ever-intensifying material treadmill, moving faster in order to stand still or in an effort to acquire more and more to provide that sense of meaning in life. The question is: does this path really satisfy? Is security and meaning to be found in larger houses, more cars, an expanding bank balance, more expensive furniture and exotic holidays abroad?

Obviously a good standard of living and comfort is a goal to aim towards, and indeed, the Aquarian spiritual movement is emerging from a worldwide group of people who live relatively affluent lifestyles, and who have sufficient time and freedom from preoccupation with eking out a subsistence level for survival. We do not suffer starvation, go cold or experience natural disasters as a common experience. Such relative freedom from essential physical necessities gives us the opportunity and responsibility to use our assets more positively, for our own development and for the betterment of others, and to help raise others above a mere survival level of existence.

The transit of Neptune through this 2nd house can begin to confront you with the issues of your personal and social value systems, and the resulting attitudes and philosophies. It can challenge you to question your life direction, especially in the context of your material-level objectives, and in your inner attitudes to money and resources, both in a personal sense and a broader global relationship. This involves the issues of investing external possessions with qualities of security and personal meaning and displacing your personal identity into the possession of status-fulfilling cult objects. In placing 'security' in external objects, you run the risk of becoming insecure if that object is damaged, stolen or lost. Neptune is interested in confronting you with the consequences of your value system, with the conditioning influence of this system on your decisions and life options; it is asking you to take another look and to change your values in some way. Perhaps more than asking you, Neptune is forcing you to reconsider, as it proceeds to dissolve those spurious external identifications, and to challenge the view that the worth of a man is measured by the value of his material possessions.

Through the images and social attitudes that condition the West and its communication and advertising media, we are encouraged to desire, to feel dissatisfied with whatever we have; there is always a new vastly improved model to move on to, new technological advances to provide better cars, videos, computers, stereos. We are stimulated to want more and more, to replace, to quickly bore of household furniture, to change our cars; after all, we are led to believe that the point of living is to consume, isn't it?

In itself, consumerism is not wrong. Where the problems arise is in the elevation of consumerism as a meaningful way of life, where the focus is always externally pointed. The empty inner space is filled with more objects and possessions; when discontent strikes, 'buy more' is the whispered mantra of our society. In possession lies fulfilment. But is it a demonic possession?

Resources are not just external. Everyone has inner resources and talents, but our society does not really encourage personal development. Lip service is paid to this but as a way of life and as individual unfolding it is not emphasised, because creating a society of autonomous, creative, aware and assertive individuals can be disturbing to the status quo. So development is often restricted along certain acceptable channels, those which can be easily absorbed and manipulated by the powerful establishment elites. Most people are unsure of their own personal value and worth, rarely recognising their hidden gifts and potential. One of the most important messages of the Aquarian vision is that of personal potential, and the release of techniques to unfold and access latent potential.

Neptune will act as a stimulant to this issue of possessions, hoping to encourage a re-orientation towards a more inner focus, so that you can begin to 'possess' those fulfilling qualities that lie within your own nature. This may be created by external difficulties concerning your reliance on possessions. Financial losses through business or divorce settlements may occur; imprudent financial decisions could lead to the collapse of companies, with resulting redundancies. Certainly you will need to be alert, practical and careful regarding your finances and material possessions or, through mismanagement, you may create future problems for yourself.

Depending upon the nature of the lesson needed, you may display either of two extremes of attitude towards material values, money and possessions. You may become more attached to them than before, intensifying the chasing of dreams, being strongly motivated to make as much money as possible, seeing it as a fulfilment in itself, and possibly cutting across ethical or social concerns in your pursuit. Or alternatively, the other extreme is a rejection of materialistic concerns or a loss of interest in adopting consumerism as a guiding and motivating light, as you come to privately consider such a preoccupation as personally meaningless. Then the focus may begin to turn inwards. Much depends on the existing balance in each person, and the distance that the pendulum of values may need to swing in order to create a suitable confrontation with the lessons indicated for each person. Neither point of extreme attitude is a station to stay; either can become troublesome as neither presents a really healthy and sensible attitude in the real world; the middle path between the two offers the clearest vision, beglamoured by neither extreme state of unbalance. Yet Neptune has a distorting effect on perceptions and values, so clarity may take some time to emerge.

Trying to keep up with some assumed level of social status can be unwise at this time, especially if you are starting to become financially overstretched, as your evaluation of your financial position can also fall prey to Neptunian distortion. Similarly your perception of potential business viability may also be less acute due to an over-estimation of your business acumen. You could be wise to seek an objective evaluation and advice from independent business and financial consultants. Also, you may discover that you are unable to take full advantage of your assets due to your lack of a clear purpose; do not force action or make irrevocable decisions unless you are really sure of what you intend doing.

Above all, learn to look within your own nature for the security that you are projecting outwards into the world. Excavate your own hidden treasures, and you'll discover that in the inner worlds there are riches beyond the dreams of avarice, and that this inner treasure house is your own heritage, awaiting the claim and arrival of its rightful owner – yourself!

NEPTUNE TRANSITING 3RD HOUSE

During this transit, you are likely to observe that your intellect and mental attitudes are being strongly influenced by more socially orientated values and issues. You are awakening more to the intrinsic relationships with society, and your role or responsibilities to humanity.

This can lead to a greater personal involvement with others in society who are active in dealing with or influencing such causes for human betterment. It is a step towards asserting that you can have a broader social influence, and that individuals are not inevitably passive and ineffective. In several ways it reflects the statement that 'the personal is the political', that personal choices and decisions reflect an underlying political attitude or sympathy, and that individuals can influence collective attitudes. This can be a new or a renewed interest in such concerns, and whilst Neptune is not so associated with the mind and intellect, it is reflective of a visionary social dream of utopian life.

You may need to guard against losing perspective and proportion in respect of everyday life, or by incorporating delusions and distortions into your intellectual thinking as a consequence of the influence of powerful social issues. It can be very enriching and valuable to become a part of national or international causes for social change, very exciting to feel a part of something which is needed for the well-being of people; it can be emotionally and intellectually satisfying. Yet fundamental change does not occur overnight; anyone involved in such movements is in for a long and difficult haul, so a degree of 'pacing' may be required, and no single person can change the world at once! There may be times when individuals move to the forefront, and maybe other times when they need to retreat a little in order to recharge their inner batteries.

Coming under the Neptunian influence of utopian dreams, there may be a danger in losing the ability to be a free thinker, independent in your own analysis of needs and actions, especially if you align yourself with specific cause-oriented groups. Such minority or pressure groups can play an invaluable role in awakening public attention to areas of world or governmental ignorance and evasion; the ecology groups such as Friends of the Earth and Greenpeace have been extremely effective in alerting the world to environmental threats. Yet it can be that 'all of your thinking' is done for you, and your role reverts into a more passive one of reflecting 'policy'. Certainly some of the more spiritual or occult groupings can reflect this tendency. Always be yourself and think for yourself – which may be easy to say and sloganise, but is very difficult and virtually impossible in practice! But the effort to achieve it is well worth the struggle.

At this time, however, once the initial burst of enthusiasm and direction has worn off a little, you may notice that the actual quality of thought is erratic, ranging from the occasionally inspirational to the confused and contradictory, and even showing undercurrents of fear and anxiety. Neptune is still attempting to provoke more underlying and subtle changes in you; the social transformation in your life is only just starting . . .

You may need to be wary of the tendency to proselytise, especially if you have been 'bitten by the bug' of social transformation for the first time. Generally, people pass through this phase of ostentatiously displaying their newly found allegiance to a vital cause and interest – as they succeed in integrating it deeper into their whole lives – but you could find that it may tend to antagonise or alienate friends and family if your expression becomes too over the top!

In your everyday life, you may begin to take on new duties and responsibilities – whether actively looked for by you or not – and you are likely to find that others begin to make additional demands upon you, and you may need to discriminate between obligation and imposition. In some cases, this new responsibility can involve children and perhaps conflicts between that social vision and the family demands at home. Changing society and the world is not just a task to be performed 'out there'; it can also be performed within the family and through our children's lives. There can be many ways to participate in the Aquarian revolution; sacrificing family and home life does not have to be one of them.

NEPTUNE TRANSITING 4TH HOUSE

As Neptune moves into the 4th house, there will be a dissolving of that sense of permanence and confidence in the deeply anchored inner roots of your personal identity. Those firm foundations which have been developed over the years – and which you trust and rely upon for inner stability and security – will begin to crumble as their crystallised cohesiveness breaks down under the Neptunian impact.

This will be a dissolving of 'parental patterns' established in your personality; those attitudes, beliefs, motivations and world view that have programmed you through social and parental conditioning. There is likely to be some experience or event in your life which serves as a trigger to reflect the commencing of this process. In some cases, this can be a crisis (turning point, decision time) within your home environment, marriage or family, as indicated by the concepts of roots and foundations. In other cases, it can be stimulated by some contact with a powerful ideal or idea that shakes your existing patterns, or by contact with a fascinating person who reveals a more inclusive approach to the rich experience of life, and in so doing, makes you feel discontented with your current experience.

The dissolving of such entrenched root patterns can be very difficult. You may begin to lose your sense of identity; the old motivating impulses lose their vitality, and you feel like a shell with no coherent centre. Feelings of inner uncertainty, nebulous fears and emotional anxieties and upheavals may occur as you are buffeted around by the unleashing of those inner Neptunian storms; moods will rise and fall with little obvious cause, and depressions may occur as you sink deeper into crumbling foundations. For some, their whole life can seem to fall apart; carefully erected edifices of self and lifestyle dissolve and seem like fading dreams. But this is just the preparatory stage of the Neptunian transformation. It is the disintegration part of the alchemical process and, painful as it may be, it is necessary for the 'lead to be transmuted into gold'.

Resisting the dying of the old familiar self and life patterns is an understandable reaction, especially if the individual experiencing this has no knowledge of psychological change. Yet it is an ultimately futile action; opposing the intent of the inner planetary gods is a brave but foolhardy action. Neptune will just agitate the seas more, call up a more violent storm to toss your ship of self on higher waves, crashing down lower into the troughs. As these 'parental patterns' dissolve, you may find that you begin to fantasise a yearning to return back to some idealised utopian roots of your past life, perhaps back into your childhood when life looked golden and full of exciting promise, and there were no cares or responsibilities.

It is a phase where you realise that the old foundations of self and identity are no longer suitable or adequate; they are insufficient to provide a vital and potent sense of meaning and purpose in your life. The influence of Neptune will be to bring this realisation with unavoidable clarity, to lay the new foundations for the potentially emerging and more inclusive identity, one which is capable of displaying and experiencing deeper meaning and purpose as an integral part of life. This phase will act as a stimulus for you to widen your interests, adding more depth and dimensions to your life as you begin to rebuild yourself. Freedom from imposed patterns of thought and attitude can seem disconcerting at first, but this liberation allows the opportunity to become yourself more fully, to be more integrated.

A search for new ways may commence. There is a multitude of avenues that can be explored; it is frightening to realise how much we limit ourselves during our three-score years and ten. We often choose to live as paupers in an overflowingly rich world. Hopefully, you will feel ready to open up to receive new influences, to find new directions. Maintaining an independence of thought has to be a priority now, after experiencing the casting off of the 10,000 heads on top of your own. Try to resist the temptation to absorb the first influence that makes a favourable impact upon you, just so that you can fill an aching inner void. Dip those toes into different waters, and check them out thoroughly before you become more committed; remember that one effect of the Neptunian vibration can be to cloud perceptive clarity.

Messages from the unconscious mind may be given to you during this transit, performing the role of pointing to future paths. Interesting dreams or evocative and meaningful symbols may arise, indicating areas which require resolution or directions to follow. The signposts will be there in your life, provided that you are alert enough to recognise them.

Being more receptive to Neptunian qualities such as inclusiveness and compassion can help you in steering the future course. Such intangible expressions of life as represented by spiritualism, astrology and mysticism may attract. Turning deeply within and becoming overly preoccupied with your problems can create a withdrawal from social activity although turning within to discover that new direction and foundation will be beneficial.

NEPTUNE TRANSITING 5TH HOUSE

The emphasis of the Neptunian influence during this transit is likely to be felt in the spheres of emotion, relationships and creativity. Distortion and illusions are probable in your emotional attachments and love life; your attitudes towards intimate relationships may need to be transformed.

The 5th house is often associated with love affairs and hedonistic self-centred pleasures, and there may be a deepening of your attraction towards such experiences. The presence of Neptune in this house will tend to dissolve existing patterns of behaviour, and can make you feel less satisfied and more discontented. Neptune will cast his net of glamour, permeating your emotional or sexual experiences, perhaps giving them an element of unusualness or peculiarity. Sudden infatuations may occur, inner obsessions or fantasies emerge, those inner archetypes of *anima–animus* may be activated, projected out on to a suitable recipient, who then proceeds to bewitch you. Through their eyes and body another world shines, beckoning you to follow them, ensnaring by the web of human desires and passions. As if pulled by a powerful magnet, you may feel that you have no choice but to follow. Neptune casts a heady spell.

If you are in a stable relationship, you may experience a deeper opening of your emotions, a new dimension of depth may be sensed, or new needs and desires may awaken. Tendencies to be excessively possessive over a partner may need to be released, in order for there to be mutual freedom in the relationship. A side effect of the Neptunian influence may be a reaction to grasp hold of a partner more firmly, using them as an anchor against those changing inner tides; this can often be resisted, and as such can perform a role in Neptune's subtle strategy.

Your emotions may be difficult to define and understand and may shift constantly under inner pressures and confusion. There can be an underlying sense of personal restlessness and dissatisfaction, which turns your gaze on any current relationship and re-evaluates it. Part of this may be due to a need for an idealistic perfect relationship; Neptune can stimulate almost impossible dreams at times, ones which you are unlikely to fulfil due to their unreality on this level, yet which fascinate and keep you looking, holding your emotions back from a real commitment on this level to another human being, hoping that fulfilment lies just around the corner.

You may realise that you are failing to appreciate and value what you already have, and that you are certainly not giving wholeheartedly to your partner. Yet you feel a deep aching for love, but can be afraid of revealing this until you feel confident that your love will be received and valued properly. In a way, you are expecting from another what you are resisting giving to them. It is you who has to learn to embody that form of selfless sacrificial love that you are expecting and demanding from a partner.

There are likely to be illusions in your perceptions of relationships during this phase. Evaluations and decisions concerning your real needs can be distorted, so look very carefully at any excessive and unrealistic expectations, as they may ruin your opportunities of a successful relationship. Potentially, Neptune is giving you the chance to transform your emotional life and experiences through cleansing those attitudes and values of illusions, giving you the opportunity to enjoy healthier and more intimately satisfying relationships which can be founded on reality.

You may be especially attracted towards highly Neptunian expressions during this transit – music, theatre, films, mysticism,
astrology, ideal romances – and may be tempted to experiment
with the sensual pleasures of drugs or other stimulants. Each of
these is like a doorway into 'alternative worlds', offering the potential to either forget or be enriched by the interpenetration of
your current reality by these more colourful imaginative alternative realms. The ambivalent influence of such interests depends
upon the individual; many can use them as a means of escape
from confronting areas of lack in their lives, by filling themselves
with rich imagery and imaginative dreams. Some become lost
through excessive and unwise drug abuse, seeking oblivion and
drowning in the depths of their own inner oceans, victims of the
Neptunian waters rising over their heads. Some successfully integrate the colour and vitality of creative imagination, transforming
it into a path of self-development through magical ritual and inner
pathworking. Like all of the gifts of the gods, the potential for
good is equal to their destructive qualities if misunderstood and
misused. Humanity often learns only by having its fingers burnt.

NEPTUNE TRANSITING 6TH HOUSE

Neptune is not especially comfortable moving through the 6th
house, as that sphere's emphasis is grounded too deeply in the
mundane tasks of life. The role of the 6th house is concerned with
individual functioning related to the surrounding environment
and world. Unlike either the 5th house, which is more personal,
self-centred and creative, or the focus on intimate partnerships
in relationships of the 7th house, the 6th house concerns social
obligations of service and work. It can be too down-to-earth for
the Neptunian temperament to flourish easily.

Whilst this transit will continue the process of the transformation of your emotional nature, Neptune is seeking now to dissolve
those more selfish attitudes towards work and service to society
as a whole. Types of experience may arise which require you to
fulfil essential needs of others. You are asked to look beyond your
own needs and desires, to make a connection with others who
may need your support. This can be within your close family
network, where through family obligation and mutual shared

responsibility you are expected to care for someone who falls ill, perhaps a partner or ageing parent. As Neptune often demands some form of sacrifice as part of the transformation process, such time- and energy-consuming commitment may be required, despite your own personal wishes.

Neptune is at odds with the Virgoan 6th house, and will clash with the natural characteristics of that house. The tendency of Neptune is to dissolve in order to be re-integrated, whilst the Virgoan 6th house tends to impose more fixed structures and classifications on everything, defining life into separate compartments through an analytical attitude. You are likely to feel this conflict within yourself, a part struggling to escape from the demands of the mundane disciplines of life towards some undefined nebulous realm of freedom, whilst another part looks to create stability through firm structures, conformity and predictability in lifestyle. Which way the inner pendulum swings will depend on the overall affinity in your chart. Most who respond to the Aquarian vision often favour following the sea whispers of Neptune, to escape from the binding ties of earthly demands.

It may be that such inner friction results in phases of ill health, a consequence of psychosomatic reactions to the stresses created by the movement of Neptune through this sphere. You may need to be concerned with the health, well-being and integration of your whole body–emotions–mind complex, possibly through the re-orientation of your attitudes and life related to work and service. Your inner relationship to employment could be dissolved at this time, either by 'external' decisions such as redundancy, company take-overs, lack of promotion and resulting loss of incentive and motivation; or by losing any interest in the job at all, where inwardly the 'job dies' and the connection seems severed. This can leave you with a feeling of being stranded, cast ashore on an unsuitable island, feeling in the wrong place and uncertain as to how you can be rescued. You may want a change of job, or decide to enter a new career. Certainly the sphere of work will be affected in some deep manner, as Neptune takes away fixed attachments.

Another form of this can be towards a selfless service, possibly work devoted to spiritual aims. Service can be given through the performance of mundane but essential tasks at home or work for no tangible reward. For instance, under the Neptunian influence, you could feel much more contented performing repetitive clerical work for an international charity than in doing the same work

for an engineering company, the difference lying in the visionary
ideal of the charity, which can satisfy the Neptunian compassionate qualities, helping you to feel that your work is valuable, important and personally meaningful.

A change can come by gaining a sense of satisfaction from any
help you can give to others, and by applying yourself whenever
needed to whatever task requires action. Moving in such a direction, you can discover that certain old attitudes are being transformed, and that the Neptunian influence is slowly leading you
towards a more tolerant and compassionate attitude. Different
aspects of your nature may start to emerge, qualities that can
enrich others' lives, talents that can help; and provided that you
do not weave illusions about your capacity and willingness to
help – which would arise from a self-centred standpoint – then
you can take another step towards embodying your personal
ideals, and this will be a more fulfilling direction to take.

NEPTUNE TRANSITING 7TH HOUSE

As Neptune moves into the 7th house, there is a need to reconnect
yourself to others through social and intimate relationships.
Where the 6th house transit was concerned with the birth of a
more impersonal level of social service, this transit is preoccupied
more with the issues of quality and value in your relationships,
especially with the degree that they successfully embody your
Neptunian ideals. This involves an intensification and deepening
of your awareness of others, both in the close intimate partnerships of marriage and family and in a concern with the complexity
of world humanity. How do you relate to people? What are your
conditioning attitudes? Are they racist, sexist, condemnatory, antagonistic and anti-social, or are they unifying, co-operative,
friendly, supportive and positively constructive?

In a more immediate context, situations and circumstances are
likely to develop which attract your attention towards the ways
in which you relate to others. This encourages you to take a deeper
look, to evaluate your relationships in terms of satisfaction, asking
if they fulfil their purpose, wondering if certain changes would
improve them, and trying to determine if changes in your own
approach would lead to more positive results and benefits for all
concerned. It would be a rare person who could honestly declare

that their relationship could not be improved in several ways; and even then, his listeners would rightly be sceptical!

To look at your relationships in such a stark light implies that you already have some insight into the reasons for and limits of each relationship, and are able to evaluate them dispassionately. Obviously this can be difficult, as self-centred perceptions will intrude, and the Neptunian influence can distort clarity. It may be that circumstances force you to look closely at your intimate partnership, perhaps through the Neptunian discontent, or a diminution of real connectedness with a partner as passion and mutual attraction may fade. Yet whilst such a process of analysis can seem a little impersonal, rightly done it can be valuable in gaining greater clarity and insight into your own personal meaning, purpose and life direction.

Neptune is liable to re-activate your inner noble ideal of love, that perfect romance that is totally fulfilling and satisfying, perfect on sexual, emotional, mental and possibly spiritual levels too. There is a fair chance that your current relationship does not match up to this idea and so appears to be a relative failure, but this can be misleading. It is a fallacy to believe that the grass is always greener on the other side. Undoubtedly your relationship could be improved. Why not try to do so from your half of the partnership? Make it move closer towards your ideal if possible, and make it fit your partner's needs too. Look to change yourself first rather than insist that your partner needs to be changed by you!

Underlying this are feelings of uncertainty and confusion in your relationships, especially if you have previously externally projected aspects of yourself on to a partner, parts which you have failed to integrate or accept into your own nature. This can lead to being dependent upon a partner for strength or security, and can create confusion regarding their motives or intentions at times, because what you will perceive is an odd mixture of these and your projected and unintegrated aspects shining back at you. You need to re-absorb and develop in yourself those projected aspects, and so become more whole.

Mutual misunderstandings can occur, and you can feel that something is changing within your intimate relationship, or that change is needed in order for the relationship to survive. As Neptune is busy dissolving older patterns in order to create new, revitalised approaches, pursuing a process of analysis and evaluation can be positive in that you are forced to look deeply into your relationships, creating a context to gain greater meaning, direction and clarity. If this can be achieved, you will be able to take full advantage when opportunities arise, so that benefits can be experienced by yourself and others. Potentially, a radical change can happen within your own attitudes and ways of expressing relationships during this transit. Providing it is positive and creatively orientated, this can lead to a new dimension of life as relationships are being opened for you to explore, enjoy and appreciate.

In a broader social context, you may need to be wary in your dealings with associates, as Neptune can leave you vulnerable to promises or pretences and allow you to fall prey to deceit as a result of a lack of awareness, whereby you accept the woven web of delusion. Be alert to any tendency to be taken in by glamour, or else you will discover that there is a price to be paid for your lack of insight.

Neptune may inspire you to become self-sacrificial. There are many around who are extremely willing to take advantage of such tendencies in people. Whilst you should give support and aid to others when needed, make sure that any form of sacrificial surrender does not make you a passive slave, vulnerable to exploitation. Such a situation is not really of benefit to anyone, although help can be offered to enable others to help themselves; they too have lessons to learn in life, and sometimes by offering too much you can take away the opportunity for them to learn for themselves. Rescuing people can become a never-ending task, and can certainly burn you out quicker. Helping them to help themselves is a slower but more effective approach. Remember, clarity in relationships is one of Neptune's intentions during this transit. Becoming lost in the depths of the world's suffering does not help anyone; yet clarity can help to show the most positive and creative way to be in your relationships, and this is potentially healing and beneficial to all concerned.

NEPTUNE TRANSITING 8TH HOUSE

During this transit, Neptune will be moving through a sphere deeply associated with sexuality, death and rebirth, touching extremely powerful forces that are intrinsic to life and to your own nature. Many find it difficult to fully integrate sexuality and death – the two poles of the energy of existence – as essential aspects of life. Both of these aspects carry an uneasy 'taboo' quality: sex through an unintegrated social preoccupation, and death as an almost unacceptable and embarrassing fact of human decline. The concept of rebirth is not really socially acknowledged in Western states, although in many Eastern countries the philosophy of rein-carnation is prevalent, and has been used as a means of social control for hundreds of years. It is perhaps better to consider the potential 8th house rebirth as not one of life after life, but one of personal change and growth ('rebirth') during this life. This is, after all, the only life that we can guarantee, and a philosophy that teaches 'No jam today, but we promise jam tomorrow' is not satisfying. Eventually, it is realised that tomorrow never comes; it is always today. However, postponement can keep the people happy, dreaming of the better tomorrow that is waiting for them, provided that they do not cause trouble through dissatisfaction and so accumulate more 'negative karma'.

The style of Neptune is to break free of boundaries and limita-tions, dissolving that imprisoning sense of separateness. In this 8th house, sexual activity can be one of its chosen channels, in that you can experience the union and merging with another human being, with your sexual partner. Sometimes it is only through sex that people experience a loss of control, of passionate abandonment to the intensity of the moment as they contact those highly powerful energies associated with sexuality. Yet such phys-ical activity involves a complex set of personal reactions upon several levels of the being: emotional, physical, mental, and a variety of individual needs, desires, and obsessional patterns of behaviour.

For some, Neptune's need to break through restrictions can lead to an intensification of the sexual impulse, dominating the personality more and directing lifestyle choices, perhaps through multiple partners, or a striving to be lost in ever greater sexual intensity. For others, Neptune can begin to confuse the personal sexual nature, in that the focus is more inwardly turned, causing a re-evaluation of a sexual identity and, perhaps in a few cases, a growing reaction against any personal need for sex, especially if particular religious ideals are being influential.

Certainly there will be confusion and delusions within your more intimate relationships, and you may feel more vulnerable to your emotions at this time, especially as Neptune is transiting through a water house. There may be tendencies to expect too much from your relationships, and to demand a conformity to some kind of ideal state. If you place the burden on any partner to fulfil your expectations, whilst perhaps being too passive yourself and not applying energy to make the relationship work, you may be soon be confronted by an angry rejection.

Neptune intends that you should discover more about your sexual nature, should integrate it into your whole nature, rather than keep it out on the periphery at arm's length, allowing it only periodic expression. Integrating this energy can permeate your whole being with personal power, sensitising every level, imbuing you with a sensual experience of life, and offering enhanced vitality and health. Neptune will show the other dimensions and depths that can be entered through your sexual nature, perhaps refining it to register those more subtle, higher vibrationary levels.

Death is a fact of life. One which we prefer to avoid and evade for as long as possible, as it is an ending of existence and of our dreams, or at least of the only life we really know. Confronting death may occur through this transit; you may come to terms with inevitability. Experiencing the loss of separate boundaries and entering the Neptunian realm is a very real and powerful experience of 'death during life'. We experience a variety of endings and beginnings during life, which are all minor deaths and rebirths, such as leaving school and entering the adult world, the breakdown of marriages and later new relationships. As Neptune desires to experience greater life through dissolving inhibiting barriers, death can be a passageway to liberation. Accepting death can intensify a personal life, cutting away all inessentials and time wasting, and stimulating a totally new and radical transformation in a person's nature and lifestyle. These can be the results of positive integration. A negative response to inner changes and pressures can be the development of self-destructive fantasies, the reimposing of barriers and the denial of a greater life. Morbid depression can set in, and the person can retreat deeper and deeper under the inner waters, offering himself as a sacrifice to Neptune's presence. Sacrifice of some kind may be expected by the god, yet it is never one of self-immolation; that is a misunderstanding of the nature of death required. Moving along that route, the individual can become attracted towards alcohol and drugs as a means of escape, an escape that consumes him and sends him spiralling down into deeper decline and suffering.

The 8th house is also associated with money, finances and inheritance. You may need to be cautious in your use of money and in your financial commitments, as you may be misled or deceived or may miscalculate your position at this time. Some become involved in legal affairs which can be related to inheritances in some form. It is possible that you will gain some benefit from inheritance, either through the receiving of property or money through a legacy, or by a firm promise of such in the future. You may need to remain alert and clear in your ideas and values, especially those concerned with business and relationships, where you should look for greater productivity in all partnerships. Avoid being excessively gullible, and look realistically at your relationships, especally your own expectations of others. Try to ensure that your marriage or intimate partnership expresses real love and communication, or you may discover that those legal affairs and financial problems arise as a consequence of a dissolving relationship.

NEPTUNE TRANSITING 9TH HOUSE

During this phase, you are likely to experience the Neptunian influence affecting your intellect and belief structures, dissolving their previous solidity. You are likely to feel more confused and uncertain about the validity of your beliefs and attitudes, personal values and established religious beliefs, especially those which have been unconsciously absorbed and accepted through social and parental conditioning. Neptune will cast doubt in your mind; this can be triggered by some event occurring in the external world that has an important impact upon you. Neptune's intention is that through initiating a process of inner questioning you may succeed in broadening your insight and perception into the depths of life. In this way the Neptunian effect of dissolving fixed barriers is operating, and it is good that this is happening, because the mind has a tendency to become stuck in certain ways of operating, running the same fixed programme over and over again as a habit pattern, eventually creating intellectual stagnation. Neptune will undermine your confidence in 'having things worked out enough', and will stimulate discontent, evoking vague worries and confusing dreams just to shake you out of feeling secure and comfortable.

Your own perception of personal meaning in your life and the value of your relationships may be highlighted as requiring a new approach and vision, especially in relation to applying your ideals in actual contact with people. Your ability to make judgements may be affected, possibly by your becoming indecisive or by reliance upon either common social attitudes or common religious and moral beliefs. You will tend not to decide by your own individual light, but mainly by reflecting an established group attitude. As this is an area to be transformed by Neptune, retreating into existing patterns may prove to be inadequate in a newly changing situation. You may need to be careful how this tendency is applied, as any rigid attitude can often be quite inappropriate in many situations, possibly creating even greater problems.

In feeling ready to change, or acknowledging an inner demand to do so, you will see redemption and salvation as residing in belief systems. You will tend to look for an ideal philosophy, religion or spiritual path through which you can merge with something greater than yourself. A desire to sacrifice yourself to a favoured ideal may be felt. Conversely, a dissolution of old ideals may occur, as Neptune breaks down existing patterns of attachment to an existing religion or ideal, and through deep disillusionment strips you of such supports, leaving you bereft, needing to find your own inner light, and unable to bask in the reflected light of a group belief structure.

You may be attracted towards more inclusive theories, attitudes, values and ideas, as well as unusual and psychic phenomena. It is a stretching of your perception of life that is happening, making you free to explore new realms, and is part of the inner intention to rebuild your basic intellectual approach to life. Eventually you will observe that developments have occurred which have used your previous pattern as a foundation, yet which have opened it out to new horizons that are more inclusive, personal and enriching to yourself.

There may be a decision to devote yourself to study in some form, even though you may not be fully certain as to what purpose it is leading towards. Physical horizons may be expanded through foreign travel, which can open your mind and eyes to different cultural lifestyles and social attitudes, thus dissolving any parochialism. Or you may begin to meet and associate with others who express unusual and strange ideas which contribute to your direction and the rebuilding of your personal world view.

Potentially, this can be a very positive phase which lays a new foundation for further exploration and discovery later in your life, and one which can free you to become more mentally independent, in distinction to the common tendency to meekly reflect and mimic established social attitudes and values without conscious and individual evaluation.

NEPTUNE TRANSITING 10TH HOUSE

Neptune's transit through the 10th house of career, public standing and social worth will be partly a reflection of how successful you have been in learning the Neptunian lessons of previous phases. You are likely to experience more external results which indicate your personal 'worth' in the context of the wider social community. It is both a culmination of previous efforts and a confrontation with the consequences of your choices, decisions and actions.

This can involve you in a developing growth of your influence through either a public or professional role, and you could emerge as a spokesperson for some public cause, interest, or pressure group in social, political or religious spheres. This may be dependent upon your prior progress and achievements, and upon the degree to which you hold a clear perception of your own worth and effectiveness.

If such illusions exist, then it is likely that during this transit circumstances will occur which reveal these to you. It can be difficult to perceive and estimate correctly your individual value to society, and often the natural tendency is to exaggerate or to deny your potential personal contribution. Exaggeration leads to the complex of ego inflation, and everyone can be susceptible to its influence to varying degrees. The issue is how long this can continue to dominate, as it is usually evident to others and recognised by them, but tends to become a blind spot in our own self-perception.

This transit will either intensify the development of your 'worth and importance' by unfolding situations which enable rapid progress to be made, or will thwart an onward progression by presenting situations that confront you with a brick wall. Certainly your focus on that personal career or meaningful interest in your life will be dominant. If advance occurs, then you may need to ensure that you quickly gain a correct sense of perspective and proportion, so that you do not suffer from a corresponding ego inflation which can turn a positive step forward into a negative effect on yourself and others. If an apparent failure occurs, and that brick wall confronts you, then strive to accept this and see the lessons that are indicated for you, especially if up to this point you have been constructing an inflated ego related to previous success.

In many respects, this can be turned into a very positive failure in that you are encouraged to look at yourself and any illusions, and to evaluate your attitudes, values and life direction. Considerable change can come from this process, or even the beginning of a new way of life. If success does come at a later time during this transit – as a result of such a re-evaluation – then you will be better prepared to handle it in a more mature and realistic manner.

There may be a confrontation with your current career and life direction, and disillusionment with work or social status. Neptune may encourage you to seek salvation by discovering more suitable work, or by feeling that you want to 'serve others' in the community. Finding the right expression for your real needs and talents could be essential during this phase, as a crucial part of your ongoing re-integration. Some are attracted towards devotion to a greater ideal, a voluntary sacrifice of their own separate identity to a high vision, as part of the attempt to embody principles that are personally extremely meaningful and important. Some who are exploiting any social power may over-stretch themselves and evoke the attention of the gods to their hubristic attitudes, and perhaps through avoidable scandals and indiscretions create crises which cause them to fall, stripping them of social power and approbation.

Try to avoid any temptation to slip into a retreat from any problems through indulging in dreamy illusions and idealism, as both can draw you away from confronting your challenges of success or failure.

What will dominate your inner life will be those concepts of social success and failure. Often you may have chased things in your life, believing that it is crucial for you to have them – possessions, jobs, relationships – because these are the dreams that society encourages us to have. It can happen that once a goal is achieved, it loses its fascinating allure, becoming devoid of meaning and satisfaction. Success can often turn into an experience of inner failure, where at the point of attainment the gold crumbles into dust in the hand, and the realisation dawns that it was not worth the time and effort spent. Failure can turn into succcess through lessons learnt concerning what is personally essential, true and meaningful. It is all relative, and it may be suggested that one of the lessons intended by Neptune during this transit is the understanding of this fact. Moving from a selfish standpoint to a more selfless one is the most viable transformation and one of worth to the greater community.

NEPTUNE TRANSITING 11TH HOUSE

The themes of the 10th house transit become more emphasised during Neptune's passage through the house of social brother-hood and group activity. There is likely to be an attraction towards more participation in social activities, perhaps through the glamours of a busy social life or by involvement with idealistic groups. In some cases such a whirl of activity may disguise an inner insecurity related to purpose and direction, especially if you are tending to participate in those lighter, more frivolous aspects of social life. This is not to deny their value as providing joyous fun and relaxation, but they can also act as a distracting factor, enabling you to avoid facing certain personal problems. Neptune may distort your perceptions generally, and experiences and ap-pearances may not always be what they seem. You are also liable to be influenced by current social trends and fashions.

Neptune is intending to open your compassionate heart towards others, so that brotherhood is not just an intellectual idea or beaut-iful ideal, but a heartfelt response to all men and women. Yet you may find that your relations with others are passing through an unsatisfactory stage, with confusion occurring in varying ways, perhaps even leading you to questioning the point of these re-lationships, and the value of your social interaction. You may feel tempted to allow some social contacts to fade away, perhaps feel-ing that the purpose behind such relationships has died away, or even feeling paranoid that your friends are turning against you. Neptune is expecting you to begin directing your own future path through awareness, and to be less dependent on the support of other people. Certain aspects of your social life are being dissolved in order to encourage you to create a renewed and wider social expression. Your present social pattern may now be restrictive and limiting, and it is time to discover greater scope and horizons within your own nature and within society.

This can be uncomfortable in several ways, yet such discomfort can be turned towards your own advantage, especially if in time it increases and enriches your perception of life, and enables you to establish more humane and compassionate values. Neptune is suggesting that service to humanity wil generate a powerful meaning to life. This altruism and a utopian vision towards social and humanitarian causes creates an expansion of self that is not egoistically inflative but inclusive and spiritual in essence.

What this may lead you towards is a new or deeper participation with ideas or groups which are dedicated to revealing the necessary next steps forward for the future of humanity, which are inspirations to encourage and create constructive social change. What particular aspect of this international movement will attract you is irrelevant, but as all aim towards creating a better life on Earth for everyone, then it is a high ideal that you are being asked to participate in by adding your own personal and unique contribution. Neptune will influence you to abandon a self-centred life to the purpose of the group endeavour; such activity offers a deep sense of purpose, meaning and direction in life and, provided that you can avoid any tendency to over-glamorise your involvement, can be a satisfying creative outlet for your energies.

NEPTUNE TRANSITING 12TH HOUSE

This is the last phase of the current Neptune transit through the wheel of houses. It represents a dissolution of the past, and points towards the next cycle. Neptune passing through the watery Piscean 12th house is at its peak in subtle disintegration and influence. It is unlikely to be an easy experience, as it challenges your attachments to existing social ideals and activities, stimulating certain doubts and fears about your own personal effectiveness, intensifying the degree of inner insecurity, a tendency which will reoccur during the new 1st house transit.

Whilst you may be attracted towards a process of withdrawal from parts of your social activity in order to remain with your favourite dreams or illusions, Neptune is indicating a clear and stark look at yourself and life. Ideally, you will succeed in dropping any aspects which are obviously illusory; otherwise, being under their influence will only create additional problems. It is inevitable that everyone has some illusions in their lives; the most difficult illusion to dispel is that of the separate self, and each of the transpersonal planets is dedicated to shattering that illusion. There may be unintegrated parts of your nature that act as Shadow aspects, which you prefer not to look at very often, aspects of relationships that are not satisfying yet are also ignored. Often though, a direct approach towards such problem areas with a positive creative spirit can seem to work wonders. Light is shone on an area of darkness, and the fact that the problem has been acknowledged as existing becomes the first step towards a positive resolution and release. At this final stage of this Neptune cycle, such a process can be extremely beneficial and in tune with the redemptive energies of this house; hopefully it can be an end to old problems and can offer the opportunity to commence the new 1st house cycle without its negative influence permeating your life.

Be prepared to be confronted with the consequences of the previous Neptune cycle of transits. A sense of crisis may be felt, as you encounter the accumulation of choices and decisions. Some consider this to be the weight of karma which requires balancing through acts of restitution. You may begin to realise that you have failed to take full advantage of your potential, or you may query your actual capabilities; you may feel that your personal contribution in relationships was not as honest or committed as it could have been. Whatever part of your life you feel could have been more fulfilling – especially where you are responsible for being less effective than you could have been – needs to be accepted as a 'failing' without unnecessary guilt or remorse, provided you seriously resolve to apply your energies in a more conscious and aware manner in the future.

Some may experience sensitivity to psychic undercurrents in life, intangible intuitions revealing unsuspected depths and subtleties. Some may feel almost swamped by emotional feelings and subterranean agitation in the oceanic depths of the unconscious mind. A rare few may experience Neptune breaking down all ego boundaries, dissolving the illusion of separateness and opening the door into an inner realm, where access to inner wisdom and guidance is given. Some, in an attempt at self-evasion, may precipitate a nervous breakdown under the effort to restrain inner pressures, movement and challenges, afraid of the darkness that is welling up inside them. Similar to every movement and activation

Visionary Dreamer

of the transpersonal planets of Uranus, Neptune and Pluto, their impacts can be as negative as positive, depending upon the ways in which the individual deals with the transformatory vibrations, and how he chooses to respond to the demands of personal change.

Remember that however you choose to deal with this final phase it will tend to condition the next Neptune cycle, so time spent now in evaluating your life, needs, intentions, values and attitudes can reap positive benefits. There are always areas in every life that can be improved by conscious effort, where enjoyment can be enhanced, and where life can be more self-created and self-directed. This is the potential which Neptune holds out for you if you choose to take the god's hand and listen to the whispered guidance.

NEPTUNE TRANSITING THROUGH THE SIGNS

The passage of the transpersonal planets through the signs has an impact on the generation born at that time, and influences necessary changes and progression within those cultures, societies and civilisations so that outworn and limiting social structures and established ways of thinking, attitudes, values and beliefs can become transformed and not stagnate. The transit cycle of Neptune through two signs (twenty-eight years) and Pluto (between twelve and thirty years for each sign) spans the emergence of a new generation which will have a new collective role to perform in the evolutionary pattern.

Each generation possesses possible solutions to previously created social challenges, as well as leaving future challenges to be faced by those who will follow. Often these indicate both the lower, more negative qualities of a planet mediated as unconscious 'fates' sweeping across the social collective and also the higher, more positive qualities which are mediated through smaller responsive groups who serve as seminal groups for a new visionary impulse to be anchored in the world. Such groups include artists of various shades, scientists, social planners, occultists, a few politicians, and radical pressure groups.

The signs in which transiting Neptune and Pluto are placed will indicate ways in which the generation born then – and those adults responsive to the higher energies – will eventually attempt to resolve social problems. This is often displayed in examples where individuals express a heretical, pioneering and controversial set of ideas to solve social issues which are opposed at the time of expression, yet by the time the corresponding generation has matured have been absorbed into mainstream thinking. Annie Beasant's early social work related to the need for contraception and women's rights is one such example. Though she was vilified at the time of expressing her social ideals, and even taken to court over the issue of publishing her writings, time has demonstrated that her vision was in the spirit of the evolutionary social vanguard.

Neptune in Aries 1861/2–1874/5

This is the start of the current Neptune transit cycle, and Neptune slowly begins to dissolve the entrenched social system in the Western nations. The concepts of state and monarchy are already dying, since the emergence of Uranus in the previous century, and the discovery of Neptune in 1846 is hastening these changes. Discovering a planet is like activating a corresponding archetype within the collective and individual psyche, whose influence may take some time to become apparent. Neptune has a particularly elusive nature, yet one which has such a potent and subtle vibration that foundations are dissolved before awareness has acknowledged that something is happening; it is only when the collapse comes that the realisation is made.

Aries is a pioneering energy, impetuous, striving for leadership and excitement; essentially what occurred in the West at this phase was an undermining of the establishment, the state, the churches and patterns of traditional thinking. Two main thrusts of this came from pioneering scientific enquiry and spiritual enquiry.

Darwin's work on the evolution of species began to dissolve traditional reliance on the factuality of the Bible and Christian teaching, which stimulated a collapse in the power of the Church over the people, many of whom were ready to recommence thinking for themselves and to develop their own spiritual and ethical attitudes.

The birth of spiritualism and mediumistic contacts from the beyond attracted many, and grew ever stronger since the Fox sisters case in America, helping to lay a foundation on which the later groups of occult derivations could be born, like the Theosophical Society.

Another agent of dissolution came from Marx's *Das Kapital*, his political and economic theories becoming the base for a new impulse of more modern political thought. With this, the emphasis on the power and role of the proletariat indicated immense shifts in the balance of national power, both internationally and within nations as workers began to demand greater influence and rewards for their endeavours. Each of these three trends was transformative, and their repercussions are still being felt today, although these pioneering and controversial impulses are now becoming ripe for further advanced redefinitions.

Neptune in Taurus 1874/5–1887/8

In a Western world that was essentially materialistic at this time, with the focus placed on increasing industrialisation and the new consumer demand of the townships, Neptune began to oppose the prevailing trend. The intent was to bring through a new spiritual impulse to impregnate the Western mind. The Victorian empire was reaching its peak, influencing and controlling many corners of the world; it was inevitable that cross-fertilisation would occur, and this began to happen through public imaginative response to the glamours and mysteries of the Orient.

In a society looking for security, stability and adherence to the old traditional values and beliefs, those trusted foundations were secretly dissolving beneath their feet. Blavatsky and theosophy brought through an immense amount of material and unknown teachings, confronting both Christian and scientific thought head on. The Hermetic Order of the Golden Dawn attracted many of the intelligentsia and artistic talents of the time, and emerged in 1887. Such occult groups have an odd role in society, far beyond their more obvious limited influence. They serve to open up channels in the collective mind, so that new and different impressions can be made on the mind of man; they reflect imminent evolutionary changes, giving invocatory voice to the human need for regeneration and change. These groups, and the many more that have been formed in their wake, opened doors for a revitalisation of the contemporary spiritual attitude of the time, flinging the doors wide open to all the world's religious thinking; Buddhism, Hinduism, Zen and Taoism all entered Western thought and imagination. Our generation has matured with such a broadness of thought readily available, and we often take it for granted, but barely a century ago this was not the case. The restoration of old gods, as invoked by the Golden Dawn, is reminiscent of the Christian belief that at the end of the age all the dead shall rise again.

This phase was a seminal time for our modern world. The progress made in developing resources and in applying scientific materialism to create, for example, the basis of our electrical technology, the fertilisation of religious thinking by other cultures, and the realisation that Christianity had parallels in myth and teaching with Eastern spiritual ways and that there were other Sons of God in different cultures, dissolved Western certainties again. The absorption of Eastern spirituality preceded the absorption of racial and ethnic minorities through immigration which in itself has transformed and is transforming our society and world into a more cosmopolitan and representative mixture of the one humanity. It is as though the idea had to precede the reality.

Neptune in Gemini 1888/9–1901/2

This transit also coincides with the commencement of the 500-year cycle of Neptune–Pluto, with the conjunction occurring in 1888. This conjunction indicates a turning point in world societies and cultures, where the death of old inhibiting concepts commences a sequence of progressive social disintegration and conflict. In Gemini, the battlefield was primarily that of the mind level, partly as a result of the stimulation of scientific enquiry of previous phases and the diminution of the religious hold over the collective mind.

In fact, it was the realm of science that was becoming the new priesthood, elevating logic and rational objective thinking as the goal to be achieved and the way forward for mankind. The collective mind was highly stimulated to search, explore and understand, and the most influential areas of exploration concerned human nature and the universe. Intellect became highly rated in the Western world, and there was a parallel growth in the awareness of the importance of education.

Major social influences that emerged out of this mental influence guided by imaginative leaps to discover new directions include the Quantum Theory of Max Planck, Einstein's preliminary work of the Theory of Relativity which would destroy the previous

Newtonian concept of the mechanical universe, as well as laying foundations for the atomic age, and Sigmund Freud's development of psychoanalysis and enquiry into the root patterns of human nature and psychology. This was the seminal period for such developments, and would emerge more fully during the Cancer transit and later phases. The value of the mind and intellect shone brightly, but with a glamorous taint, often ignoring other equally vital aspects of the human nature, especially as to how this developing scientific knowledge would be used.

Neptune in Cancer 1901/2–1914/15

There seems to be an observable pattern that the major steps of development or transformation occur and emerge during the last few years of Neptune's passage through a sign. This is where time is spent on slowly dissolving those restrictive foundations prior to the next step suddenly emerging at the end of the process. During this transit through Cancer, Neptune is dissolving the emotional and physical security of the Western states, the culmination of which was World War I.

It is a stripping away of all the old assumptions of the social fabric that has been previously established, and a reminder that there is no real security in life; if nature does not provide occasional prompts, then humanity will periodically wake itself through deliberate self-inflicted suffering. The power of the Victorian empire peaked, yet had created a model for other ambitious nations to emulate and desire. Families, societies and nations sleepwalked towards the cruel desecration of their dreams and ideals in the trenches of Europe, as nations tore each other apart in a paroxysm of nationalistic greed and madness. Here was Neptune operating and possessing the collective emotional nature through Cancer. It was the first culmination of the changes demanded by Neptune, where sacrifice, victims and martyrs co-existed in their millions throughout the West; it was an international redemptive purification and release of the established social order, where traditional values died with the cannon fodder of loyal men, and the old social rulerships and class distinctions dissolved in mutual agony.

There was no shell to retreat into; changes could not be avoided any longer. One important development from this culmination at the end of the Cancer transit and into that of Leo was the restoration of some degree of social power to women, and a re-balancing of social influence, a phase which is still going on as entrenched attitudes can sometimes take a long time to die.

Neptune in Leo 1914/15–1928/9

Once the traumas of the war years had passed, Western nations attempted to return to the old structures with which they were familiar. Obviously, several of these had suffered terminal blows, but there was still some life left in those patterns of collective behaviour. It was an uneasy period, often uncertain of what direction to move towards, still dependent on an old momentum to restore national stabilities and identity. But the process of dissolution was not to be denied, and the established patterns derived from the Victorian phase collapsed in disarray.

Collective relief and lack of social clarity led to a relaxation in tightly held attitudes, and a more *laissez-faire* climate became the vogue in artistic and cultural leanings as relative permissiveness spread across society. Leo, as the sign of individuality, enhanced this sense of hedonistic pleasure that people were looking for, a chance to play and have fun again after the repressions of the war. Escapism and pleasure attracted the young, who also responded to the fascinations of a more Bohemian lifestyle, and to the romantic idealism that was creeping back into life. Music became one focus for this, with the Jazz Age, and major occult figures flourished within the liberated atmosphere, like Crowley, Gurdjieff, Steiner, Bailey, and Fortune, who drew to them those intellectuals and seekers who were searching for more meaning and purpose in life, and who had recognised that the established value structure was dying and needed a new path to take. Artistic and cultural expressions, drama, theatre and literature all benefited from this social relaxation, and progress was made in breaking free of previous inhibitions, especially in the realms of sexual morality and in the development of new political thinking.

The social balance of power was shifting, as women gained the vote as a result of the suffragette and women's rights movements and their collective role during war time performing many types of employment that had previously been the domain of men. The ex-soldiers, returning from the fields of Europe, also had a different perspective on life and their social position. They were less willing to submit to the status of the higher class, and with the developing of the collective trade union movement, began to realise the real strength of their united will.

The world war had broken the power of the social class distinctions and nearly ruined several European nations, diminishing their world power and influence. This allowed other nations to become more assertive and independent, especially as economic powers; this was particularly the case with America, which had been relatively immune from the European struggle. The old nationalistic attitudes were showing signs of change – if only through necessity – and reformulations of national identity were occurring in several states. This also stimulated new political themes such as Socialism, Communism and Fascism to become stronger and to become dominant ideologies in countries like the USSR and Italy.

New developments in man's psychological understanding of himself proceeded through a greater absorption of Freud's theories and the branches created by Adler and Jung.

Eventually, the extravagant pursuit of change within an unintegrated social collective, flying high after the tensions of war but with little sense of control or direction, began to fall to earth. The economic crash at the end of the Roaring Twenties, and the collapse of the financial stock markets led to the Great Depression and widespread economic deprivation and unemployment. Neptune's changes were still proceeding, sometimes quietly and subtly, but with devastating effect.

Neptune in Virgo 1928/9–1942/3

Neptune is in detriment in Virgo, and this is an uneasy part of the transit phase. It is like a direct clash with attempts to maintain control and order in society, where illusions come crashing down in heaps of rubble, or sow the seeds of their own eventual decline. It was a period of unconvincing hope set against the growing storm clouds of social tension and the undercurrents of pressure ready to erupt.

For those living or born at this time, expressing the higher Neptunian qualities was inhibited by the social climate. Material deprivation was common for many, issues of survival were the main challenges, and the ability to indulge in imaginative flights

of fancy was denied to many youngsters. The Depression, unemployment, and economic fluctuation cast a heavy shadow over
nations, and seemed to be like another vindictive laugh from a
dark god who had teased with the apparent prosperity of the
earlier twenties as nations worked hard to renew their social fabric.

International suspicions mingled with idealistic hopes, social
visionaries emerged offering their panaceas for social transformation, politically active pressure groups jockeyed for position as
each nation experienced a series of internal reactions to the cul-
minative disasters of the previous phases. Fascism and National
Socialism gained power in Italy and Germany, and spurious scientific arguments emerged associated with concepts of racial
supremacy and nationalistic virtues. Aryan purity became a political policy, attempting to eradicate other despised minorities.
Fanaticism gained an upper hand, dominating the political
dialogue in several nations, and the use of media propaganda
became skilful and effective in persuading the minds of many
listeners of the aptness of their conditioning arguments.

In the clash between Neptune and Virgo, the battle of water
and earth resembled the spray cast off by a waterfall, distorting
the perception of the sudden change in levels that had precipa-
tated the descent of water over the edge. The lessons had still
not be learnt. The collective separatist mind was still dominant
and resistant to acknowledging the facts that nationalistic antagonism was dangerous and futile, and that it would be only
through international co-operation that progress could be made.
The dictatorships of Italy and Germany, and the rising sun of
Japan, would plunge the world over the edge of another precipice,
for reasons of national aggrandisement and power seeking. The
illusions and glamours were still strong.

Neptune in Libra 1942/3–1956/7

World War II was even more devastating to a greater part of the
globe than the first one, stretching beyond Europe into many
more countries and creating a pivotal pause in the affairs of the
twentieth century. Libra as the sign of balance indicates a shift
in the function of Neptune. Almost eighty years of slow erosion
of the traditional ways of society had now reached a peak, and
were reflected externally in the physical struggle of the world

war. What was to emerge at this time involved a more positive dimension of energy, pointing the way towards what may be considered to be Neptune's underlying vision and intention.

Whilst dissolution was still important in the restoration of a new balance, the creative visionary dreaming aspect of Neptune was being revealed. This was through the post-war generation, those who will guide society into the next millennium. It is a transition phase, reflecting great social confusion, conflicts and uncertainty; issues of human rights and freedoms were all in the melting pot after the war ended with the awesome destructive power of the atomic bombs at Hiroshima and Nagasaki. Since then, the threat of nuclear holocaust has hung over the world, as the technology to make the weapons has proliferated and been developed by several countries.

The vision of Neptune has been revealed in the emphasis on social relationship, which is a Libran theme. Whilst there have been degrees of confusion associated with this, and a shifting understanding of interpersonal and international relationships, this is the way forward. During this phase, the tendency was to create international affinity blocs – NATO, SEATO, the Warsaw Pact, the EEC, the United Nations and subsidiary bodies like Unesco and WHO – for mutual security and protection, for greater economic markets, for international aid to nations in need. On the individual level, civil rights emerged as a social issue, developing into the civil rights movement in America and seeking equality for minority groups in society.

A sub-culture emerged founded on youth, hedonistic and idealistic, which would flower during the Scorpio transit as the hippy generation, focused around the musical pied pipers who expressed Neptunian ideals of love, and personal creativity fused with collective social action, as in the attempts to stop the Vietnam War. It would be a generation that would become politicised, where the 'personal is the political'. Youth culture was born in the early phase of rock and roll, and is now an established fact of modern life, renewed every few years by a new fashionable style of rebellion and youth attitude. However, much of this has been badly tainted by its connections with drug and alcohol abuse, which is the negative face of Neptune unintegrated into the collective, and symptomatic of a lack of meaning, direction and purpose.

The nature of relationships has been questioned, and society is confronted by an escalation of the dissolution of traditional marriage structures and commitment, with consequences for families and children. People are challenged to evolve their own unique understanding and expression of traditional social ways because blind obedience to the old ways is creating friction and greater difficulty. In addition, it is this generation that has become the 'narcissistic seekers', looking for greater self-understanding, peering into the mirror of their own natures, trying to determine what, if anything, is really there; peeling away layers of themselves as if peeling an onion. This is the New Age generation, embodying optimistic dreams for the future, many illusions and glamours, yet also trying to bring a better world into being through social and political activity by pressure groups.

The Neptune–Libra vision is one of global relationship and responsibility, as embodied in the symbol of the United Nations, a great ideal of unity and common purpose, and one which we are still a long way from manifesting. Yet always the idea has to come first; in striving towards its shining vision lies the path of transformation, and it serves as a global image of the future of humanity, just as enlightenment attracts the individual seeker.

Neptune in Scorpio 1956/7–1970/1

The period of Neptune's transit through Scorpio inaugurated a post-war phase in Western societies, where many social attitudes which had been formed before the war were challenged by a new generation, and the concept of the generation gap became revitalised.

Much of this confrontational energy flowed through the expanding youth culture that began to group itself around an affinity for the music of rock and roll. Youngsters had money from greater employment opportunities, and started to indulge in the extended consumer market that was devoted to catering for everyone's desires. In England, these were the Macmillan years of 'You've never had it so good'.

The spheres that Neptune was to dissolve were traditional Scorpio associations. Sexual morality was turned upside down with more social promiscuity in the 'swinging sixties'; pornography began to flourish and almost became respectable as a symbol of liberation. Homosexuality emerged on to the world scene in a more assertive and open fashion. The glamours of media fame were more prolific as television became increasingly influential in society, and media stars were quickly made by appearances on the small screen.

Drugs spread throughout the West, especially the psychedelic type of drugs, where Leary's message of 'Turn on, tune in and drop out' spoke volumes of apparent wisdom to many. The role of drugs was extremely important to many at that time, opening doors of perception and insight into levels of reality that were previously unknown. Musicians adopted roles as spokesmen for the blossoming youth culture, acting as role models for a generation to emulate. The friction between youth and the establishment intensified in America, Britain and Europe, and the counterculture slowly formed as hippies and yippies gathered together for mutual support.

In true Neptunian fashion, image symbols helped to differentiate them from their parents and contemporaries: music, hair, fashion, attitudes and the use of drugs often set them apart. The dream of 'Peace and Love' and the spread of electronic music generated a new collective grouping and internationally famous hero figures from top musicians and movement leaders. The drug generation – a Neptunian phenomenon – allowed many to have personal experience of alternative inner realities, especially that of heightened unity with all life, and artificially forcing open psychic channels led to a perception of the outer planet's sublime vibrations. Many experienced mystical states of perception which consequently changed and redirected their lives, laying the foundations for much of the modern attention devoted to transformation techniques, which are less potentially harmful to the unfolding person.

A political awareness deepened as youth were often threatened as a minority group and discriminated against in various ways for their refusal to think, act and dress like their more sober elders. Youth affirmed life, exploration and pleasure, perceiving the straight society as upholders of Saturn-like restrictions and prohibitions. Street demonstrations, sit-ins and racial riots erupted; society passed through a period of great confusion as the old clashed with the youth impulse. Freedom became important, and protests against the American involvement in Vietnam grew more powerful. Death as a means of political change was re-adopted over the sixties, with the assassinations of the Kennedy brothers and Martin Luther King shaking social structures and stability.

The dangers of nuclear confrontation reached a peak in the Bay of Pigs affair and the stand-off between Kennedy and Krushchev. Terrorism became popular in an attempt to force social change or international policies through violent threats.

The phase was very Neptunian and Scorpionic; interest in mysticism and occult teachings burst through the youth culture, and Leary associated the psychedelic drug experience with Hindu and Tibetan spiritual experiences. Pilgrimages to India in search of gurus started *en masse*, and Eastern teachers established their base in the more lucrative land of America. Self-knowledge became the vogue, and youth found more to interest them in exotic Eastern teachings than in the more staid Christian teachings, so breaking free of their initial social conditioning. Counter-culture groups formed and became more influential, and there was a spirit that real and radical change was happening; dreams ran riot as deceptive enthusiasms ignored the need for practical thinking in their idealistic inspirations.

But this was a very powerful seminal period, changing the lives of many who had been born in the post-war generation, and creating social splits that offered both new opportunities and new dangers which we still have to face. The level of drug abuse that exists today is one consequence of that door being opened, especially as the drugs are much more physically harmful and addictive now and have led to an intensification of street crime, especially in America. Yet this need for a spiritual regeneration was stimulated at this time, and distorted as it may have become, is still active and demanding progress. Neptune in Scorpio stirred those unconscious depths and, like Pandora opening her forbidden box, unleashed a disruptive energy of transformation whose consequences are still to be fully realised.

This would later create the foundation for the New Age generation who as a minority group are responsive to the vibrations of the transpersonal planets of Uranus, Neptune and Pluto. What identifies this group are qualities associated with a bridging role between cultures and societies, between our contemporary world and the world which is waiting for our arrival after AD 2000. In addition, most of these are the post-war generation 'baby boomers', and have been part of the influential youth movement or counterculture since the early sixties. The influence of Uranus, Neptune and Pluto is powerful in their charts, and they serve as a planetary bridge between the old Piscean state of mind and the emerging Aquarian vision.

Neptune in Sagittarius 1970/1–1984/5

The almost primal energy that burst through the Scorpio transit had peaked by the start of the seventies, and the bubble of idealism had burst after the 1968 crescendo of student revolt had failed to ignite total social revolution. Yet what began to occur during this Sagittarius period was a refinement of this impulse. The same tendencies were present, but it was like a pause to reconsider, to analyse and think more carefully and deeply about the nature of social transformation and the individual and group role that was required. After the extroverted passion and high of freedom of the sixties, a more mature introverted period was needed for assimilation.

Materialistic consumerism was still expanding and promoted as the source of fulfilment in life; resources and the environment were still perceived as ripe for human exploitation and greed. Scientific progress intensified with technological advancement, knowledge and information began to explode throughout the world as human enquiry became more effective with the aid of modern scientific instruments, and quantum mechanics started to emerge as the cutting edge of contemporary investigation into the nature of the universe. New sciences were evolving, often synthetic mergings of previously disparate disciplines, and re-search into the human genome became feasible.

It was a phase of Sagittarian higher thinking, where the need for a more spiritual, philosophical and aware society became evident. Exploring the mind through either brain research or by individual meditation increased, and psychoanalysis or personal psychotherapy were popularised. As societies became more cosmopolitan, and were confronted with those challenges of social integration, so foreign travel and the flow of intercultural ideas increased too. 'The search' became acceptable: the search for self, the search for a new social system, the search for ecological balance and stewardship of living on Earth all expanded into recognisable patterns in human life. The opportunity for personal experience of the spiritual dimension or God was available to all those who desired to follow ancient paths and techniques; the need for a mediating priesthood was dissolved. Yet this too could find distortions in the initial needs for a guide and teacher, where many became dependent on guru figures and dubious cults.

Neptune–Sagittarian ideals infiltrated those who were responsive to them in society, where the global vision rose slowly into view as offering the only viable solution to contemporary problems. For many, the quality of life became more personally important than mere material possessions and physical existence. Concepts of revolution began to fade, and were replaced by ideas of transforming society from within, through social activism and involvement in radical groups or through inner spiritual work in meditation. Utopian dreams began to be resurrected, although their degree of practicality is often questionable; but if a finger points the way, then a way forward can be determined. Threaded through the levels of social confusion is a golden thread which points towards concepts of unity; slowly more people are growing conscious of its presence and are attempting to make it a reality on Earth.

Neptune in Capricorn 1984/5–1998/9

Capricorn is an Earth sign, and this phase is noticeably different from the previous transits which in Scorpio influenced a more emotional need for freedom in the collective, and in Sagittarius affected the mental level.

It is a crucial decision time confronting humanity. Social structures are steadily disintegrating in several major respects, and we are becoming increasingly aware of what we are doing to the planet, with ecological disaster looming, the ozone layers being depleted, forests disappearing at a rapid rate and a world economy based on an unbalanced distribution. The inevitability of essential change is slowly dawning even on resistant Western governments, who because of social pressure are having to acknowledge that problems like pollution do actually exist, even though they are still resistant to seriously tackling the problems.

As the possibility of chaos seems to intensify, there has been a corresponding reaction towards older types of attitude and social security. Fundamentalist attitudes have re-emerged, fuelled by reactionary tendencies. Bigotry and racism are stirring under the surface, and many of the apparent steps of social liberation gained in the previous two transits are under threat; for example, homosexuality is threatened again by social reactions to the dangers of AIDS. Authoritarian state attitudes have regained some power again, as people believe that through strong dictatorial leadership stability and security can be restored against the floods of permissiveness that stimulate uneasy changes.

The issues of ecology have now hit the media headlines, and survival instincts alone will probably urge the public to ensure that governments begin to take the necessary steps to resolve the international challenges. But in a global culture now, we still need to acknowledge what that means in terms of co-operative international policies. A form of practical spirituality has to emerge; not just a fanciful image of Secret Masters, because that is superfluous, but one which seriously deals with the challenges of mankind inspired by a vision of global unity. Neptune in Capricorn will stimulate again this concept of world government, reinvigorate slowly forming conceptions of the new politics, like the ideal of pneumatocracy, where politics is inspired by the inner spirit.

Signs of this are occurring, and one example is the work of Mikhail Gorbachev in the USSR. He is trying both to transform a stagnating and repressed nation of many states and minority groupings and, in his public pronouncements to the world concerning greater disarmament and more international co-operation, to solve world problems. It is an immense task, but changes are essential to prevent us falling over the precipice into the abyss.

Like the individual poised to expand into the Aquarian group consciousness, the collective is poised to develop more universal types of social organisation. This trend started with the current Pluto and Neptune cycles, and should reach a culmination over the next seventy years as both Pluto and Neptune complete their total cycles. 1992 may well be an important year as both Uranus and Neptune enter a conjunction in Capricorn, which should release additional inspirational and visionary energies. Fusing and integrating matter and spirit is the hidden theme, both for individuals and the collective, and as we approach the next millennium there will be a greater emphasis placed on considering what type of world we wish to create and live in after AD 2000. Each of us can help in bringing the overshadowing vision closer to the awareness of humanity.

Neptune in Aquarius 1998/9–2011/12

In the previous transit cycle of Neptune, the planet was discovered whilst in the sign of Aquarius, so this phase is likely to hold considerable significance, as well as Neptune joining Uranus in that sign by 1998-9. The crossing into the new millennium may well indicate the passage into the Aquarian Age.

Mental idealism and activity will be stimulated during this transit, where the collective tendency of Neptune unites with the concepts of social universal brotherhood that is reflected by Aquarius. The need for group consciousness will dominate the collective level of mind, and world awareness of the need for new cultures, civilisations and a transformed humanity will intensify. This will involve a higher turn of the spiral that initiated the development of early tribal group societies, where for mutual support and protection small groups of individuals banded together in order to survive. We face essentially the same problem, but our sphere is that of a global co-operation that needs to be achieved. Even if change occurs for purely pragmatic reasons of survival, the need for a more altruistic humanitarian spirit will become obvious. Through worldwide media communications, we cannot ignore suffering in other parts of the world; we have little excuse for turning a blind eye and pretending that it isn't happening, for retreating into our comfortable homes to illusory womb-like security.

It is likely that scientific breakthroughs will occur during this transit, both enhancing the developing web of instant communication networks, and probably showing the potential for new forms of energy production which are less dangerous to the world ecology. Solar power and nuclear fusion are likely areas for additional development. Satellite and space technology will become more important. Science and technology, especially in medicine, will become more effective, and serious attempts will be made to resolve several of the major health problems in deprived countries, as less finance is poured into the pit of armaments spending, and is instead used for more humanitarian concerns.

Neptune in Pisces 2011/12–2024/5

This is the final phase in the current Neptune cycle, and hopefully should see a culmination of the more positive qualities of the Neptunian vibration. The phase of necessary dissolution has been achieved by the turning point during the Libra transit, followed by the more visionary and positive qualities making their impact on more receptive individuals

Each end of a cycle is the seeding time for the new one, and Neptune is comfortable working through the sign of Pisces. The phase is likely to have its share of confusion and vacillation, where the world is still poised for many radical changes still to happen, and where there is a disparity existing between the more modern states and those which still have a long way to develop before progress is secured. Tensions will exist between those economically powerful nations and the weaker areas in the world, although a more equitable and less exploitative distribution will be slowly occurring.

There will still be a dawning realisation of the progress that has been made in the world since Neptune was discovered, as well as the direction that humanity has basically chosen to follow. Planetary consciousness and environmental responsibility will be well established in many nations and great efforts applied towards ecological redemption; world pressure will be put on nations who still persist in ecological damage, and a general emphasis will be placed on the value of global and international co-operation to solve world problems, recognising that for individual nations the task is too great to tackle alone.

It is likely that new forms of imaginative creativity will emerge, forms which have a majestic and uplifting quality, and which are designed to promote feelings of unity and to heal the planet. Having made it this far, social visionaries will be dreaming greater dreams for humanity to move towards, and utopian ideals will shine even stronger and appeal to the heart of humanity.

CHAPTER 7

The Esoteric Neptune

IN EXPLORING THE NATURE OF the astrological Neptune it is often illuminating to consider associated esoteric teachings, especially those which emphasise the transpersonal function and the impact of the Neptunian energies on the individual and society.

The system of occult teaching which is commonly known as 'The Seven Rays' is a major source of additional research. These concepts of seven creative rays of energy being the foundations of manifested life in this solar system were initially indicated in Madame Blavatsky's books *Isis Unveiled* and *The Secret Doctrine*. These were the seminal books for the formation in 1875 of the Theosophical Society and its later development. Further expositions of these teachings were made by Alice Bailey working as the amanuensis of the Tibetan teacher D.K. from the trans-Himalayan occult brotherhood, and have been made more publicly available through the efforts of those groups that she initiated, the Lucis Trust, the Arcane School, World Goodwill and Triangles. The legacy of the Bailey books is considerable and highly influential in this phase of anchoring the new Aquarian vision; they are, however, more suited for the advanced occult or astrology student. Nevertheless, a familiarity with those teachings can be very beneficial. Contacting the Lucis Trust for their newsletters and pamphlets can be an easier introduction for anyone who is interested in this approach to the Ageless Wisdom.

THE 6TH RAY

In the system of 'the Seven Rays', Neptune is associated with the 6th Ray of Idealism and Devotion. Esoterically, this ray governs the astral plane, and so the images that are connected are those

of Neptune as the 'God of the Waters', the 'Ocean of Life' and
the 'Waters of Substance'. In this context, 'waters' are associated
with esoteric wisdom and as we will shortly observe, are related
to the purifying effect of water, as in the experience of spiritual
baptism at the 2nd Initiation.

The astral plane is often visualised as a watery realm where
matter is less 'solid' and more pliable to influence by desire and
thought. Like water, it is fluid, prone to storms, and reflects all
impressions made upon its surface; reacting to these impressions
can stimulate the phenomenon of mists and fogs (glamours and
illusions) rising. This is the world of dreams, visions, desires and
powerful emotions and is often the hidden battleground of humanity. As we all should recognise, the power of the emotions is
currently more direct and immediate than thought or intellectual
complexity; most of humanity is ruled by their emotional response
to experience and circumstance, and rarely by a truly intelligent
reaction to real life. In the word 'emotions', there is the implicit
indication of motion, of being moved, and all of us are familiar
with the experience of being swept by an e-motional response,
through the whole range of pleasurable and painful e-motions
that we can confront. Desire triggers an e-motion, a movement
towards possessing or experiencing the object of our desire, and
gives the motivating impulse to direct our attention towards the
external world which appears to be the source of all fulfilment.

For a humanity which is strongly focused within a desire–
emotional nature, the effects of the 6th Ray are extremely potent,
and have been intensified since the emergence into conscious
recognition of the outer planets with the discovery first of Uranus
and then especially of Neptune in 1846. Indications of this range
from both the transformation created by the Industrial Revolution
– the building of factories which mass-produce items of consumer
desire, all of which are socially accepted and encouraged as necessary for individual fulfilment and contentment (whether actually
necessary or not for the well-being of life) – to the formulation of
world political ideologies such as Marxist communism.

In several ways, there has been a revitalisation of this 6th Ray
influence on humanity since the discovery of Neptune. Generally,
this 6th Ray is more attuned to the passing Piscean Age, where
the great world religions of Christianity and Islam spread and
influenced many cultures and societies. It has been during the
Piscean Age that many have realised 'that men are as fishes,

immersed in the sea of emotions', a phrase which evokes the older imagery of the early Christians and Christ as the 'fisher of men (or the Fisher King of the Grail legends). At this phase of the transition from the Piscean Age into that of Aquarius, a fusion of the energies has occurred, almost as if acting as a bridge towards the global vision of Aquarius and its emphasis on the virtues of group consciousness. It is suggestive to realise that whilst Pisces is associated with water imagery, Aquarius too is a symbol involving water in the form of a representative of the coming Christ awareness carrying and pouring the water from the urn: 'Waters of Life am I, poured forth for thirsty men.'

Over the last 150 years, we have seen the emergence of powerful ideologies which attempt to unite both emotion and mind so that they have a total resonance within the individual. These are then fused into potent groups of workers and idealistic thinkers who are committed to transforming an 'old order' and moving beyond negative social divisions. Such major examples of this include communism, socialism, humanitarianism, trade unionism, the women's movement, civil liberties, the Baha'i movement, the emerging New Age politics and the mass goodwill of the common man through altruistic sharing.

As the 6th Ray is that of Idealism and Devotion, such causes have generated great commitment from their believers, and have been a powerful cause of social change leading towards the birth of the global vision. What has occurred is the tendency of Neptunian idealistic singlemindedness to work through the revitalised 6th Ray, so that devotion to an objective has become a guiding light for many. Those latent ideological tendencies of humanity have emerged into the world through the unfolding of man's intellect, forcing desires for social improvement to create mass concepts of achieving social betterment.

For the individual or spiritual seeker, the 6th Ray characteristics are close to those of Neptune. Positive ones include: devotion, spiritual idealism and religious instincts, prayer, visionary mysticism, feelings of unity and of the immanence of divinity in life, reverence, loyalty, aspiration, beneficent sensitivity and tender compassion. Ambivalent characteristics include: singlemindedness, highly sensitised personal feelings and emotions, renunciatory tendencies. More negative characteristics due to misunderstood, misapplied and separatist individual expressions include: jealous love, partiality, sectarianism and prejudicial bias, self-deception, fanatical zeal, misplaced devotion, vagueness, over-receptivity to external influences, emotional and desire fantasies, reclusive escapism, mediumistic psychism on lower delusive levels, possessive and dependent love.

The difficulty facing the individual with a pronounced 6th Ray attunement is to express the higher qualities in a consistent manner, without becoming lost in the miasmic turmoil of the astral plane and his own emotional reactions. That quality of a singleminded visionary zeal and fiery aspiration committed towards achieving that ideal is a major 6th Ray characteristic. Neptune helps the individual to connect to that idealistic and heart-felt vision, absorbing his mental focus within the overshadowing goal, and then activates both Mars and Jupiter as energies necessary to pursue that ambition and make it real on Earth.

There are, in fact, two planets associated with this 6th Ray, Neptune and Mars, with the signs of Virgo, Sagittarius and Pisces especially involved. The mixture of Neptune and Mars is revealing in the 6th Ray tendencies that result; it depends upon the actual astrological chart of the individual as to which of the two planets is more dominant. In the less evolved it is the Mars energy that predominates, colouring the mediatory quality of that ray, making the expression more aggressive, extremist, direct and combative; the war-like tendencies within both Christianity and Islam are evidence of this in the Holy Wars over Jerusalem and the Holy Lands, as well as in the Inquisition phase in European Catholicism. The higher aspect involves the Neptunian energy, which is essentially the more pacific aspect of these religions, the Christian 'turning of the other cheek' attitude and that of community service and loving your neighbour as yourself – a universal heart vision that we are still attempting to embody.

Responding to this Neptune/6th Ray influence encourages the aspirant to be devoted both to higher spiritualised values and human welfare. This may take the form of adherence to a spiritual plan or purpose, requiring personal characteristics of loyalty and dedication, probably selfless service and personal sacrifice too. The mystical dimension of Neptune always stimulates a sensitivity and intuition of an ideal reality that is held as a potential within matter and form, awaiting the appropriate time before it is capable of manifestation. This commitment to actualising the ideal often takes the form of 'my truth, peace, dream, vision of reality, limited ideal, finite thoughts of God – for these I struggle, fight and die'.*

One danger inherent in this is an indiscriminate devotion to an ideal or person, whether encouraged by a state or a religion or self-created and imposed. What has occurred in the past is the rising of the extremist tendencies in people, where the dualistic consciousness and potent personal emotions have resulted in division between peoples and nations. Attitudes of 'we are holy and right, God is on our side, and they are evil and of the devil', and 'we are moral and righteous and they are immoral and should be penalised' as well as ideological and religious disputes are the inevitable consequence of separatist reactions to this energy.

Most are unaware of the controlling illusions that distort clear perception, especially where the ground of contention involves theological or spiritual differences, and such reasons for disagreements are still associated with the negative aspect of the Piscean Age. The 6th Ray has been termed the 'ray of blind procedure, where the individual has been blinded by the fragments of the whole, believing it to be total and exclusive'.*

Responding to the Neptunian vibration can leave the individual more introspective, gentle and probably over-sensitive, especially liable to an empathic registration of the feelings and emotions of others, like the traditional concept of Piscean psychic sensitivity. If this is not handled correctly, then through an excessive and sentimental sympathy the individual can become lost within the problems of another by an unwise identification with his plight; the result of this is an inability to serve and be of help. It is a 'hard compassion' and not a 'sentimental compassion' that is usually required; the hard compassion of the soul is considered only within the principle of the greatest good for the greatest number, and takes a much broader view of long-term repercussions and effects. Sometimes the lessons that are given from a soul level are painful, but soul or spiritual love seeks to truly evoke the spiritual life within individuals and society, rather than flattering and supporting personalities alone.

The 6th Ray reflects that eternal conflict between the lower and higher self, between the separate self of body–emotions–mind and the inclusive self of soul and spirit; the battleground of realisation is that of the emotional nature and astral plane. In *Esoteric Astrology* it is suggested that in the mass mind, Neptune is veiled by both Cancer and the Moon, where the created veils prohibit the individual from registering those many higher impacts and influences of which the 'true man' is sensitive. Breaking free of the constraints of the Cancerian mass-group existence and from the personal instinctive past of the Moon enables alignment with Neptune to occur. What becomes open then is a more mystical consciousness, an open sensitive heart which conveys the feeling experience of the higher vision, where there is the recognition of the underlying inter-relationship within the world process of manifested duality. The personal role is then to act as a mediator for this truer world to be displayed and expressed. In esoteric terms, this has been described as the obliteration of the power of Moon, Cancer and Neptune influences by the power and light of soul control. 'The initiate is no longer ruled by the Mother of Forms or the God of the Waters; when the waters break and are carried away, the Mother gives birth to the Son and the individual spiritual entity stands free'.*

The effect of the 6th Ray playing upon the agitated astral plane (created by mankind's desires, emotions and dreams) is to stimulate a vortex of force which magnetically evokes the descent of higher mental energy. This is true both of society and the individual aspirant, and the impact of the more refined mental energy tends to provoke the experience of conflicting ideologies and group dreams. During this century we have seen the consequences of this precipitated on to the physical plane through the tensions and crises of two world wars, as well as more localised areas of stress and conflict. The effects of the 6th Ray on the mental level tend to crystallise thought, creating a fanatical devotion to an obsessive mass ideal and becoming imprisoned by the dominating ideology until free thought becomes impossible, and the mind closes to other alternative perceptions and interpretations.

THE 2ND INITIATION: THE BAPTISM

In the Seven Rays system, Neptune is associated with the 2nd Initiation, commonly known as the Baptism, as was demonstrated in the biblical story of Jesus receiving the overshadowing Christ at his immersion in the River Jordan by John the Baptist. This represents a further stage in the transformation of mass consciousness into that of the inclusive sensitivity of the spiritual 'disciple' or initiate.

In the concepts of esoteric astrology, the Solar Logos as embodied in the Sun focuses higher energy and influences through the transpersonal planets of Neptune and Uranus, using them as a stepping-down transmitter and focusing lens to enter and affect life on Earth. Neptune has been described as the 'heart of the Sun' which when called into activity pours spiritual energies via Neptune upon humanity. The intended result of this activity is to transform emotion-desire into love-aspiration, which is orientated and dedicated to the inner soul. Once the emotional-feeling nature of the aspirant is responsive to the nature of the energies emanating from the 'heart of the Sun', then the indication is present that the seeker is ready to proceed through the 2nd Initiation, which involves the sublimation of the influences of the Moon and Cancer. The 6th Ray comes both from and through Neptune, who with Jupiter is the co-ruler of Pisces. Jupiter is also associated with the 6th Ray channel and rules Sagittarius too, and has a tendency to express this ray energy with more of an active and dynamic style than the more contemplative Neptune. Both Neptune and Jupiter are exalted in Cancer, which is the sign of mass incarnation and where the desire for incarnation eventually finds fulfilment and liberation. In *Esoteric Astrology* it is suggested that in the ordinary mass-directed man the ordinary astrological relationships are Cancer ruled by the Moon, 4th Ray, and Pisces ruled by Jupiter, 2nd Ray. In the unorthodox attributions and especially for disciples and initiates, Cancer is ruled by Neptune, 6th Ray, and Pisces by Pluto, 1st Ray.

The influence of Neptune is both to create true individuals out of mass humanity, and to enable them to take their place within the Aquarian group mental consciousness that is slowly emerging. This is the concept of world servers, who act as a mediatory group between the inner spiritual vision and the needs and demands of mass humanity. 'Disciples' are those individuals who are inspired by a progressive and humanitarian group ideal and who are learning how to embody, transmit and express this to illumine the way for others. Usually such groups work under the initiating aegis and organisational management of the 'ashram of a Master', in full affinity with their individual and group purpose.

During this transitional phase in world evolution, and in respect particularly of the Western world, Neptune is known esoterically as the Initiator: 'In certain ancient formulas, the great Teacher of the West and the present World Initiator, Christ, is spoken of as Neptune, Who rules the ocean, whose trident and astrological symbol signifies the Trinity in manifestation, and Who is the ruler of the Piscean Age.'*

At the time of the 1st Initiation, the inner Christ (soul or spiritual life) is born within the individual; this was discussed in *Phoenix Rising: Exploring the Astrological Pluto*. The 2nd Initiation is the point of crisis in becoming capable of controlling the astral–emotional–desire nature.

There has been a reorientation of the personal life towards the spirit and aspirational ideas as a consequence of the 1st orBirth Initiation. This second stage is reached through an intensification of the energy of aspiration and humanitarian dreams. The seeker is often beglamoured by his own powerful and almost fanatical adherence to the unfolding of his ideals and his devotion to what he perceives as 'good'. He desires to serve. His ideal is world transformation. But as he moves along his path, he is shocked and horrified to become aware of his own inner astral nature, and the complexity of the world astral level.

He sees that the astral plane is perpetually agitated by constant separatist desires, that storms rage across the waters caused by the clash of opposing desires and dreams, that deceptive thought forms are reflected into the minds of men, and that the malleable astral matter reacts to every impulse, desire and magnetic pull from both good and evil sources, from visions of unity and of separateness. Rarely does tranquillity persist; the nature of the astral level is instability, the waters moved by the hidden currents and the strength of the wind. He sees that these energies are fluid, drifting, often undefined, and that the water is the closest and most appropriate symbol from the physical plane.

He realises too that he contributes to this chaotic realm, through his own uncontrolled and unintegrated emotional and desire responses; that he too is a victim of his own personal glamours and illusions. The light dawns upon him of his own responsibility, that he too needs to clear his own nature of excessive and unconscious emotionally based reactions. He understands his own contribution to the 'storms aroused by his emotional nature, the dark clouds and mists in which he constantly walks'.* It is a salutary and sobering realisation that confronts the seeker. Mystical glamours have been considered in Chapter 3, but it is at this point of the process of the 2nd Initiation that the seeker faces the door created by the electrical energy of the sum total of all his glamours. By now, these glamours are becoming more potent and intensified, and signs of this should be reflected back from the outer life. His perception and clarity is clouded and distorted by these deceptive yet illusory energy forms that act as an obstacle and impede further progress. Essentially he tends to create his own diversionary paths to travel along, deviating along ways formed by old habits, often expressing himself in such a way as to actually inhibit his own intended direction, undermining his own purpose.

He realises that a sacrifice of his own separatist desires needs to be achieved, and that his focus must be transferred towards emphasising only the good of the whole. Slowly, through great personal struggle between his lower and higher self as on the battleground of Kurushektra between Arjuna and Krishna in the *Bhagavad Gita*, he begins to make progress in understanding, integrating and reorientating his emotional nature. Some degree of emotional adjustment and control needs to be demonstrated, and a knowledge of how to apply spiritual energies to dissipate those glamours. He needs to pass through the transition from an emotionally based aspirational position into that of applied intelligence founded on a clarity of perception. Old desires, habits and patterns of automatic response lose their power to dominate him, and he learns how to become increasingly responsive to the demands of the soul centre. By using mental illumination focused on the more quiescent astral–emotional nature, applying this as a transmitter of the inner soul light, he sees that glamours can be dispelled and that 'it is the struggle to clear the world atmosphere which will confront humanity after the first initiation'.*

Once that inner battle for supremacy is won by the spiritual nature, the waters of the emotions and personal astral nature become quietened, capable of being a more accurate reflector of those higher impulses and the universal vision. Emotions are purified through the fires of self-created suffering and resistance, and his lower separate nature is subservient to his higher self.

Breaking free of the immersion in glamour opens the door to greater insight. His ability to serve is amplified, his inner influence as a transpersonal channel is intensified, and more powerful energies pour constantly through him as his life becomes sacrificial. A more expanded insight into the evolutionary Plan is revealed and the world's need is experienced more acutely. Increasingly he will be expected to sacrifice his own personal needs to those of the world; service will be his guiding light in whatever way it can be rendered. He becomes a *kama-manasic* initiate, in whom there is an ever-intensifying awareness of inter-relationship, of unity within the One Life, a fact that he is dedicated to express into the world. Humanity or group consciousness become paramount, and he is imbued with an enhanced creative vision and with his role to perform as he enters a phase of world service. As he moves into the greater clarity of the mental-level focus, he sees that one ongoing task is the reor-ganisation of the astral–psychic–emotional life of humanity, so that this level can be cleansed, enabling the spiritual light to shine through more easily, and the energy of goodwill to be released to achieve purposes connected to right human relationships.

This phase of the 2nd Initiation is under the esoteric influence of Vulcan, Neptune and Jupiter, and directly involves the solar plexus, heart and throat energy chakras in the human etheric body. It involves a peculiar purification by 'fire' which is released by the light penetrating through the mental level into the astral plane, and is the occult application of 'fire to water'. The water is transformed into steam, and the candidate for initiation is 'im-mersed in the fogs and miasmas, the glamours and the mists'* as we have seen.

This is termed the 'Baptism', and the biblical account of the washing and purification by water apparently reflects an ancient Atlantean tradition within the initiatory process, where a descent is made into water and, coupled with a word of occult power, the candidate is reborn. One Buddhist connection to this stage is known as 'entering the stream'. Stepping into the baptismal waters is an intense purification, as occultly it 'enables him for ever to step out of the waters and be no longer in danger of drowning or submergence; he can now "walk on the surface of the sea"and with safety proceed onward towards his goal'.* This was symbol-ically demonstrated for the disciples by Christ walking on and calming the stormy seas, a ruler of the oceans of life, and as the higher manifestation of the Neptune ideal.

ATLANTIS

Madame Blavatsky's *The Secret Doctrine* clearly regards Neptune–Poseidon as a powerful symbol of Atlantean magic. Poseidon was considered to be the personification of the Spirit or Race of Atlantis, both positive and negative tendencies. The modern image of Atlantis is that of a large island or continent surrounded by the ocean, which is believed to have been submerged due to either a great flood or earthquakes, with volcanic activity eventually causing the island to break apart. Traditionally, continents 'perish' by either fire or water, through sinking, floods, or by earthquakes or volcanoes which transform the shape of the land masses under the pressures of shifts deep in the earth.

There is considerable occult lore and speculation concerning Atlantis, and it is often seen as the source of archaic wisdom and esoteric teaching. Atlantis is perceived as an ideal, where a 'golden age' existed of magic, harmony and mystery. Ancient Egypt was supposed to have been one repository of Atlantean knowledge which was retained after the death of the island, and there are persistent indications that much of the earlier Western magical tradition has roots from prior Atlantean migrations. Dion Fortune and her group often attempted to explore such connections in their work of reformulating the Western tradition.

Amongst the Atlantean symbols of magical power and authority was that of the 'Dragon', an ancient symbol associated with the 'Serpent' which reccurs in many old religions. Poseidon was recognised as a Dragon, and was adopted as the patron deity in the later city of Poseidonis in Atlantis. Plato actually commenced his story of Atlantis by the division of the continent by Poseidon, who was the grandson of Ouranos. The status of Dragon–Serpent was given to the 'Initiators' and this is reminiscent of that current function of Christ to which the Tibetan referred.

Concepts of dragon and serpent wisdom are found across the world in many of the older religions, and this is either an archetypal pattern that was active then and registered independently throughout the world, or else the symbols and teachings did emanate from one particular source. The Babylonian and Egyptian hierophants were known as the 'Sons of the Serpent', 'Sons of the Dragon', and the Western druids also claimed a similar title: 'I am a Serpent, I am a Druid'. In Mexico as a continuance of Aztec traditions, the national deity symbol is Quetzalcoatl, the flying plumed serpent, who is a God acknowledged as the civiliser of mankind through sharing his knowledge to raise the level of an ancient humanity. The symbols of serpent and dragon were always associated with the mystery wisdom teachings and immortality, and the elevation of man into the godhead, and were not considered to have any connection with evil as our Christian heritage has stated. In the Bible's Old Testament, Genesis has the story of the Tree of Knowledge, where the serpent is the disguise for the Devil-Satan, tricking Eve into persuading Adam to taste the forbidden fruit, leading to the banishment from the paradisal Garden of Eden. The serpent serves again in the role of Initiator, helping to discover the wisdom that is ever present through self-knowledge. Unfortunately, much of later Christian teaching and action tends to prohibit the search for personal *gnosis* and generally does not encourage individual realisation outside the boundaries of Christian theology.

QABALAH AND ALCHEMY

In the Qabalistic esoteric system, Neptune is often associated with the highest Sephirah, Kether. This has been termed the 'Crown of Creation' and is placed on the central Pillar of Equilibrium on the Qabalistic Tree of Life. Whilst Kether has primarily a spiritual context, there are parallels with the theory of life emerging from the physical seas on Earth. It is the Fount of Creation, the point where life wells up from the depths of the unmanifested original chaos plenum-void. In mythology, Kether is aligned with those primal creators who emerge into active being from the apparent abysses of vast waters or space, and in this sense connect to the role of Poseidon. One Qabalistic image relevant to Kether and Poseidon is that of the 'Vast Countenance', a great head rising from the depths of a calm sea until it completely covers the space above the horizon, with the image reflected by the surface of the sea. For the individual seeker, Kether is a point where union with the godhead is achieved, and the anointing crown is received. As Kether is essentially formless, contacting that energy leads to a gradual dissolution of separateness as fusion is realised with the inner spark of divinity.

It is this aspect of dissolution that links Neptune, Kether and the spiritual dimension of the alchemical quest through the concept of 'the universal solvent'. A stripping away of all veils is involved, of all accretions of manifestation in dense matter until the essence is revealed. The Philosopher's Stone is the aim of many alchemists, and is a symbol of some mystery that can only be discovered within the psyche of man, yet is often guarded by using imagery pertaining to the transformation of baser metals into gold. This Stone is something that can never be lost or dissolved, and is thus impervious to the impact of Kether or Neptune. The process includes the reduction of the separate form into 'primal matter' which is indivisible and whole in its own nature. The limits of time are broken and the possessor of the Stone enters eternity. For the alchemists searching for the spiritual secrets this imagery implied the mystical experience of encountering God within their own soul, and this was the culmination of many prolonged attempts to burn away all those inhibitory veils, glamours and illusions of separate identity within themselves. Once this was achieved, then the Stone glowed brightly, and the base metal had been transformed into gold. In the process, the alchemist had also dissolved, melted down into a more fluidic nature as those barriers dissipated under the intense heat of his spiritual crucible.

* Quotes reprinted with permission from Alice A. Bailey, *A Treatise on the Seven Rays*, Vol. III, *Esoteric Astrology*, and *A Treatise on the Seven Rays*, Vol. V, *The Rays and The Initiations* (Lucis Trust).

CHAPTER 8

Neptune and the Awakening Heart of Humanity

SINCE THE DISCOVERY of Neptune in 1846, there has been a remarkable shift in human consciousness and social humanitarian development, which has paralleled the slowly dawning awareness of the planetary unity of humanity. Whilst Uranus ushered in the age of intellectual and mental unfolding, Neptune has stimulated the birth of the opened and compassionate heart, seeking to ensure that a wise application and direction of mankind's knowledge is made. We are still standing at a cultural crossroads, where national leaderships are confronted with the need to adopt more inclusive and internationally co-operative and beneficial policies, in distinction to the older established patterns of favouring powerful social and political elites, or furthering separative party and international policies.

Neptune has been considered to be the higher vibrational octave of the energy which is embodied in the planet Venus, and represents the more universalised love vibration which compassionately embraces the world and humanity – a more inclusive development of Venus, which is more limited to the love for a partner or immediate family. Neptune is the love that dissolves barriers between the individual and the collective: in the social sense it is an encompassing energy, reaching out to unite and integrate through the transformation of illusory boundaries and separative attitudes. Neptune symbolises a possible consummation that stretches out as an aim for humanity, the search for a human brotherhood and a relationship of the heart.

Whilst Uranus can be considered to be associated with the Illuminated Grail of the Mind, Neptune is the Inspired Heart of the Grail. Both need to work together in harmony and synchronisation so that the Phoenix resurrection and rebirth symbolised by Pluto can occur. Neptune is the apotheosis of the vision of the World Heart.

By the mid nineteenth century, signs were emerging of a shift in social awareness. In English Victorian society members of the middle class were turning compassionate eyes towards those less fortunate in their society, and humanitarian and philanthropic projects began to be developed in an attempt to improve the standard of living for those who were impoverished. The work of Charles Dickens played a role in this slow awakening; his novels concerned with social themes had a noticeable impact on his readers at that time. Dickens performed as a social commentator through his fiction, influencing people through his shrewd and perceptive insights into the climate of the times and revealing the hypocrisy of much of his society and the impact of poverty and social alienation on disadvantaged souls. Many creative people adopted social concerns as foundational ideas for their personal expression, attempting to steer social attention towards looking into the darker corners of life and trying to prick the Christian conscience. We have already discussed the intent of an artistic movement, the Pre-Raphaelites, during this phase. This interpenetration of creative expression and society has continued to deepen since then, and reflects a sensitive, feeling response to the level of social care, an awareness of the disparity of social fortune and the apparent reliance on luck as to where and to whom you are born.

The philanthropic spirit took firm root during this period, and a strand was anchored in the human heart and mind that caring brotherhood was the progressive way forward. The International Red Cross was established in 1864 at the Geneva Convention to offer an international organisation for the relief and treatment of the sick and wounded in war, and was staffed by nurses and doctors who received the injured from the Red Cross ambulances. Another social order is the St John's Ambulance Association, formed in 1877 to provide first-aid, nursing and welfare services. Even many factory owners adopted an attitude of concern for their workers, although compared to today, this was relatively minimal and arguably for their own interests, yet the effects were an increase in the workers' standard of work and life. Some, like Robert Owen, went even further and developed styles of utopian communities, and greatly influenced the later socialist and co-operative movements. The key point to these developments is the growing awareness of the other, a dissolving of self-centred interests and perceptions, and a sensitive response to the suffering of people linked to a desire to alleviate this suffering to some degree.

Within international politics, Abraham Lincoln and the Northern States in America fought against the southern Confederacy over the issue of freeing negro slaves shipped over from Africa, a confict that eventually led to radical changes in the role and position of a minority group in America, even though the struggle still continues and reached one level of focus in the Civil Rights Movement at the time of Martin Luther King's 'I have a dream . . . ' vision. In Russia, a corresponding social change was to occur with Czar Alexander II's efforts to emancipate the serfs. For their attempts at freeing a socially abused people, and for responding to their own intrinsic feelings of right and wrong, both Lincoln and Alexander were assassinated. Two international political and economic movements were also born during this latter half of the nineteenth century, both evocative of an intellectual reaction to social compassion; these were Marxism and socialism, and whilst the initial impetus may have become distorted the original foundations were visionary and associated with the Neptunian resonance with the collective.

During this century, we have seen the ongoing development of broader international movements, all of which have a core vision of the one humanity. The prime example of this is the United Nations, which came into existence in 1945-6. Its initial conception was the maintenance of international peace and security, but this has expanded to include the Universal Declaration of Human Rights, which defines the natural rights inherent in the human condition regardless of race, creed, nationality, sex, age, or religion, and which supports economic and religious freedom, as well as the rights of women and children. This holds a vision for mankind to gauge its progress against, and is a reminder of the goal that we should be seeking. The United Nations has also become a major influence in the sharing of international aid, attempting to heal deprived nations and improve the standard of living for millions across the globe through its World Health Organisation and its educational programmes run by Unesco.

Such examples have also had a profound effect on socially aware individuals throughout the world. There has been a rapid increase in 'grassroot groups' springing up, dedicated to social influence and pressure activity on governments. This reflects the developing of that enlightened public opinion which is so crucial to the unfolding of the Aquarian vision; the future of humanity is too vital to be left to politicians alone.

Recent examples include charity aid rising from the power of the youth culture and music. Band Aid, Live Aid and Comic Relief have dissolved many barriers and given a taste of what public response can provide in terms of money and support when the heart is touched. Save the Children is given millions of pounds to fund its programmes of care, and the media have become the transmitters of a global eye that demands the awakening of a heart response to suffering. Groups like Oxfam, War on Want and the Hunger Project are devoted to reducing the threat of starvation in Third World nations. Amnesty International is dedicated to helping prisoners who are in unjust incarceration, and is promoting worldwide human rights. CND and END work towards enlightening public opinion against the dangerous threats of world nuclear war, and there are many anti-nuclear groups in every country. Friends of the Earth, Greenpeace and the World Wide Fund for Nature are devoted to environmental protection and healing, and to preserving endangered species of plant and animal life; today the once-derided ecology groups are now respected and socially established groups, whose informed knowledge is widely sought after for media comment – their words of warning are being revealed to be prophetically correct. There are many, many more concerned groups, all of whom do valiant and crucial work in the world.

All of these groups work from the heart, and share in the vision of the transpersonal planets in building a new world order, a new culture and civilisation approach to life on Earth. The role of Neptune is to stimulate the awakening heart of humanity. This transforms the level of love that exists as an unconscious compulsion, a biological instinct, a physical and psychological passion towards that of a conscious socialised form of spiritual service to the whole. It is an impulse to reach beyond, to grasp the hand of others in a mutual celebration and conscious unity. Love is the emerging conditioning energy that is urging humanity to recognise the essential inter-relatedness of life, and to take steps to reach world goodwill aand harmony. It may be an impossible dream and vision, but striving to reach it will bring constructive and positive change in our wake, and so make it a step closer to attainment.

Love partakes of the nature of fire – as anyone who has suffered in love knows – and God has been described as a 'consuming fire'. Limits are consumed, barriers and boundaries transcended as love perceives beyond superficial appearances, and relates to the secret and hidden heart centre where the love of the spiritual soul is released. In our twentieth century, we have released the atomic fire through science; now we need to release the spiritual fire of transformative love, so that through heat the individual and the collective are transfigured. The Christian ideal of *agape* needs to be revitalised, where unconditional love becomes the aim, the limitations of self are extended for the serving and benefit of others, and where through mutual support, co-operation and trust we encourage the dreams of potential, empowering one other with high visions which dissolve the separatist ego.

The heart is the point of a sensitive, feeling response to the world; an open heart is the point of alignment, where the integrating unifying power streams outwards as a compassionate act of impersonal love for mankind, synthesising multiplicity and diversity into realised unity. The transpersonal planets open the individual to the spirit, which permeates the individual life with inner purpose and power. Bridges can be established which cross racial, political, religious, cultural, ideological and psychological divides through the radiance of the heart.

. . . and Visions

What is it that inspires individuals to act, to pour their vital energies into achieving something that is motivating them? It may be desires of fortune and fame, or perhaps more ordinary and mundane needs, but the vitalising energy inspiring any effort arises from personal dreams and visions. It is these that make the world go round, the source of individual and collective evolutionary development.

Neptune is the planet of dreams and visions, and there can be a narrow dividing line separating the nature of such inner images; between the realms of illusions and illumination many spiritual aspirants are dissolved by that universal solvent only to reappear with a visionary insight into the underlying universal reality.

Everyone has personal dreams of fulfilment and achievement, needs and desires that ideally will be satisfied; these are the searches for the perfect, interesting and well-paying job or position of seniority; for the most beautiful home, family and marriage partner; the search for physicial and spiritual wholeness; the need for public recognition, acknowledgement and fame. Dreams of desire are innumerable, and many devote their lives to chasing after them in the hopes that when achieved they can then relax and bask in the glow of attainment.

People can be filled with personal dreams and visions, and many of them will be frustrated by the impasse provided by the reality of life. Perhaps personal commitment to achieving them is not sufficient to overcome those inevitable obstacles standing in the way; perhaps the intention is not clearly defined; perhaps personal characteristics and talents are inadequate to attain an impractical dream. Yet much human energy is expended in dreaming and chasing those dreams, sometimes to a successful conclusion, but more often it is just dissipated and all ambitions are stillborn.

For the individual, dreams serve to compel action. They are the impulse and impetus to direct the attention of the self towards achieving that specific dream; initially, the dream may appear to be impossible to actualise, but there is always the chance that it can be made real through personal choice, commitment and dedicated effort. The dream is the 'maybe I can . . .' that activates the Sun, Mercury, Venus and Mars into concentrated focus, as imagination stimulates the belief that a desire can be satisfied. This becomes a path towards creating a new reality in personal life, opening up new opportunities and new horizons to explore, and the hope that the life can be re-created into the type of ideal lifestyle that has been dreamed of for so long. It is a recognition of the importance of choice in life; that doors are only closed because you have chosen not to open them, and not because they are forever locked against you. Life offers a multiplicity of options and paths; we are responsibile for limiting ourselves, by refusing to dream and have visions – we need to have faith to make them real. Through choice, we decide what to do, choose who to live with, decide how we will feel about our lives, determine where to live; if our lives are unfulfilling, then we have the free choice to change them, but only if we decide to take that transformative path.

The act of taking responsibility for our lives is crucial. By using the techniques of constructive creative visualisation we can re-shape our enjoyment of life, enhancing meaning, purpose and direction. Types of positive life visualisation are developed from the Neptunian quality of imagination and emotional resonance, and are focused through the higher mental quality of Uranus.

Whilst the touch of Neptune will stimulate dreams, the real intention is to help transform these into a more positive and constructive vision, especially one designed to enhance the quality of life for the greater whole, the collective human race and the kingdoms of nature on Earth.

Dreams begin to transform into the visionary approach, where the vision is seen as the first step in building a *pre-reality pattern* which will become manifested in due course. Those responsive to the positive vibration of Neptune will see this as forming their gifts to the world, their contribution to the quality of life, their inspiration and message irrespective of the specific channel they are working through. Always, the inspiring vision precedes the act of creation and manifestation on the physical levels.

Neptune leads us through the inner dreamscape on a magical path towards the vision quest. He inspires the human need to want, imagine, sense and desire those dimensions of life that offer the abundant life, and in so doing brings into existence those new perceptions, values, forms, structure and potentials that help us to expand beyond our self-imposed limits and to become attuned to the holistic vision. Aspiration is intensified, life is enriched and vitalised, creative potential released and the way forward stands out in a stark relief like a lighted beacon. Individual clarity and strength of purpose increases, and the belief in the option of positive change inspires the will to proceed with faith and confidence in eventual success. Visions offer the power of hope, where even in the darkness, the small flame of light still flickers, serving as an inspirational belief that there is a way out, a way forward that will validate the need for transformative suffering.

Neptune may offer a social vision, a vision of a world that could be, and which is waiting for our contribution and choice to make it real, a pre-formed reality pattern of a potential future world of unity. But to take that step, the individual has to move beyond the limits of separative image and thought and become a more inclusive consciousness. Several world-famous political figures have expressed this theme of vision, and have become historically famous; John F. Kennedy, Gandhi and Martin Luther King are three recent examples. King's 'I have a dream . . . ' speech is a classic of its kind, and still a rallying call to oppressed and disadvantaged minorities. Mikhail Gorbachev is also currently communicating a vision of dissolving the international Cold War and nuclear warhead stocks; he envisages a more united Europe and a diminishing of USSR control over satellite states; he is a Pisces ruled by Neptune.

The Neptune vision is one of heart which is dedicated to collective service, aiming to be beneficial to all, constantly expansive, enriching, inclusive and inspirational, and which attempts to empower all who fall under its spell to follow their own vision quest.

What is Neptune's higher teaching for humanity? It is a vision of a great dream, where humanity learns how to live together with all the kingdoms of life in peace and mutual harmony, where the guiding light is one of universal compassionate love. It is a great dream and a great vision. It is our choice whether or not to attempt to make this real.

And how can we co-operate with Neptune if we choose to share in his vision?

There is a simple answer, and one which has been given to us as a living example by Gandhi:

> I am . . . a practical dreamer. I want to convert my dreams into reality.

Index

PHOENIX RISING
Exploring the Astrological Pluto

Using chart analyses ranging from
Margaret Thatcher to Karl Marx,
the author examines Pluto's
influence on both the individual
and society, dealing in depth with
the Pluto myths, the psychology of
the God of the Underworld, natal
house positions, planetary aspects,
transit cycles and historical events.

ISBN 1 85230 042 6 paperback £7.95

REVOLUTIONARY SPIRIT
Exploring the Astrological Uranus

This second book of the outer
planets trilogy considers the effect
of Uranus on our contemporary
and future worlds. It examines its
influence on the individual, both
from a humanistic and a
transpersonal perspective, through
an analysis of major planetary
aspects, natal house positions and
transit movements.

ISBN 1 85230 059 0 paperback £7.95